CINDEDAUGHTER

"Orenstein is an unapologetically passionate critic of the marketing onslaught she skewers so stunningly in her latest and most masterful book. . . . [She] consistently brings an opinionated yet sensible sensibility to the hottest-button questions of contemporary feminism. . . . In *Cinderella Ate My Daughter*, we see Orenstein at her genre-busting best—and our culture's warped commercialization of girlhood at its worst."
— Meredith Maran, *San Francisco Chronicle*

"Orenstein is such a breezy, funny writer, it's easy to forget she's an important thinker too."—Judith Newman, *People*, "People Pick" (four stars)

"A feminist critique in the guise of a chat with a friend, Orenstein's book inspires parents to rethink girlie-girl culture. . . . *Cinderella Ate My Daughter* is entertaining as well as useful, not only for parents of daughters."
— Christy DeSmith, *Minneapolis Star Tribune*

"Orenstein's reflexive self-interrogation is a good match for her material. It allows her to coax fresh insights from the exhaustively analyzed subject of gender and its discontents. . . . [She] has done parents the great favor of having this important debate with herself on paper and in public; she has fashioned an argument with its seams showing and its pockets turned inside out, and this makes her book far more interesting, and more useful."
— Annie Murphy Paul, *New York Times Book Review*

"Reading *Cinderella Ate My Daughter* is like hanging out with a straight-talking, hilarious friend; taking a fascinating seminar on twenty-first-century girlhood; and discovering a compendium of wise (but never preachy) advice on raising girls. A must-read for any parent trying to stay sane in a media-saturated world."
— Rachel Simmons, author of *Odd Girl Out* and *The Curse of the Good Girl*

"The cultural critic looks at how beauty pageants, Disney princesses, and Miley Cyrus are shaping young minds. Hint: it isn't pretty."

—Karen Holt, *O, The Oprah Magazine*

"A gripping, hilariously horrifying account of battling for your child's soul in the toy aisle, one that excoriates consumer culture while sympathizing with parents trying to make sense of it all. As a mother of two young Barbie-loving daughters myself, I was riveted by Orenstein's blend of self-deprecation and outrage." —Mary Elizabeth Williams, *Salon*

"A sparkling and provocative look at the new 'girlie-girl' culture that has taken our daughters hostage." —Daphne Merkin, *More*

"[Orenstein's] writing style is engaging and conversational without being dumbed-down—an ideal combo for taking on the cultural ills that threaten our daughters. . . . There's real pleasure to be derived from reading Orenstein's sane and reasoned dissection of this phenomenon."

—Myla Goldberg, *Slate*

"A highly entertaining (and disconcerting) romp."

—Michael Mechanic, *Mother Jones*

"This is a book that not only makes you stop and think, it also at times brings tears to your eyes—tears of frustration with today's girl culture and also of relief because *somebody* finally gets it—and is speaking out on behalf of our daughters."

—Judith Warner, author of *Perfect Madness: Motherhood in the Age of Anxiety*

"Thought-provoking." —Joyce Saenz Harris, *Dallas Morning News*

"*Cinderella Ate My Daughter* will engage, inform, entertain, and surprise you. It will also forever alter the way you see the world that girls—and their parents—are, for the most part unconsciously, navigating."

—Rebecca Traister, author of *Big Girls Don't Cry: The Election that Changed Everything for American Women*

"They're back! Peggy Orenstein reacts to her daughter's embrace of the sinister Disney-princess agenda by reporting on how retro-feminist attitudes of the 50s are being hustled to innocent girls in the blood-chilling *Cinderella Ate My Daughter*." —Elissa Schappell, *Vanity Fair*

"Intelligent and richly insightful." —Kirkus Reviews (starred review)

"[Orenstein] is an excellent guide through the sparkly territory young girls increasingly inhabit. . . . In *Cinderella Ate My Daughter*, Orenstein wrestles with her own ambivalence about the princess culture. . . . And that's part of the book's considerable charm. Her forays into the mysteries of child beauty pageants and toy design are often hilarious, sometimes troubling, always real." —Kate Tuttle, *Boston Globe*

"Every mother needs to read this book."
—Ayelet Waldman, author of *Bad Mother*

About the Author

Peggy Orenstein is the author of the *New York Times* bestselling memoir *Waiting for Daisy: A Tale of Two Continents, Three Religions, Five Infertility Doctors, an Oscar, an Atomic Bomb, a Romantic Night and One Woman's Quest to Become a Mother; Schoolgirls: Young Women, Self-Esteem and the Confidence Gap*; and *Flux: Women on Sex, Work, Love, Kids and Life in a Half-Changed World*. She is a contributing writer to the *New York Times Magazine*. Her work has also appeared in the *Los Angeles Times*; *USA Today*; *Vogue*; *Elle*; *Parenting*; *O, The Oprah Magazine*; *More*; *Discover*; *Salon*; and *The New Yorker*. She lives in the San Francisco Bay Area with her husband and their daughter, Daisy. Visit her Web site at www.peggyorenstein.com; you can follow her on Twitter @peggyorenstein.

ALSO BY PEGGY ORENSTEIN

*Waiting for Daisy: A Tale of Two Continents, Three Religions,
Five Infertility Doctors, an Oscar, an Atomic Bomb, a Romantic
Night, and One Woman's Quest to Become a Mother*

*Flux: Women on Sex, Work, Love, Kids, and Life in a Half-
Changed World*

Schoolgirls: Young Women, Self-Esteem, and the Confidence Gap

CINDERELLA ATE MY DAUGHTER

DISPATCHES FROM THE FRONT LINES OF THE NEW GIRLIE-GIRL CULTURE

PEGGY ORENSTEIN

HARPER

NEW YORK · LONDON · TORONTO · SYDNEY

Names and identifying details of some individuals have been changed to protect their privacy.

HARPER

A hardcover edition of this book was published in 2011 by HarperCollins Publishers.

HarperCollins books may be purchased for educational, business, or sales promotional use. For information please write: Special Markets Department, Harper-Collins Publishers, 10 East 53rd Street, New York, NY 10022.

Portions of this book appeared in altered form in the *New York Times Magazine*.

FIRST HARPER PAPERBACK PUBLISHED 2012.

Designed by William Ruoto

The Library of Congress has catalogued the hardcover edition as follows:

Orenstein, Peggy.
  Cinderella ate my daughter : dispatches from the front lines of the new girlie-girl culture / Peggy Orenstein. — 1st ed.
    p. cm.
  Includes bibliographical references and index.
  ISBN 978-0-06-171152-7
  1. Girls—Psychology. 2. Femininity. 3. Mothers and daughters. I. Title.
  HQ777.O74 2011
  305.23082—dc22

2010028724

ISBN 978-0-06-171153-4 (pbk.)

12 13 14 15 16 ID/RRD 10 9 8 7 6 5 4 3 2 1

For Daisy

Contents

CHAPTER 1 Why I Hoped for a Boy 1

CHAPTER 2 What's Wrong with Cinderella? 11

CHAPTER 3 Pinked! 33

CHAPTER 4 What Makes Girls Girls? 55

CHAPTER 5 Sparkle, Sweetie! 73

CHAPTER 6 Guns and (Briar) Roses 95

Contents

CHAPTER 7 Wholesome to Whoresome: The *Other* Disney Princesses 113

CHAPTER 8 It's All About the Cape 133

CHAPTER 9 Just Between You, Me, and My 622 BFFs 159

CHAPTER 10 Girl Power—No, *Really* 179

Appendices

   A Conversation with Peggy Orenstein . . . 193

   Beyond Princesses (Sort of): What Girls See on Screen 201

   The New Girlie Girlhood by the Numbers. 205

Acknowledgments 207

Notes 209

Bibliography 239

Index 247

Chapter One

Why I Hoped for a Boy

*h*ere is my dirty little secret: as a journalist, I have spent nearly two decades writing about girls, thinking about girls, talking about how girls should be raised. Yet, when I finally got pregnant myself, I was terrified at the thought of having a daughter. While my friends, especially those who'd already had sons, braced themselves against disappointment should the delivery room doc announce, "It's a boy," I felt like the perpetual backseat driver who freezes when handed the wheel. I was supposed to be an *expert* on girls' behavior. I had spouted off about it everywhere from *The New York Times* to the *Los Angeles Times*, from the *Today* show to FOX TV. I had been on NPR *repeatedly*. And that was the problem: What if, after all that, I was not up to the challenge myself? What if I couldn't raise the ideal daughter? With a boy, I figured, I would be off the hook.

And truly, I thought having a son was a done deal. A few years before my daughter was born, I had read about some British guy who'd discovered that two-thirds of couples in which the husband was five or more years older than the wife had a boy as their first child. Bingo. My husband, Steven, is nearly a decade older than I am. So clearly I was covered.

Then I saw the incontrovertible proof on the sonogram (or what they said was incontrovertible proof; to me, it looked indistinguishable from, say, a nose) and I suddenly realized I had wanted a girl—desperately, passionately—all along. I had just been afraid to admit it. But I still fretted over how I would raise her, what kind of role model I would be, whether I would take my own smugly written advice on the complexities surrounding girls' beauty, body image, education, achievement. Would I embrace frilly dresses or ban Barbies? Push soccer cleats or tutus? Shopping for her layette, I grumbled over the relentless color coding of babies. Who cared whether the crib sheets were pink or glen plaid? During those months, I must have started a million sentences with "*My* daughter will never . . ."

And then I became a mother.

Daisy was, of course, the most beautiful baby ever (if you don't believe me, ask my husband). I was committed to raising her without a sense of limits: I wanted her to believe neither that some behavior or toy or profession was *not* for her sex nor that it was *mandatory* for her sex. I wanted her to be able to pick and choose the pieces of her identity freely—that was supposed to be the prerogative, the privilege, of her generation. For a while, it looked as if I were succeeding. On her first day of preschool, at age two, she wore her favorite outfit—her "engineers" (a pair of pin-striped overalls)—and proudly toted her Thomas the Tank Engine lunchbox. I complained to anyone who would listen about the shortsightedness of the Learning Curve company, which pictured only boys on its Thomas packaging and had made "Lady," its shiny mauve girl engine, smaller than the rest. (The other females among Sodor's rolling stock were passenger cars—*passenger cars*—named Annie, Clarabel, Henrietta, and, yes, Daisy. The nerve!) Really, though, my bitching was a form of bragging. *My* daughter had transcended typecasting.

Oh, how the mighty fall. All it took was one boy who, while whizzing past her on the playground, yelled, *"Girls* don't like trains!"* and Thomas was shoved to the bottom of the toy chest. Within a month, Daisy threw a tantrum when I tried to wrestle her into pants. As if by osmosis she had learned the names and gown colors of every Disney Princess—I didn't even know what a Disney Princess was. She gazed longingly into the tulle-draped windows of the local toy stores and for her third birthday begged for a "real princess dress" with matching plastic high heels. Meanwhile, one of her classmates, the one with Two Mommies, showed up to school every single day dressed in a Cinderella gown. With a bridal veil.

What was going on here? My fellow mothers, women who once swore they would never be dependent on a man, smiled indulgently at daughters who warbled "So This Is Love" or insisted on being addressed as Snow White. The supermarket checkout clerk invariably greeted Daisy with "Hi, Princess." The waitress at our local breakfast joint, a hipster with a pierced tongue and a skull tattooed on her neck, called Daisy's "funny-face pancakes" her "princess meal"; the nice lady at Longs Drugs offered us a free balloon, then said, "I bet I know your favorite color!" and handed Daisy a pink one rather than letting her choose for herself. Then, shortly after Daisy's third birthday, our high-priced pediatric dentist—the one whose practice was tricked out with comic books, DVDs, and arcade games—pointed to the exam chair and asked, "Would you like to sit in my special princess throne so I can sparkle your teeth?"

"Oh, for God's sake," I snapped. "Do you have a princess drill, too?"

She looked at me as if I were the wicked stepmother.

But honestly: since when did every little girl become a princess? It wasn't like this when I was a kid, and I was born back when feminism was still a mere twinkle in our mothers' eyes. We did not dress head to toe in pink. We did not have our own miniature high heels. What's more, I live in Berkeley, California: if princesses had infiltrated our little retro-hippie hamlet, imagine what was going on in places where women actually shaved their legs? As my little girl made her daily beeline for the dress-up corner of her preschool classroom, I fretted over what playing Little Mermaid, a character who actually gives up her *voice* to get a man, was teaching her.

On the other hand, I thought, maybe I should see princess mania as a sign of progress, an indication that girls could celebrate their predilection for pink without compromising strength or ambition; that at long last they could "have it all": be feminist *and* feminine, pretty *and* powerful; earn independence *and* male approval. Then again, maybe I should just lighten up and not read so much into it—to mangle Freud, maybe sometimes a princess is just a princess.

I ended up publishing my musings as an article called "What's Wrong with Cinderella?" which ran on Christmas Eve in *The New York Times Magazine.* I was entirely unprepared for the response. The piece immediately shot to the top of the site's "Most E-mailed" list, where it hovered for days, along with an article about the latest conflict in the Middle East. Hundreds of readers wrote in—or e-mailed me directly—to express relief, gratitude, and, nearly as often, outright contempt: "I have been waiting for a story like yours." "I pity Peggy Orenstein's daughter." "As a mother of three-year-old twin boys, I wonder what the land of princesses is doing to my sons." "I would hate to have a mother like Orenstein." "I honestly don't know how I survived all those hyped-up images of women that were all around *me* as a girl." "The genes are *so* powerful."

Apparently, I had tapped into something larger than a few dime-store tiaras. Princesses are just a phase, after all. It's not as though girls are still swanning about in their Sleeping Beauty gowns when they leave for college (at least most are not). But they did mark my daughter's first foray into the mainstream culture, the first time the influences on her extended beyond the family. And what was the first thing that culture told her about being a girl? Not that she was competent, strong, creative, or smart but that every little girl wants—or should want—to be the Fairest of Them All.

It was confusing: images of girls' successes abounded—they were flooding the playing field, excelling in school, outnumbering boys in college. At the same time, the push to make their appearance the epicenter of their identities did not seem to have abated one whit. If anything, it had intensified, extending younger (and, as the unnaturally smooth brows of midlife women attest, stretching far later). I had read stacks of books devoted to girls' adolescence, but where was I to turn to understand the new culture of *little* girls, from toddler to "tween," to help decipher the potential impact—if any—of the images and ideas they were absorbing about who they should be, what they should buy, what made them *girls*? Did playing Cinderella shield them from early sexualization or prime them for it? Was walking around town dressed as Jasmine harmless fun, or did it instill an unhealthy fixation on appearance? Was there a direct line from Prince Charming to *Twilight*'s Edward Cullen to distorted expectations of intimate relationships?

It is tempting, as a parent, to give the new pink-and-pretty a pass. There is already so much to be vigilant about, and the limits of our tolerance, along with our energy, slip a little with each child we have. So if a spa birthday party would make your six-year-old happy (and get her to leave you alone), really, what is the big deal? After all, girls will be girls, right? I agree, they will—and that is exactly why we need to pay more, rather than less, attention to what is happening in their world. According to the American Psychological Association, the girlie-girl culture's emphasis on beauty and play-sexiness can increase girls' vulnerability to the pitfalls that most concern parents: depression, eating disorders, distorted body image, risky sexual behavior. In one study of eighth-grade girls, for instance, self-objectification—judging your body by how you think it looks to others— accounted for half the differential in girls' reports of depression and more than two-thirds of the variance in their self-esteem. Another linked the focus on appearance among girls that age to heightened shame and anxiety about their bodies. Even brief exposure to the typical, idealized images of women that we all see every day has been shown to lower girls' opinion of themselves, both physically and academically. Nor, as they get older, does the new sexiness lead to greater sexual entitlement. According to Deborah Tolman, a professor at Hunter College who studies teenage girls' desire, "They respond to questions about how their bodies feel—questions about sexuality or arousal—by describing how they think they look. I have to remind them that looking good is *not* a feeling."

All of that does not suddenly kick in when a girl blows out the candles on her thirteenth birthday cake. From the time she is born—in truth, well before—parents are bombarded with zillions of little decisions, made consciously or not, that will shape their daughter's ideas and understanding of her femininity, her sexuality, her self. How do you instill pride and resilience in her? Do you shower her with pink heart-strewn onesies? Reject the Disney Princess Pull-Ups for Lightning McQueen? Should you let your three-year-old wear her child-friendly nail polish to preschool? What's your policy on the latest Disney Channel "it" girl? Old Dora versus New Dora? Does a pink soccer ball celebrate girlhood? Do pink TinkerToys expand or contract its definition? And even if you think the message telegraphed by a pink Scrabble set with tiles on the box top that spell "F-A-S-H-I-O-N" is a tad retrograde, what are you supposed to do about it? Lock your daughter in a tower? Rely on the tedious "teachable moment" in which Mom natters on about how if Barbie were life-sized she'd pitch forward smack onto her bowling ball boobs (cue the eye rolling, please)?

Answering such questions has, surprisingly, become *more* complicated since the mid-1990s, when the war whoop of "Girl Power" celebrated ability over body. Somewhere along the line, that message became its own opposite. The pursuit of physical perfection was recast as a source—often *the* source—of young women's "empowerment." Rather than freedom *from* traditional constraints, then, girls were now free *to* "choose" them. Yet the line between "get to" and "have to" blurs awfully fast. Even as new educational and professional opportunities unfurl before my daughter and her peers, so does the path that encourages them to equate identity with image, self-expression with appearance, femininity with performance, pleasure with pleasing, and sexuality with sexualization. It feels both easier and harder to raise a girl in that new reality—and easier and harder to be one.

I didn't know whether Disney Princesses would be the first salvo in a Hundred Years' War of dieting, plucking, and painting (and perpetual dissatisfaction with the results). But for me they became a trigger for the larger question of how to help our daughters with the contradictions they will inevitably face as girls, the dissonance that is as endemic as ever to growing up female. It seemed, then, that I was not done, not only with the princesses but with the whole culture of little girlhood: what it had become, how it had changed in the decades since I was a child, what those changes meant, and how to navigate them as a parent.

I'm the first to admit that I do not have all the answers. Who could? But as a mother who also happens to be a journalist (or perhaps vice versa), I believed it was important to lay out the context—the marketing, science, history, culture—in which we make our choices, to provide information that would help parents to approach their decisions more wisely.

So I returned to the land of Disney, but I also traveled to American Girl Place and the American International Toy Fair (the industry's largest trade show, where all the hot new products are introduced). I trolled Pottery Barn Kids and Toys "R" Us. I talked to historians, marketers, psychologists, neuroscientists, parents, and children themselves. I considered the value of the original fairy tales; pondered the meaning of child beauty pageants; went online as a "virtual" girl; even attended a Miley Cyrus concert (so you know I was dedicated). And I faced down my own confusion as a mother, as a woman, about the issues that raising a girl raises in me about my own femininity.

As with all of us, what I want for my daughter seems so simple: for her to grow up healthy, happy, and confident, with a clear sense of her own potential and the opportunity to fulfill it. Yet she lives in a world that tells her, whether she is three or thirty-three, that the surest way to get there is to look, well, like Cinderella.

But I'm getting ahead of myself. Let's go back and begin where all good stories start.

Once upon a time.

Chapter Two

What's Wrong with Cinderella?

When Daisy was three, I lost her. Or, more precisely, I allowed her to get lost. She dashed off into the crowd at a reception after my niece's bat mitzvah, and I did not stop her. How much trouble could she get into, I reasoned: there were at least fifty Jewish mothers in the room. On the other hand, there was also a steep flight of marble stairs, doors that opened onto a dark parking lot leading to a reedy swamp, and a kitchen full of unattended chefs' knives. So when twenty minutes passed and she hadn't checked in, I began to get a little edgy. Okay, I panicked.

I pushed through the crowd shouting her name, leaving riled-up grandmothers in my wake. Then one of my niece's friends tugged at my sleeve. "She's over there," the girl said, pointing to a knot of ten or so teenagers.

I still did not see my child. So I stepped closer and peered over a boy's shoulder. There was Daisy, lying on the ground, her arms folded corpselike across her chest, her lips pursed, her expression somber.

"What about Isaac?" asked a girl, pushing forward a skinny six-year-old boy.

Without opening her eyes, Daisy shook her head.

"Michael?" a second girl tried. Another terse shake.

"Jeff?" Again the wordless dismissal.

I asked the boy in front of me what was going on.

"She's Snow White," he explained. "She ate the poison apple, and now we're trying to find the right prince to wake her."

I had never told Daisy the story of Snow White. I had purposely kept it from her because, even setting aside the obvious sexism, Snow herself is such an incredible pill. Her sole virtue, as far as I can tell, is tidiness—she is forever scrubbing, dusting, nagging the dwarves to wash their filthy mitts. (Okay, the girl has an ear for a catchy melody, I'll give you that. But that's where it ends.) She is everything I imagined my daughter would reject, would not, in fact, ever encounter or even understand if she did, let alone embrace: the passive, personality-free princess swept off by a prince (who is enchanted solely by her beauty) to live in a happily-ever-after that he ultimately controls. Yet here was my girl, somehow having learned the plotline anyway, blissfully lying in wait for Love's First Kiss.

Daisy lifted a hand. *"Harry!"* she announced. *"Harry* has to be the prince." Two girls instantly peeled off to search for her eleven-year-old cousin, while everyone else remained standing there, gazing at my princess, enthralled.

She was so confident of their presence that she still hadn't opened her eyes.

ᕲᜃᜃᕲ

God knows, I was a Disney kid. I still have my bona fide mouse ears from 1970, monogrammed with an embroidered, loopy yellow PEGGY. I wore out my Close 'n Play on my Magic Mirror storybook records of *Peter Pan*, *Alice in Wonderland*, and even *Cinderella*. But until I had a daughter, I had never heard of the Disney Princesses. As a concept, I mean. It turns out there was a reason for that. They did not exist until 2000. That's when a former Nike executive named Andy Mooney rode into Disney on a metaphoric white horse to rescue its ailing consumer products division.

I spoke with Mooney one day in his fittingly palatial office in Burbank, California. In a rolling Scottish burr that was pretty darned Charming, he told me the now-legendary story: how, about a month into his tenure, he had flown to Phoenix to check out a "Disney on Ice" show and found himself surrounded by little girls in princess costumes. Princess costumes that were— horrors!—*homemade*. How had such a massive branding opportunity been overlooked? The very next day he called together his team and they began working on what would become known in-house as "Princess." It was a risky move: Disney had never marketed its characters separately from a film's release, and old-timers like Roy Disney considered it heresy to lump together those from different stories. That is why, these days, when the ladies appear on the same item, they never make eye contact. Each stares off in a slightly different direction, as if unaware of the others' presence. Now that I have told you, you'll always notice it. And let me tell you, it's freaky.

It is also worth noting that not all of the eight DPs are of royal extraction. Part of the genius of "Princess," Mooney admitted, is that its meaning is so broadly constructed that it actually has no meaning. Even Tinker Bell was originally a Princess, though her reign did not last. Meanwhile, although Mulan (the protofeminist young woman who poses as a boy to save China) and Pocahontas (an Indian chief's daughter) are officially part of the club, I defy you to find them in the stores. They were, until late 2009, the brownest-skinned princesses, as well as the ones with the least bling potential. You can gussy up Pocahontas's eagle feathers only so much. As for Mulan, when she does show up, it's in a kimono-like *hanfu*, the one that makes her miserable in the movie, rather than in her warrior's gear. Really, when you're talking Princess, you're talking Cinderella, Sleeping Beauty, Ariel, and Belle (the "modern" Princess, whose story shows that the right woman can turn a beast into a prince). Snow White and Jasmine are in the pantheon, too, though slightly less popular.

The first Princess items, released with no marketing plan, no focus groups, no advertising, sold as if blessed by a fairy godmother. Within a year, sales had soared to $300 million. By 2009, they were at $4 billion. Four *billion* dollars! There are more than twenty-six thousand Disney Princess items on the market, a number which, particularly when you exclude cigarettes, liquor, cars, and antidepressants, is staggering. "Princess" has not only become the fastest-growing brand the company has ever created, it is the largest franchise on the planet for girls ages two to six.

To this day, Disney conducts little market research on the Princess line, relying instead on the power of its legacy among mothers as well as the instant-read sales barometer of the theme parks and Disney Stores (Tiana, the much-ballyhooed "first African-American Princess," was somewhat of an exception, but we will get to her in a later chapter). "We simply gave girls what they wanted," Mooney said of the line's success, "although I don't think any of us grasped how much they wanted this. I wish I could sit here and take credit for having some grand scheme to develop this, but all we did was envision a little girl's room and think about how she could live out the princess fantasy. The counsel we gave to licensees was: What type of bedding would a princess want to sleep in? What kind of alarm clock would a princess want to wake up to? What type of television would a princess like to see? It's a rare case where you find a girl who has every aspect of her room bedecked in Princess, but if she ends up with three or four of these items, well, then, you have a very healthy business." Healthy, indeed. It has become nearly impossible for girls of a certain age *not* to own a few Princess trinkets. Even in our home, where neither Steven nor I have personally purchased a Princess item, several coloring books, a set of pencils, a Snow White doll, and a blow-up mattress have managed to infiltrate.

Meanwhile, by 2001, Mattel had brought out its own "world of girl" line of princess Barbie dolls, DVDs, toys, clothing, home decor, and myriad other products. At a time when Barbie sales were declining domestically, they became instant best sellers. Even Dora the Explorer, the intrepid, dirty-kneed adventurer, ascended to the throne: in 2004, after a two-part episode in which she turns into a "true princess," the Nickelodeon and Viacom consumer products division released a satin-gowned Magic Hair Fairytale Dora with hair that grows or shortens when her crown is touched. Among other phrases the bilingual doll utters: "Vámonos! Let's go to fairy-tale land!" and "Will you brush my hair?"

I do not question that little girls like to play princess: as a child, I certainly availed myself of my mom's cast-off rhinestone tiara from time to time. But when you're talking about 26,000 items (and that's just Disney), it's a little hard to say where "want" ends and "coercion" begins. Mooney was prepared for that concern and for my overall discomfort with the Princesses, who, particularly in his consumer products versions, are all about clothes, jewelry, makeup, and snaring a handsome husband.

"Look," he said, "I have friends whose son went through the Power Rangers phase who castigated themselves over what they must've done wrong. Then they talked to other parents whose kids had gone through it. The boy passes through. The girl passes through. I see girls expanding their imagination through visualizing themselves as princesses, and then they pass through that phase and end up becoming lawyers, doctors, mothers, or princesses, whatever the case may be."

He had a point. I have never seen a study proving that playing princess *specifically* damages girls' self-esteem or dampens other aspirations. And trust me, I've looked. There is, however, ample evidence that the more mainstream media girls consume, the more importance they place on being pretty and sexy. And a ream of studies shows that teenage girls and college students who hold conventional beliefs about femininity—especially those that emphasize beauty and pleasing behavior—are less ambitious and more likely to be depressed than their peers. They are also less likely to report that they enjoy sex or insist that their partners use condoms. None of that bodes well for Snow White's long-term mental health.

Perhaps you are now picturing poor, hapless girls who are submissive, low-achieving, easily influenced: the kind whose hair hangs in front of their faces as they recede into the background.

I know I have a hard time connecting such passivity to my own vibrant, vital daughter. Yet even can-do girls can be derailed—and surprisingly quickly—by exposure to stereotypes. Take the female college students, all good at math, all enrolled in advanced calculus, who were asked to view a series of television commercials: four neutral ads (showing, say, cell phones or animals) were interspersed with two depicting clichés (a girl in raptures over acne medicine; a woman drooling over a brownie mix). Afterward they completed a survey and—*bing!*—the group who'd seen the stereotyped ads expressed less interest in math- and science-related careers than classmates who had seen only the neutral ones. Let me repeat: the effect was demonstrable after watching *two ads.* And guess who performed better on a math test, coeds who took it after being asked to try on a bathing suit or those who had been asked to try on a sweater? (Hint: the latter group; interestingly, male students showed no such disparity.)

Meanwhile, according to a 2006 survey of more than two thousand school-aged children, girls repeatedly described a paralyzing pressure to be "perfect": not only to get straight As and be the student body president, editor of the newspaper, and captain of the swim team but also to be "kind and caring," "please everyone, be very thin, and dress right." Rather than living the dream, then, those girls were straddling a contradiction: struggling to fulfill all the new expectations we have for them without letting go of the old ones. Instead of feeling greater latitude and choice in how to be female—which is what one would hope—they now feel they must not only "have it all" but *be* it all: Cinderella *and* Supergirl. Aggressive *and* agreeable. Smart *and* stunning. Does that make them the beneficiaries of new opportunities or victims of a massive con job?

The answer is yes. That is, both are true, and that is what's so insidious. It would be one thing if the goal were more realistic or if girls were stoked about creating a new femininity, but it's not and they aren't. The number of girls who fretted excessively about their looks and weight actually *rose* between 2000 and 2006 (topping their concern over schoolwork), as did their reported stress levels and their rates of depression and suicide. It is as if the more girls achieve the more obsessed they become with appearance—not dissimilar to the way the ideal of the "good mother" was ratcheted up just as adult women flooded the workforce. In her brilliant book *Enlightened Sexism*, Susan Douglas refers to this as the bargain girls and women strike, the price of success, the way they unconsciously defuse the threat their progress poses to male dominance. "We can excel in school, play sports, go to college, aspire to—and get—jobs previously reserved for men, be working mothers, and so forth. But in exchange we must obsess about our faces, weight, breast size, clothing brands, decorating, perfectly calibrated child-rearing, about pleasing men and being envied by other women."

A new banner unfurled over the entrance of Daisy's preschool when I dropped by one fall morning: a little girl, adorned with a glittering plastic-and-rhinestone tiara and matching earrings, grinned down from it. WELCOME TO OUR CAMPUS, the banner read. The image might have irritated me in any case—even my kid's *school* had bought into the idea that all girls should aspire to the throne—but what was really cringe-making was the fact that this was part of a Jewish temple. When I was growing up, the last thing you wanted to be called was a "princess": it conjured up images of a spoiled, self-centered brat with a freshly bobbed nose who runs to "Daddy" at the least provocation. The Jewish American Princess was the repository for my community's self-hatred, its ambivalence over assimilation—it was Jews turning against their girls as a way to turn against themselves. Was this photograph a sign we had so transcended the *Goodbye, Columbus* stereotype that we could now embrace it?

"What about Queen Esther?" asked Julie, the mother of one of Daisy's classmates, when I questioned the picture's subtext. "She saved the Jewish people. Shouldn't girls try to be like her?"

Julie, a forty-five-year-old owner of a Web consulting company, was among several mothers I had asked to join me after drop-off for a chat about princess culture. Each one had a preschool-aged daughter obsessed with Disney royalty. They also knew I had my qualms about the subject, which they did not necessarily share. I wanted to know, from a mother's perspective, why they allowed—in some cases even encouraged—their girls to play princess. Did they think it was innocuous? Beneficial? Worrisome? Healthy?

"I think feminism erred in the 1960s by negating femininity," announced Mara, a thirty-six-year-old education consultant who was currently home with her kids. Her voice sounded tight, almost defiant. "That was a mistake. I want my daughter to have a strong identity as a girl, as a woman, as a *female*. And being pretty in our culture is very important. I don't want her to ever doubt that she's pretty. So if she wants to wear a princess dress and explore that side of herself, I don't want to stand in the way."

She folded her arms and collapsed back on her chair, as if she had said her piece. But before I could respond, she cocked her head and added, "On the other hand, I also have a son, and we really encourage his intelligence. I worry about that. A reward for her is 'You look so pretty, you look so beautiful.' People tell her that all the time, and we do, too. We tell *him*, 'You're so smart.'"

Dana, a thirty-eight-year-old stay-at-home mom, who had been watching Mara with a slightly awestruck expression, spoke up. "For me it's a matter of practicality," she said. "Having those Disney Princess outfits around the house is really helpful for the endless playdates. And Eleanor loves to swim, so she identifies with Ariel."

I began to ask Dana how she felt about the rest of the *Little Mermaid* story, but she cut me off. "Oh, I don't let the actual *story* in the house," she said. "Just the *costumes*. Eleanor doesn't know the stories."

That turned out to be Mara's policy, too. The issue to her was not princesses, it was plotlines. "Those stories are horrible," she said, making a face. "Every single one is the same: it's about romance, love, and being rescued by the prince. I *will* protect my daughter from that."

Thinking back on my own girl's inexplicable acquaintance with the Snow White story, I had to wonder whether that was possible. I'd believed I could keep out the tales *and* the toys but had failed on both counts. What were the odds, then, that you could permit one without the other? I had spent a lot of time with Dana's daughter and already knew she could give a full recitation of Ariel's story. Dana shrugged. "Well, yeah, she hears it from her friends," she admitted. "But at least not at home."

What gave those mothers pause, then, was the fantasy the stories promoted that a man would take care of you. Yet the tales also provide the characters with some context, a narrative arc. Cinderella may ride off with the prince, but before that, she spends much of her time dressed in tatters, offering children object lessons about kindness, forbearance, and humility. Without that backstory, what was left? What did they imagine a storyless "princess" represented to the girls?

That's when Julie piped up. "I think it's all about being looked at," she said, "being admired. And about special treatment." She rolled her eyes. "Receiving it, not giving it."

"And it's *fun*," Dana pointed out.

Hell, yeah, it's fun. Who doesn't love nail polish with flower appliqués? Who doesn't like to play dress-up now and again, swoosh about in silk and velvet? Daisy once whispered conspiratorially to me, "Mom, did you know that girls can choose all kinds of things to wear, but boys can only wear pants?" There it was: dressing up fancy, at least for now, was something she felt she *got* to do, not something she *had* to do. It was a source of power and privilege, much like her game of Snow White in which the action revolved around and was controlled by her.

Whereas boys . . . even here in Berkeley, a friend's seven-year-old son was teased so ruthlessly about his new, beloved pink bike that within a week he refused to ride it. It is quite possible that boys, too, would wear sequins if only they could. Isabelle Cherney, a professor of psychology at Creighton University, found that nearly half of boys aged five to thirteen, when ushered alone into a room and told they could play with anything, chose "girls'" toys as frequently as "boys'"—provided they believed nobody would find out. Particularly, their fathers: boys as young as four said their daddies would think it was "bad" if they played with "girls'" toys, even something as innocuous as miniature dishes. Boys were also more likely to sort playthings based on how they perceived gender roles (such as "Dad uses tools, so hammers are for boys"), whereas girls figured that if they themselves enjoyed a toy—*any* toy—it was, ipso facto, for girls. So it seems that, even as they have loosened up on their daughters, dads continue to vigorously police masculinity in their sons. I believe it: consider the progressive pal of mine who proudly showed off the Hot Wheels set he had bought for his girl but balked when his boy begged for a tutu. Who's to say, then, which sex has greater freedom?

I am almost willing to buy that argument: that boys are the ones who are more limited; that little girls *need* to feel beautiful; that being on display, being admired for how they look, is critical to their developing femininity and fragile self-esteem; that princess sets their imaginations soaring; that its popularity is evidence that we've moved past 1970s feminist rigidity. Except that, before meeting with the preschool moms, I had flipped through a stack of drawings each child in Daisy's class had made to complete the sentence "If I were a [blank], I'd [blank] to the store." (One might say, for instance, "If I were a ball, I'd bounce to the store.") The boys had chosen to be a whole host of things: firemen, spiders, superheroes, puppies, tigers, birds, athletes, raisins. The girls fell into exactly four camps: princess, fairy, butterfly, and ballerina (one especially enthusiastic girl claimed them all: a "princess, butterfly, fairy ballerina"). How, precisely, does that, as Disney's Andy Mooney suggested, expand their horizons? The boys seemed to be exploring the world; the girls were exploring femininity. What they "got" to do may have been uniquely theirs, but it was awfully circumscribed. "Yeah, I was surprised," the teacher admitted when I asked about it. "The girls had so little range in their ideas. We tried to encourage them to choose other things, but they wouldn't."

Of course, girls are not buying the 24/7 princess culture all on their own. So the question is not only why *they* like it (which is fairly obvious) but what it offers their parents. Julie may have been onto something on that front: princesses are, by definition, special, elevated creatures. And don't we all feel our girls are extraordinary, unique, and beautiful? Don't we want them to share that belief for as long as possible, to think that—just by their existence, by birthright—they are the chosen ones? Wouldn't we like their lives to be forever charmed, infused with magic and sparkle? I know I want that for my daughter.

Or do I? Among other things, princesses tend to be rather isolated in their singularity. Navigating the new world of friendships is what preschool is all about, yet the DPs, you will recall, won't even *look* at one another. Daisy had only one fight with her best friend during their three years of preschool—a conflict so devastating that, at pickup time, I found the other girl sobbing in the hallway, barely able to breathe. The source of their disagreement? My darling daughter had insisted that there could be only *one* Cinderella in their games—only *one* girl who reigned supreme—and it was she. Several hours and a small tantrum later, she apologized to the girl, saying that from now on there could be *two* Cinderellas. But the truth was, Daisy had gotten it right the first time: there *is* only one princess in the Disney tales, one girl who gets to be exalted. Princesses may confide in a sympathetic mouse or teacup, but, at least among the best-known stories, they do not have girlfriends. God forbid Snow White should give Sleeping Beauty a little support.

Let's review: princesses avoid female bonding. Their goals are to be saved by a prince, get married (among the DP picture books at Barnes & Noble: *My Perfect Wedding* and *Happily Ever After Stories*) and be taken care of for the rest of their lives. Their value derives largely from their appearance. They are rabid materialists. They *might* affect your daughter's interest in math. And yet . . . parents cannot resist them. Princesses seem to have tapped into our unspoken, nonrational wishes. They may also assuage our fears: Cinderella and Sleeping Beauty may be sources of comfort, of stability in a rapidly changing world. Our daughters will shortly be tweeting and Facebooking and doing things that have yet to be invented, things that are beyond our ken. Princesses are uncomplicated, classic, something solid that we can understand and share with them, even if they are a bit problematic. They provide a way to play with our girls that is similar to how we played, a common language of childhood fun. That certainly fits into what Disney found in a survey of preschool girls' mothers: rather than "beautiful," the women more strongly associate princesses with "creating fantasy," "inspiring," "compassionate."

And "safe." That one piqued my interest. By "safe," I would wager that they mean that being a Princess fends off premature sexualization, or what parents often refer to as the pressure "to grow up too soon." There is that undeniable sweetness, that poignancy of seeing girls clomp off to the "ball" in their incongruous heels and gowns. They are so gleeful, so guileless, so delightfully delighted. The historian Gary Cross, who writes extensively on childhood and consumption, calls such parental response "wondrous innocence." Children's wide-eyed excitement over the products we buy them pierces through our own boredom as consumers and as adults, reconnecting us to our childhoods: it makes us *feel* again. The problem is that our very dependence on our children's joy erodes it: over time, they become as jaded as we are by new purchases—perhaps more so. They rebel against the "cuteness" in which we've indulged them—and, if we're honest, imposed upon them—by taking on the studied irony and indifferent affect of "cool."

Though both boys and girls engage in that cute-to-cool trajectory, for girls specifically, being "cool" means looking hot. Given that, then, there may indeed be, or at least *could* be, a link between princess diadems and Lindsay Lohan's panties (or lack thereof). But in the short term, when you're watching your preschooler earnestly waving her wand, it sure doesn't feel that way. To the contrary: princess play feels like proof of our daughters' innocence, protection against the sexualization it may actually be courting. It reassures us that, despite the pressure to be precocious, little girls are still—and ever will be—little girls. And that knowledge restores our faith not only in wonder but, quite possibly, in goodness itself. Recall that the current princess craze took off right around the terrorist attacks of September 11, 2001, and continued its rise through the recession: maybe, as another cultural historian suggested to me, the desire to encourage our girls' imperial fantasies is, at least in part, a reaction to a newly unstable world. We *need* their innocence not only for consumerist but for *spiritual* redemption.

Sound far-fetched? This is not the first time princess obsession has cropped up during a time of societal crisis. The original European fairy tales rose from a medieval culture that faced all manner of economic and social upheaval. Frances Hodgson Burnett's book *A Little Princess* was published in 1905, a time of rapid urbanization, immigration, and spiraling poverty; Shirley Temple's film version was a hit during the Great Depression. Little Shirley may actually be the ultimate example of girlish innocence conferring adult salvation (with the comic pages' *Little Orphan Annie* a close second). A mere six years old when she starred in her first film, with her irrepressible, childlike optimism she gave Americans hope during a desperate era: President Franklin Roosevelt even reportedly proclaimed, "As long as our country has Shirley Temple, we will be all right." Imagine! Her cinematic formula—which typically included at least one dead parent so adults in the audience could project themselves into that vacant role—put her at the top of the box office for three years running, beating out Clark Gable, Joan Crawford, and Gary Cooper. She remains the most popular child star of all time. She also became the first celebrity aggressively marketed to little girls. During the height of her fame, there were Shirley Temple songbooks, handkerchiefs, jewelry, handbags, sewing cards, coloring books, soap, mugs, dresses, hair bows, records—anything that could carry her image did, and the appetite for her seemed endless. Like the Disney Princesses, the first Shirley Temple doll was released independently of a movie—in time for Christmas 1934. Within a year, it accounted for a third of all doll sales. Another doll, released to coincide with both a film and Shirley's eighth birthday, was, according to the company that manufactured it, "the biggest non-Christmas toy event in history." Though I doubt parents in that era were (consciously or not) trying to prolong girls' innocence through those dolls, they were surely celebrating it—perhaps, after a fashion, even feeding off it: if Shirley herself gave the country's morale a boost during hard times, perhaps her likeness, cradled in the arms of a beaming daughter, gave heart to individual families.

Unlike animated royalty, however, Shirley Temple was a flesh-and-blood girl, whose reign could not go on indefinitely—she had no choice but to relinquish the crown once she entered puberty. What's more, unlike much of today's princess schlock, Shirley Temple dolls were synonymous with quality: they ran a whopping $4.49, which was almost quadruple the price of competing dolls. In that way, they were less like the Disney Princesses and closer to what seems—at least at first glance—like the princess antidote: the upscale, down-to-earth American Girl collection.

Ten-year-old Sophie is no longer into American Girl. That's what her mother, my friend Karen, reported apologetically when I invited them to join me for a jaunt to American Girl Place, the brand's Mecca-like store in Manhattan. Eventually Sophie agreed to go, if reluctantly. For research. Because, as I said, she was no longer into American Girl. She was no longer into it—until she got there.

American Girl Place, which sits on the corner of Fifth Avenue and 49th Street, across from Saks, contains three stories of dolls, dresses, books, and the most cunning miniature furniture you have ever seen. It houses a doll hospital (where, after "treatment," repaired dolls are returned with a hospital gown, an identification bracelet, a "Get Well Soon" balloon, and a certificate of good health) and a hair salon (where stylists strap dolls into tiny barber's chairs for facials and new 'dos). There is also a café, where I had cadged a coveted reservation for the three of us plus Sophie's doll Kaya.

There was no line around the block when we arrived, as there routinely had been several years before when the store first opened, but, on a dreary winter afternoon, there were still throngs of little girls streaming in, most of them already clutching dolls or toting them in specially designed backpacks.

"Mama, *look*!" Sophie cried, pointing to a blue wrought-iron daybed with butterfly-themed linen and its own trundle.

"Sophie, *look*!" Karen replied half jokingly, pointing at a book with a pink-and-turquoise cover titled *Clutter Control.*

Sophie ignored her, looking eagerly around. "Can I get *two* things?" she asked.

"Let's see what you choose," Karen said firmly. But Sophie was already running toward the escalator to check out the second floor.

American Girl was born in 1986, started by a former teacher, TV reporter, and textbook editor named—I kid you not—Pleasant Rowland. Pleasant conceived of her dolls one holiday season while shopping for presents for her nieces. Every doll she saw seemed to be either cheaply made, unattractive, or fashion-obsessed. And nothing, she felt, communicated "anything about what it meant to be a girl growing up in America." Rather than a bucket of Barbies, Rowland dreamed of offering girls a doll they would treasure, that would forge a bond between mothers and daughters, that could even become an heirloom, passed from generation to generation. She wanted her dolls to offer an alternative, morally inspiring vision of girlhood, one that would, in the process, express her own passion for history. The American Girl dolls in the historical line, then, represented different eras in the country's past: among them were Kirsten, "a pioneer girl of strength and spirit"; Felicity, "a spunky Colonial girl"; Addy, a "courageous girl" who escapes slavery (who is still the *only* black girl in the historical line); and Kaya, Sophie's doll, a Nez Percé Indian from the mid–eighteenth century. The dolls are eighteen inches high with notably realistic, childlike proportions—no Barbie bosoms here, though at a hefty $110 per doll, they are also up to twenty times as expensive. Six books (purchased separately) tell each doll's story. Their worlds can be re-created with astonishingly detailed period clothing, furniture, and other paraphernalia. The kit for Kit, a Depression-era girl who dreams of being a journalist, includes a miniature "reporter's set" with an authentic-looking leather-bound notebook, tiny pencil, and eraser; a period camera (complete with box of Kodak film and five preshot photos); and a stack of newspapers, tied with twine, showing her byline splashed across the front page.

Be still, my heart! I thought, leaning in to get a closer look.

Eavesdropping as we strolled through the store, I noticed that, like me, the mothers were captivated by the tiny jars of canned peaches, the realistic 1930s cookstove, the wee 1940s-style chifforobe with its faux cut-glass mirrors and hanging quilted dress bag.

The girls, on the other hand, were into the clothes.

"I want the pink dress!" a blond four-year-old screeched twenty-four times in the space of thirty seconds. Her mother finally grabbed it off the rack.

The formula was brilliant: moms were hooked by the patina of homespun values and the *Antique Road Show* aesthetic of the accessories; then the girls angled for fashions. Most walked out laden with some of each.

By 1998, the Pleasant Company was pulling down more than $300 million in annual sales. That year brought two changes: the first American Girl Place opened (the dolls had previously been sold exclusively through mail order), and Pleasant sold her empire to Mattel—the maker of the same disposable doll she had been trying to combat. You can't really blame the woman, though: who wouldn't compromise an ideal or two for a $700 million payday? Mattel has since added the Just Like You line, which jettisons the historical format, letting girls customize dolls with hair, eye color, and skin tone that matches their own (outfits and furnishings to bring the dolls' "stories" alive sold separately). They also partnered with Bath & Body Works to produce a Real Beauty product line, though that did not last: maybe even Mattel recognized the contradiction in telling an eight-year-old that a perfume called "Truly Me" would help her feel good about "just being yourself."

Before my visit, I was familiar with American Girl only through the books, which I had flipped through at the public library. The titles in each series are identical: *Meet* [doll's name];

[doll's name] *Learns a Lesson*; [doll's name]*'s Surprise*; *Happy Birthday,* [doll's name]; [doll's name] *Saves the Day*; and *Changes for* [doll's name]. In one typical story, Molly, a "loveable, patriotic girl growing up on the home front during World War II" whose father is fighting in Europe, plays a series of pranks on her pesky brother. Eventually the stakes escalate, and she learns that peace can be harder than war. Our heroines may confront a smidgen of sexism, racism, or even, on occasion, tragedy, but nothing a little pluck and ingenuity can't conquer. Which is fine with me: it's not as though I would want my seven-year-old exposed to the details of the Triangle Shirtwaist Factory fire. Reading the books, though, I was struck by their presentation of the past as a time not only in which girls were improbably independent, feisty, and apparently without constraint but, in a certain way, in which they were *more* free than they are today: a time when their character mattered more than their clothing, when a girl's actions were more important than how she looked or what she owned—a time before girlhood was consumed and defined by consumerism. I found myself comparing Kit, the courageous, impoverished Depression-era girl who is committed to becoming a muckraking reporter, to Yasmin, a character from Bratz.com, which competes for the same six- to eleven-year-old demographic: Yasmin has "got a lot of strong opinions and loves to share them," "enjoys curling up with a cool autobiography about celebs she admires," and blogs about "staying involved with your community while still doing fun things like getting makeovers."

Suddenly American Girl's price tag didn't look so bad.

And maybe it wouldn't be, if the doll and books were the end of it. But that little cookstove would set you back $68 and the chifforobe another $175. For *doll* furniture. Therein lies the paradox of American Girl: the books preach against materialism, but you could blow the college fund on the gear. In fact, Kit, Addy, Molly, and their friends could never afford the dolls that represent them—an irony that became particularly piquant in fall 2009 with the introduction of Gwen, a $95 limited-edition doll who was supposed to be *homeless*. The truth is, I asked Sophie and Karen to join me on this outing because Daisy had not yet heard about American Girl, and I was not eager to hasten her discovery. It's not that I object to the dolls, exactly, and I surely understand supporting a girl's interest in the line, but I would prefer to stave it off, if not avoid it entirely: there has to be a less expensive way to encourage old-fashioned values.

We headed up the escalator to the café, a black-and-white-striped confection iced with pink daisies and whimsical mirrors. Inside, dolls were seated in clip-on "treat seats" and given their own striped cups and saucers. *Everything* was for sale: the doll seat ($24), the tea set ($16), the pot that held the daisies ($8). All around us mothers were smiling, nibbling their quiche, reveling in this New York reprieve from the pressures of Paris (Hilton, that is). While my gaze was elsewhere, Sophie took a bite of a cucumber slice and slipped it onto Kaya's plate, then pretended the doll had eaten it. She was ten years old but, swept away by the moment, was willing to believe in the kind of magic she already knew was not real. They might as well have put up a sign: check your cynicism at the door. I was happy to comply.

Almost. It turned out that Kaya, like Disney's Pocahontas, did not inspire a lot in the way of outfits or accessories. Not fun. Sophie asked if she could buy a new doll using money she had been saving from her birthday and allowance. Karen hesitated—this was the child who wasn't "into" American Girl anymore—but then agreed. She even sprang for matching girl-doll outfits ($107) as well as a $20 salon appointment for Kaya. Then she bought the daybed and trundle ($68) because, well . . . even Karen didn't know why. "I can't believe I'm succumbing!" she moaned. When we got to the cash register, she was told the butterfly bedding was sold separately—for another $26. Karen sighed in disgust. "Are you writing this down?" she said to me. She turned to the salesclerk. "Okay, I'll get the bedding."

She slapped down her AmEx. "My husband is going to think I've lost my mind," she muttered.

I glanced across the street to the window display at Saks Fifth Avenue. It held a hypnotically spinning red-and-white-striped disc with two words in the center in tall black letters: WANT IT. The same phrase ran endlessly around the window's edge. At least, I thought, that store was up front about its agenda.

Pleasant Rowland herself has called the dolls something mothers can "do" for their girls. But as Sophie, Karen, and I trudged eastward on 49th Street, our arms weighted down by giant shopping bags, it occurred to me that you don't "do" $500 worth of merchandise. You buy it. It is a peculiar inversion: the simplicity of American Girl is expensive, while the finery of Princess comes cheap. In the end, though, the appeal to parents is the same: both lines tacitly promise to keep girls young and "safe" from sexualization. Yet they also introduce them to a consumer culture that will ultimately encourage the opposite—one in which Mattel and Disney (the parent companies, respectively, of the two brands) play a major role. Both Princess and American Girl promote shopping as the path to intimacy between mothers and daughters; as an expression, even for five-year-olds, of female identity. Both, above all, are selling innocence. And nothing illustrates the gold mine it has become—or the contradictions it represents—better than the color pink.

Chapter Three

Pinked!

*t*he annual Toy Fair at New York's Javits Center is the industry's largest trade show, with 100,000 products spread over 350,000 feet of exhibition space. And I swear, at *least* 75,000 of those items were pink. I lost count of the myriad pink wands and crowns (feathered, sequined, and otherwise bedazzled) and infinite permutations of pink poodles in purses (with names like Pucci Pups, Fancy Schmancy, Sassy Pets, Pawparazzi . . .). The Disney Princesses reigned over a new pink Royal Interactive Kitchen with accompanying pink Royal Appliances and pink Royal Pots and Pans set (though I would have thought one of the perks of monarchy would be that someone else did the cooking). There were pink dinnerware sets emblazoned with the word PRINCESS; pink fun fur stoles and boas; pink princess beds; pink diaries (embossed with PRINCESS, BALLE-RINA, or butterflies); pink jewelry boxes; pink vanity mirrors, pink brushes, and toy pink blow-dryers; pink telephones; pink bunny ears; pink gowns; pink height charts; a pink Princess and the Pea board game (one square instructed, "Wave like a princess, pretty as you can be"); My Little Pink Book Board Game ("a cool game for girls in which they secretly choose a dream date from their Little Pink Book of guys and then try to be the first to guess who everyone else is dating"); and a pink toy washing machine. All of those, however, were perhaps to be expected. Less explicable were the pink spy kits; pink roll-aboard suitcases; pink cameras; a giant pink plush squid (which, from behind, looked exactly like a giant penis); a pink plush boa constrictor; a pink plush beanstalk (or really *any* plush beanstalk); pink rocking horses; pink cow-girl hats ("There's something wrong here," I heard one toy store buyer comment, "it needs rhinestones or glitter or something to sell"); pink gardening gloves; pink electric pianos; pink punching balls; pink gumball machines (with pink gumballs); pink kites; pink pool toys; pink golf clubs, sleds, tricycles, bicycles, scooters, and motorcycles, and even a pink tractor. Oh, and one pink neon bar sign flashing LIVE NUDES.

It's not that pink is intrinsically bad, but it is such a tiny slice of the rainbow, and, though it may celebrate girlhood in one way, it also repeatedly and firmly fuses girls' identity to appearance. Then it presents that connection, even among two-year-olds, not only as innocent but as *evidence* of innocence. Looking around, I despaired at the singular lack of imagination about girls' lives and interests, at the rows and rows of make-your-own jewelry/lip gloss/nail polish/fashion show craft kits at the drumbeat of the consumer feminine.

Pinked!

"Is all this pink really necessary?" I asked a bored-looking sales rep hawking something called Cast and Paint Princess Party.

"Only if you want to make money," he said, chuckling. Then he shrugged. "I guess girls are born loving pink."

Are they? Judging by today's girls, that would seem to be true—the color draws them like heat-seeking missiles. Yet adult women I have asked do not remember being so obsessed with pink as children, nor do they recall it being so pervasively pimped to them. I remember thinking my fuchsia-and-white-striped Danskin shirt with its matching stirrup pants was totally bitchin', but I also loved the same outfit in purple, navy, green, and red (yes, I had them all—there must have been a sale at Sears). My toys spanned the color spectrum, as did my hair ribbons, school notebooks, and lunchboxes. The original Easy-Bake oven, which I begged for (and, dang it, never got), was turquoise, and the Suzy Homemaker line—I had the iron, which really worked!—was teal. I can't imagine you would see that today. What happened? Why has girlhood become so monochromatic?

Girls' attraction to pink may seem unavoidable, somehow en-coded in their DNA, but according to Jo Paoletti, an associate professor of American studies at the University of Maryland, it's not. Children weren't color-coded at all until the early twenti-eth century: in the era before Maytag, all babies wore white as a practical matter, since the only way of getting clothes clean was to boil them. What's more, both boys and girls wore what were thought of as gender-neutral dresses. When nursery colors were introduced, pink was actually considered the more masculine hue, a pastel version of red, which was associated with strength. Blue, with its intimations of the Virgin Mary, constancy, and faithful-ness, symbolized femininity. (That may explain a portrait that has always befuddled me, of my father as an infant in 1926 wearing a pink dress.) Why or when that switched is not clear, but as late as the 1930s, in a poll of its customers conducted by the New York City department store Lord & Taylor, a solid quarter of adults still held to that split. I doubt anyone would get it "wrong" today. Perhaps that is why so many of the early Disney heroines—Cinderella, Sleeping Beauty, Wendy, Alice in Wonderland, *Mary Poppins*'s Jane Banks—were dressed in various shades of azure. (When the company introduced the Princess line, it deliberately changed Sleeping Beauty's gown to pink, supposedly to distinguish her from Cinderella.) It was not until the mid-1980s, when amplifying age and sex differences became a dominant children's marketing strategy, that pink fully came into its own, when it began to seem innately attractive to girls, part of what defined them as female, at least for the first few critical years.

I hadn't realized how profoundly marketing trends dictated our perception of what is natural to kids, including our core beliefs about their psychological development. Take the toddler. I assumed that phase was something experts—people with PhDs at the very least—developed after years of research into children's behavior: wrong-o. Turns out, according to Daniel Cook, a historian of childhood consumerism, it was popularized as a marketing gimmick by clothing manufacturers in the 1930s. Trade publications counseled department stores that, in order to increase sales, they should create a "third stepping-stone" between infant wear and older kids' clothes. They also advised segregating girls' and boys' clothing no later than age two: parents whose sons were "treated like a little man" were thought to be looser with their purse strings. It was only *after* "toddler" became common shoppers' parlance that it evolved into a broadly accepted developmental stage. If that seems impossible to believe, consider the trajectory of "tween," which was also coined, in the mid-1980s, as a marketing contrivance (originally describing children aged eight to fifteen). Within ten years, it was considered a full-blown psychological, physical, and emotional phase, abetted, in no small part, by the classic marketing bible *What Kids Buy and Why*. Its author confidently embedded "tween" in biology and evolution, marked by a child's "shift from right brain focus to left brain focus" and ending with a "neural 'housecleaning'" in which "millions of unmyelinated neurons are literally swept out of existence." Whatever *that* means. Scientifically proven or not, as phases go, "tween" is a conveniently elastic one: depending on who is talking, it now stretches from children as young as seven (when, according to the cosmetic company Bonne Bell, girls become "adept at using a lip gloss wand") to as old as twelve. That is hardly a span that has much common ground—nor, I would argue as a parent, *should* it have.

Splitting kids, or adults, or for that matter penguins, into ever-tinier categories has proved a surefire way to boost profits. So, where there was once a big group that was simply called "kids," we now have toddlers, preschoolers, tweens, young adolescents, and older adolescents, each with their own developmental/marketing profile. For instance, because of their new "perceptual filters," *What Kids Buy and Why* counsels, thirteen- to fifteen-year-olds may still appreciate the wisecracks of Bugs Bunny, but a new passion for "realism" draws them to sports figures such as Michael Jordan; no accident, then, that those two were teamed up to shill for Nike in the mid-1990s. Even children one year old and under are being hailed as "a more informed, influential and compelling audience than ever before." *Informed?* An article published by the Advertising Educational Foundation stated, "Computer interaction and television viewing make this kid segment very savvy, and has led to dramatic changes in today's American families." Children as young as twelve to eighteen months can recognize brands, it went on, and are "strongly influenced" by advertising and marketing. *Yikes!* Meanwhile, I have seen the improbable term "pre-tween" ("pre"-between *what*, exactly?) floated to describe—and target—the five-year-old girl who has a discerning fashion sense and her own Lip Smackers collection.

One of the easiest ways to segment a market is to magnify gender differences—or invent them where they did not previously exist. That explained the token pink or lavender building sets, skateboards, tool belts, and science kits scattered throughout the Toy Fair. (The exception was Tonka, which had given up on girls altogether with its slogan "Boys: They're Just Built Different.") That pinkification could, I suppose, be read as a good-faith attempt at progress. The advent of pink TinkerToys, "designed especially for girls" (who can construct "a flower garden, a butterfly, a microphone and more"), might encourage preschool girls to use mechanical and spatial skills that might otherwise lie fallow. Or it might reinforce the idea that the "real" toy is for boys while that one measly pink Lego kit *in the whole darned store* is girls' consolation prize. It could even remind girls to shun anything that *isn't* pink and pretty as not for them, a mind-set that could eventually prove limiting. And what about the girl who chooses something else? I recalled taking Daisy to the park one day with a friend who had a pink Hello Kitty scooter and matching helmet. Daisy's scooter was silver; her helmet sported a green fire-breathing dragon.

"How come your helmet's not pink?" her friend asked. "It's not a girls' one."

Daisy furrowed her brow, considering, then said, "It's for girls *or* boys." Her friend looked skeptical. Even though I was relieved by Daisy's answer, I found the question itself disturbing. Would other girls view her with suspicion—even exclude her—if she did not display the proper colors? I hoped her friend would get the message and broaden her repertoire. I hoped Daisy would resist the pressure to narrow hers.

⟨∞⟩

I took a break from the Toy Fair and strolled uptown to Times Square, home of the international flagship Toys "R" Us store. Part emporium, part amusement park, the post–FAO Schwarz monolith (Toys "R" Us swallowed up that venerable vendor in 2009) features a three-story neon-lit Ferris wheel at the entrance. Each car has a different theme: *Toy Story*, Mr. and Mrs. Potato Head, Monopoly, a fire truck. There are also a five-ton animatronics T. rex (which scared the bejeezus out of several toddlers during my brief visit), the New York skyline constructed entirely from Legos, and a two-story "Barbie Mansion" painted the iconic Pantone 219, often referred to as "Barbie Pink."

I paused in front of a display of plush Abby Cadabby dolls: throughout the store, I had noted Abby bath sets, costumes, books, party packs, sing-along CDs, backpacks—the typical array of licensed gimcracks. A resident of *Sesame Street*, Abby is a three-year-old "fairy in training" with cotton-candy-colored skin, a button nose, sparkly purple pigtails, pink wings, and a wand. She was launched in 2006; her presence in the neighborhood brought the grand total of female Muppets, after thirty-seven seasons, to five (Miss Piggy was on *The Muppet Show*, not *Sesame Street*, and, by the way, was voiced by Frank Oz, a man).

That in itself is astonishing—*Sesame Street*, which has skillfully tackled differences involving race, language, disability, and culture, can't figure out gender?

Not that it hasn't tried. The show has introduced a new female Muppet nearly every year, only to see them fizzle. Just as with real women, audiences seem to judge them by different standards than the males. "If Cookie Monster was a female character, she'd be accused of being anorexic or bulimic," the show's executive producer, Carol-Lynn Parente, has quipped. And, she added, were he a girl, Elmo's "whimsy" might be misread as "ditziness." But the real fur ceiling has to do with appearance. Lulu, a shy, scruffy-looking monster introduced in 2000, was a flat-out flop—mainly because "she wasn't that attractive" (unlike that dreamboat Grover?). The most successful female Muppet has been Zoe, who was the first character entirely conceived of by Sesame Workshop executives rather than the creative team, as well as the first one intentionally designed to be good-looking. Apparently, though, they did not go far enough. While Zoe is cute, in a radioactive orange kind of way, her release fell short of expectations, the—*ka-ching!*—hope of creating a female Elmo. Even slapping a tutu on her did not help. Perhaps, one of her creators later mused, the problem was that she wasn't pink. The Workshop was not going to make that mistake again. With Abby, every detail was researched, scrutinized, and tested. Designers labored over the size of her nose (large may be funny, but it's not *pretty*) as well as its shape (too snoutlike in one version). Her eyelids were an issue, too—how much should show? In the end, they cover only the outermost part of her exaggerated, circular whites, giving the character a vulnerable, slightly cross-eyed appearance. Her lashes are long and dreamy. Her voice is sibilant, babyish in its pitch, and her catchphrase is "That's so magic!" She practically begs to be hugged.

Workshop executives have denied they created Abby with a licensing bonanza in mind; the fact that she is so infinitely marketable, that she dovetailed precisely with the pink-fairy-princess megatrend among girls, was apparently a mere happy coincidence. Besides, as Liz Nealon, the executive vice president and creative director of Sesame Workshop, has explained, the company was simply following the logic of dramatic convention. "If you think about *The Mary Tyler Moore Show*," she said. "Some girls relate to Rhoda, who's our Zoe, and some girls really relate to Mary, who's a girly girl." I don't know which reruns she's been watching, but the last I checked, that description fit not Mary but the airheaded Georgette—and who wants their daughters "relating" to *her*? No matter. Workshop execs claimed that Abby's character was ideal for exploring the challenges children face when they are new at school or different from other kids. That makes all kinds of sense—because everyone knows it's easy to fit in when you are snaggle-toothed and fat and have bad fur. What is really, really hard for a girl is being cute, sparkly, and magical.

I hate to sound like Peggy the Grouch, but it seemed disingenuous to spin the same old sweet-and-cute, pink-and-sparkly version of girlhood as an attempt at diversity or redress for some perceived historical slight. I was annoyed that the show I admired—and had loved as a child—for celebrating differences and stomping stereotypes so blithely upheld, even defended, this one. Yet it wasn't the first time I had heard that argument. At every geographic outpost from Disneyland to Sesame Street, executives described the same "taboo-breaking" vision, with an identical self-righteous justification about "honoring the range of play patterns girls have." All this pink-and-pretty, they claimed, was about giving girls *more* choices, not fewer. Like Disney's Andy Mooney, marketers would tell me, "We're only giving girls what they want," as if magnifying kids' desires is less coercive than instigating them. Even Dora the Explorer, who, according to Brown Johnson, the president of animation for Nickelodeon, was consciously developed as an alternative to the "Barbie image of girlhood," morphs into something else in the toy store. During a phone conversation, Johnson told me that Dora was drawn to resemble a real child, "not tall or elongated." She was envisioned as powerful, brave, indifferent to beauty. Her clothes were loose and functional, her hair cut in a simple bob. "Part of the DNA of Nickelodeon when it comes to gender portrayal," Johnson said, "is to not have everyone be perfect-looking."

But how did that square with what fans find on the shelves of Target and Claire's: the Dora Star Catcher Lip Gloss Bracelets; Dora's Let's Get Ready Vanity; Dora hair care kit; Dora Style Your Own Cellphone; Dress and Style Dora? The "adorable" boogie board? Wow! Way to counteract Barbie! I could almost hear Johnson purse her lips through the phone as she prepped the corporate damage control. "There's a delicate tension between the consumer products group and the production group," she said crisply. Followed by the familiar phrase "One of the important aspects of Dora's success is to not deny certain play patterns kids have."

In 2009, Nick introduced a "new" Dora aimed at five- to eight-year-olds, whom the company referred to as tweens. This Dora was, um, tall and elongated with long, luscious hair and round doe eyes. Her backpack and map had disappeared. Rather than shorts and sneaks, she sported a fashionable pink baby-doll tunic with purple leggings and ballet flats. The character's makeover set the Momosphere angrily abuzz: was Dora becoming a "Whora"? That was not, I imagine, the response Nick and Mattel were hoping for. But to my mind, sluttiness was not the issue. New Dora wasn't sexy, not at all—she was *pretty*, and that prettiness was now inextricable from her other traits. No longer did she turn "gender portrayal" on its head by "not looking perfect." New Dora stands as a reminder to her rugged little sister that she better get with the program, apparently by age five.

There's no question that new Dora is appealing. Of course she is, just as Abby Cadabby is the quintessence of adorable. Girls love them. In a vacuum, I might love them, too. And perhaps the problem is not so much that *they* exist as what still does *not*. Abby would trouble me far less if there could be a female Muppet as surly as Oscar or as id-driven as Cookie or as goofy as Grover: if there were more "play patterns" to "honor" than just this one.

I get why manufacturers play to pink—it makes good business sense. A marketing executive I spoke with at LeapFrog, which is based in Emeryville, California, told me that her company even had a name for it: "the pink factor." "If you make a pink baseball bat, parents will buy one for their daughter," she explained. "Then, if they subsequently have a son, they'll have to buy a second bat in a different color. Or, if they have a boy first and then a daughter, they'll want to buy a pink one for their precious little girl. Either way, you double your sales." But as a parent, I wonder what all that pinkness—the color, the dominance of the play pattern it signals—is teaching girls about who they are, what they should value, what it means to be female?

⌒﹏﹏⌒

A family portrait hangs near the front door of the home of a friend of mine. It is a bright, playful, almost cartoonlike painting in which they are surrounded by their worldly belongings. There is my friend, dressed in jeans and a T-shirt, pressing a cell phone to her ear with one hand, her computer perched on a table close by. She and her husband are both writers; their books stand at their feet like additional family members. Their younger daughter sits cross-legged on a couch wearing a frothy tutu; their older daughter carries their son piggyback-style. The windows implausibly reflect the facade of their two-story home, as well as the kids' wooden play structure in the backyard. You have never met them, you don't know who they are, but those clues are enough for you to deduce their class, education, lifestyle. You can imagine them now, put them into context, can't you?

I thought about that portrait as I wandered back to the Javits Center. It's so tempting to say these are just toys. Some scholars would indeed argue that I'm projecting my own adult apprehension onto Fashion Angels or My Bling Bling Barbie that has nothing to do with a child's experience of the dolls or how she plays with them. And to a point I agree: just because little girls wear the tulle does not mean they've drunk the Kool-Aid. Plenty of them shoot baskets in ball gowns or cast themselves as the powerful evil stepsister bossing around the sniveling Cinderella. Yet even if girls stray from the prescribed script, doesn't it exert its influence? Don't our possessions reflect who we are; shape, even define, our experience? The belongings surrounding my friends in their portrait form a shorthand statement about their identities—and, I might add, a pretty accurate one. So what do the toys we give our girls, the pinkness in which they are steeped, tell us about what we are telling *them*? What do they say about who *we* think they are and ought to be?

At one time, playthings were expressly intended to communicate parental values and expectations, to train children for their future adult roles. Because of that, they can serve as a Rorschach for cultural anxieties. Take baby dolls. In the late nineteenth century, industrialization shifted the source of the family income outside the home. Without the need for free labor, middle-class couples no longer felt compelled to have more than one child. Nor were girls of the era particularly enamored with dolls: less than 25 percent in an 1898 survey cited them as their favorite toy. A few years later, however, President Theodore Roosevelt, who was obsessed with the waning birth rates among white Anglo-Saxon women, began waging a campaign against "race suicide." When women "feared motherhood," he warned, our country "trembled on the brink of doom." Baby dolls were seen as a way to revive the flagging maternal instinct of white girls, to remind them of their patriotic duty to conceive; within a few years dolls were ubiquitous, synonymous with girlhood itself. Miniature brooms, dustpans, and stoves tutored those same young ladies in the skills of homemaking, while "companion" dolls—including the decidedly straight-bodied Patsy, who came with a wardrobe of little dresses—provided lessons in the feminine arts of grooming, intimacy, and caretaking. Boys, by contrast, were plied with Tinker-Toys and blocks, Erector sets and model trains, preparing them to step into a new world of science and industry.

That division continued, more or less, until the cultural upheavals of the 1960s. Suddenly sex roles were thrown into flux. Expectations for girls were less clear, the paths to both manhood and womanhood muddled. To what, exactly, were girls now supposed to aspire? With what should they play? What would supplant washing machines and irons as preparation for their futures?

Enter Barbie.

It's hard to imagine now, but when she was introduced in 1959, the bombshell with the high-heeled feet was considered a rebel: single and childless, she lived a glamorous life replete with boyfriends (hinting at the possibility of recreational sex). She had a beach house in Malibu (which she had apparently paid for herself), a host of exciting careers (Fashion Editor! Tennis Pro! Stewardess!), and no evidence of parents (Barbie Millicent Roberts was initially supposed to be a teenager, though her age has become nonspecific). Sure, she had a wedding gown (which was to die for), but she was not about to be trapped in a soapbox of domestic drudgery like the baby-boomer girls' dissatisfied mothers. There is, it's worth noting, no "Mom-with-three-ungrateful-children Barbie." In that sense, the doll represented a new, independent vision of womanhood, an escape from "the problem that had no name." She was a feminist icon! The hitch, of course, was that her liberation was predicated on near-constant attention to her appearance. Long before Elle Woods or Carrie Bradshaw, Barbie was the first "I am woman, see me shop" feminist, with all the inconsistencies that implied.

Whether you love or loathe Barbie, you cannot have grown up in the last half century untouched by her influence. Movies have been made about her (check out the bootlegs of Todd Haynes's banned film *Superstar: The Karen Carpenter Story* on YouTube); books have been penned (*Forever Barbie* is a must). What other toy can make such claims? In one 11.5-inch polyvinyl chloride package, she embodies fifty years of cultural ambivalence over standards of beauty and appropriate role models for girls. My own relationship with the doll has evolved from desperately wanting one as a kid (my mom, an instinctive anticonsumerist, forbade any plaything that you had to add to, ruling out not only Barbie but Lego, Hot Wheels, and nearly everything else fun) to, in the apotheosis of my "wymyn's studies" phase, condemning the doll as a tool of the patriarchy to, these days, finding her kind of quaint.

Maybe "quaint" is the wrong word. What Barbie has become is "cute," in the way I described earlier: in which the toys we buy for our kids jump-start our own moribund sense of wonder. It is an interesting twist—when Barbie was introduced, moms disapproved of her, looking askance at her pinup proportions. That was precisely her appeal to girls: she helped them to stake out their turf in the land of "cool." Fifty years later, baby boomers and Gen Xers who had treasured the doll were so eager to share her with their own daughters that they didn't wait until the girls were eight to twelve (Barbie's original demographic); they presented her to their three-year-olds. That instantaneously made her anathema to her intended market. A headline-grabbing 2005 British study revealed that girls aged six to twelve enjoyed torturing, mutilating, and microwaving their Barbies nearly as much as they liked dressing them up for the prom. What interested me about the report, though, was the reason the researchers offered for that behavior: girls "saw her as representing their younger childhood out of which they felt they had now grown." Rather than sexuality or sophistication, then, Barbie was now associated with baby stuff.

As her audience dipped younger, Barbie herself began to change. Today's pleasantly open-faced dolls barely resemble the original. Yes, the vintage version was based on a German sex toy, but the effect was urbane rather than tawdry. Early Barbie exuded a self-knowing poise; her eyes cut to the side as if she harbored a secret. She was not even especially beautiful: the effect was more of a Grace Kelly–like elegance. I *still* wouldn't mind having one of those. Twenty-first-century Barbie's eyes are rounder and wider and point directly forward; the fire engine red pout has transformed into a friendly pink smile; the curves of her face have softened; her hair is shinier and blonder. All of this has made the doll look warmer, younger, *prettier*. Even her breasts have shrunk (at least a little) while her waist has been broadened. The astronauts, surgeons, and presidents of her glory days have been largely replaced by fairies, butterflies, ballerinas, mermaids, and princesses whose wardrobes are almost exclusively pink and lavender (with the occasional foray into turquoise). Original Barbie would be appalled: her palette was never so narrow—even her tutu was silver lamé. Yet the "cuter" Barbie became, the lower her sales fell: in the fourth quarter of 2008 alone, they sank by 21 percent. Some of that was a by-product of the tanked economy, but the exodus had begun long before. Following the cute-begets-cool formula (with "cool" carrying increasingly "hot" connotations), girls as young as six were rejecting the watered-down, mom-approved doll for something edgier, something called, appropriately enough, Bratz.

Bratz dolls were released in 2001 by a small, privately owned company called MGA—just months, as it happened, after the debut of the Disney Princesses—and they aimed to catch girls just as they aged out of that line, to seamlessly usher them into a new, more mature fantasy. With their sultry expressions, thickly shadowed eyes, and collagen-puffed moues, Bratz were tailor-made for the girl itching to distance herself from all things rose petal pink, Princess-y, or Barbie-ish. Their hottie-pink "passion for fashion" conveyed "attitude" and "sassiness," which, anyone will tell you, is little-girl marketing-speak for "sexy." Rather than donning a Cinderella gown and tripping off to the ball themselves, which would be woefully juvenile, seven-year-olds could send their Bratz Princess doll—rocking a tiara, purple fitted corset, and black net skirt—off in her limo to party in a Vegas Bratz pal's hot tub. How awesome was that? Bratz brilliantly distilled Barbie's acquisitiveness while casting off the rest: why be a role model when you can be simply a model?

Bratz, in short, were cool.

Even if moms didn't like the dolls—and generally, they did not—they bought them anyway, much as their own mothers had once bought Barbies: perhaps they succumbed to what marketers call the "nag factor," or they were afraid of the "forbidden fruit" effect in which the denied toy becomes all the more alluring. Or maybe they couldn't resist the Tokyo-A-Go-Go! Sushi Lounge, which, I have to say, was pretty special. At any rate, for seven years, Bratz gave Barbie a run for her money, gobbling up a full 40 percent of the fashion doll market. Then, in 2008, Mattel struck back, suing MGA for copyright infringement: Bratz's creator, it seemed, had been in Mattel's employ when he had designed the dolls. Mattel initially won the case and, within a year, had all but stripped the shelves of its competitor.

Bratz's downfall, then, had nothing to do with a drop in popularity or parental objections. Nor did it mark the end of the grade school diva. Consider the "girls' editions" of classic board games, each of which appears to have been dipped in Pepto-Bismol. The sparkly pink Ouija board includes a deck of seventy-two cards that "Ask the questions that girls want to know." ("Who will text me next?" "Will I be a famous actress someday?") Pink Yahtzee includes a fuzzy shaker and dice that boast, rather than numbers, hearts, butterflies, flowers, cell phones, flip-flops, and dresses. Monopoly Pink Boutique Edition claims to be "All about the things girls love! Buy boutiques and malls, go on a shopping spree, pay your cell phone bill, and get text and instant messages." The raspberry-tinted fantasy these products peddle assumes, like Disney Princess, that all girls long to be the fairest of them all (and the best dressed and the most popular), but something, somewhere, has shifted. The innocence that pink signaled during the Princess years, which seemed so benign, even protective, has receded, leaving behind narcissism and materialism as the hallmarks of feminine identity. The customization of these toys verges on parody; it also discourages the possibility of cross-sex friendship. Could you share your Pink Glam Magic 8 Ball with a pal who happened to be a boy? My sources say no.

With Bratz on ice, the similar My Scene and Fashionista Barbie sales soared, and the doll's earnings rebounded. Meanwhile, in 2009 MGA rolled out Moxie Girlz, which it positioned as a toned-down Bratz for a more economically somber era. And it's true, the clothing, though garish, is less revealing; the accessories are somewhat less excessive. But the dolls still wear the same provocative expression as their predecessors: they have similar shadow-rimmed eyes, and their lips are still freakishly full and lacquered to a high gloss. Their tagline may be "Be true * Be you," but, like pink products all along the age span that urge girls to "be yourself," "celebrate you," "express yourself," they define individuality entirely through appearance and consumption. I suspect that if Bratz had never existed, Moxies would create similar controversy, but the aesthetic of the former permanently pushed the frontiers of propriety; it effectively desensitized parents, dulled our shockability, so that now anything less bootylicious, even by just a smidgen, seems reasonable. The bigger surprise was that Mattel has skewed so hard in the other direction. In 2010, the company launched Monster High—a line of dolls, apparel, Halloween costumes, Webisodes, and eventually a television show and feature film, all aimed at girls ages six and up. Made up of the "children of legendary monsters," the school's student bodies resemble undead streetwalkers, only less demure. Take Clawdeen Wolf, "a fierce fashionista with a confident no-nonsense attitude" whose favorite activities are "shopping and flirting with the boys." Her least favorite school subject is gym, because "they won't let me participate in my platform heels." The company's timing was fortuitous: that summer, a federal appeals court overturned the $100 million verdict against MGA, paving the runway for the comeback of Bratz. The doll wars are *on*. Honestly, it is enough to make a mom beg for the days of little dustpans and baby bottles.

❦

On the Toy Fair's last day, I visited the Fisher-Price showroom, for which I needed a special pass: not just anyone can sneak a peek at next year's Talking Elmo. The preschool girls' section was decorated with a banner on which the words BEAUTIFUL, PRETTY, COLORFUL were repeated over and over (and over) in pink script. The display included a pink DVD player, a pink camera, stick-on jewelry that could be colored with pink or orange pens (and stored in a pink purse or pink jewelry box), a Cuddle and Care Baby Abby Cadabby, and a Dora the Explorer "styling head." In the next room, a banner over the boys' section, scripted in blue, exclaimed, ENERGY, HEROES, POWER. Among the multicolored toys were "planet heroes" action figures, a robotic dinosaur, a jungle adventure set, and a Diego Animal Rescue Railway. Outside, on the streets of Manhattan, it was the twenty-first century, but the scene here in toy land was straight out of *Mad Men*, as if the feminist movement had never happened.

I'm not saying that Fisher-Price (or Mattel or Disney or even MGA) is engaged in some nefarious scheme to brainwash our daughters—or, for that matter, our sons. They wouldn't make those products or spin those sales pitches if they didn't work, and it's not as though little girls themselves are laying down the cash. So again I found myself mulling over why we parents want to—

even need to—amplify the differences between boys and girls. If the baby doll propaganda of the early twentieth century reflected adult fears that white girls would reject maternity, what anxieties account for the contemporary surge of pink-and-pretty? The desire to prolong innocence, to avoid early sexualization, may be part of it, but that does not explain the spike in cosmetics sales for preschoolers, press-on nails for six-year-olds, or R-rated fashion dolls. There is some evidence that the more freedom women have, the more polarized a culture's ideas about the sexes become: an annual survey administered to students at the University of Akron since the 1970s, for instance, found *greater* differences in perceived gender-related traits over time, especially when it came to femininity. The conviction that women are more "sympathetic," "talkative," and "friendly" rose significantly among both male and female respondents. And although women no longer saw "athleticism" or "decisiveness" as inherently masculine, men still did. Men also felt that women had become both more domineering *and* more timid, while associating masculinity more strongly than ever with the adjectives "adventurous," "aggressive," "competitive," and "self-confident."

How is one to interpret that trend? Does it indicate a need to keep the sexes distinct, one we eagerly reinforce in our youngest children? A deep-seated fear that equality between men and women will create an unappealing sameness? Or could it be that, with other factors stripped away, so many barriers broken down, we can finally admit to difference without defensiveness? Maybe even if girls aren't born loving pink, precisely, their behaviors, tastes, and responses are nonetheless hardwired, at least to a degree, and today's parents are able to accept that without judgment, even savor it. Perhaps the segregation of girl and boy cultures is inevitable. Biologically driven.

Clearly, before going any further, I needed to understand, once and for all, how much of children's gender behavior was truly inborn and how much was learned. Yet, as I left the Fisher-Price showroom, I wondered: even if nature proved dominant, what impact might this new separate-but-equal mentality have on children's perceptions of themselves, one another, and their future choices?

Chapter Four

What Makes Girls Girls?

$\mathcal{W}$hen I was in seventh grade, my English teacher assigned our class "X: A Fabulous Child's Story." Originally published in *Ms.* magazine and later as a stand-alone picture book, it was a kind of sci-fi fable about a child, code-named X, whose sex would not be revealed until it announced itself at puberty. The scientists conducting this "Very Important Xperiment" provided X's parents with a manual containing tens of thousands of pages of instructions (there were "246½ pages on the first day of school alone!"). Mom and Dad cared for X equally; both parents played dolls and trucks with the child, shot marbles, and jumped rope. And guess what? It turned out that X "Xcelled" at everything—spelling, running, baking, football, playing house! Under X's influence, X's classmates threw off the yoke of gender tyranny: boys ran vacuums and girls ran lawn mowers. Irate parents demanded that X be evaluated by a shrink, who, tears of joy streaming down his (yes, *his*) cheeks, declared that X was "the least mixed-up child I've ever Xamined."

And they all lived neutrally ever after.

The story was supposed to illustrate how gender, really, is all a bunch of socially constructed hooey, which was the prevailing belief of the time. We were, our teacher told us, totally Free to Be You and Me (a play, as it happens, I would be cast in a few years later, performing in shorts, toe socks, and "Mork from Ork" rainbow-striped suspenders). Or were we? Flash forward three decades to 2009, when a real-life story of X caromed across the Internet: a Swedish couple had decided to indefinitely conceal their child's gender. Pop (the pseudonym they gave the child in interviews to protect the family's privacy) was two years old when the story broke. According to the newspaper *Svenska Dagbladet*, Pop's wardrobe included dresses and trousers; Pop's parents changed the child's hairstyle regularly. Pop was free to play with whatever Pop wished. "It's cruel to bring a child into this world with a blue or pink stamp on its forehead," Pop's mother proclaimed.

My sister journalists disagreed. Strongly, and not just because of the challenge posed by avoiding a definite pronoun in writing. Attitudes had shifted profoundly. Not only were there no second-wave feminist huzzahs for Pop's parents' courage in attempting to buck the new pressures of hypergendered childhood (less than a century ago—when, if you recall, all children wore frilly white dresses and unshorn hair until at least age three—Pop's androgyny would have been no biggie), but one writer decried the "violence committed on the child's sense of self" in denying Pop overt knowledge of Pop's sex, calling what the parents were doing tantamount to "child abuse." Another grimly invoked the example of a "militant feminist friend" who let her daughter play only with cars and trucks—until the day she found the girl rocking a blanket-wrapped Tonka while feeding it a bottle through its chassis. Several cited the classic 1967 case of David Reimer, one of a pair of twin boys, who was raised as "Brenda" after a bungled circumcision left him—whoops!—without a penis. When he discovered the truth as a teenager, David underwent reconstructive surgery and received testosterone injections to become a boy again, saying he had felt male all along; at age thirty-eight, he declared the experiment of his life a failure and committed suicide.

Why such rancor? It wasn't as if Pop's parents were physically reassigning their child's sex. Nor were they dictating Pop's choice of toys or clothing. Besides, banning dolls and insisting a girl play solely with trucks is hardly an exercise in equality. Quite the contrary: it disparages the feminine, signals that boys' traditional toys and activities are superior to girls'. Leaving that misconstrual aside, however, this was not the first time I'd heard the cautionary tale of the over-the-top mother forcing trucks on her despairing daughter in the name of feminism. Always attributed to "a friend of a friend," it invariably ended with—triumphant drumroll, please!—the girl swaddling and bottle-feeding her truck "babies" (though if conventionally feminine toys were verboten, how did the girls get the bottles anyhow?). It has always smacked to me of urban legend, like the story about poisonous spiders under airplane toilet seats or cell phones sparking fires in gas stations: something that *seems* as though it ought to be true because it confirms our suspicions about the unnatural consequences that will result from meddling with the natural order of things. Either way, it illustrates how fully biological determinism has come roaring back into fashion.

Doing the math, I realized that the journalists who were most outraged by Pop were the ones who would've been the daughters—metaphorically or literally—of 1970s feminists, girls who had been stuffed into endless pairs of shapeless overalls (which in itself would scar a person for life). Their moms had doubtless been well meaning, but their ideals were misguided. And boring. And they backfired: there was no way all those Carries, Terris, Randis, and Jos were going to inflict that neutered femininity on their daughters. When they had children, then—which coincided with marketers' discovery of the power of microsegmentation by age and sex—they were primed, eager, to embrace the new "postfeminist" girlie-girl. They were beyond the notion of "gender-free" childhood; they no longer needed to squash kids' inborn preferences in the name of equality, they could *vive la différence* as Mama N. intended. Good-bye, X; hello, Cinderella.

It is impossible—or at the very least unwise—to explore the culture of girlhood without confronting the question of "nature or nurture" head-on. There *have* to be innate differences between the sexes, right? How else to explain the Machiavellian manipulations of three-year-old girls or the perpetual motion of preschool boys? How else to understand the male attraction to all things that roll or the female fascination with faces? For most of us, such beliefs are a matter of life experience, grounded in instinct and personal observation rather than a bibliography of double-blind studies. I wanted to know whether there was really something essential and immutable about maleness and femaleness. Are boys and girls destined to be miniature Martians and Venusians? Or are they more like Canadians and Americans: mostly alike except for some weird little quirks, such as how they pronounce the word "about"? And even if the latter turns out to be true and the disparities are minimal, how much—if at all—do we really want to mess with them; how much do we want our children to be products of social engineering? As long as we don't consider the behaviors and interests of one sex as *inferior* to the other's, who cares? Does gender segregation matter, for either the good or the ill? What, I wondered, could science tell me about the stubbornly separate cultures of boys and girls?

꧁꧂

To begin to answer those questions, I consulted Lise Eliot, a neuroscientist and the author of *Pink Brain, Blue Brain*, a fascinating book for which she sifted through more than a thousand studies comparing males' and females' brains and behaviors. She was kind enough to offer me a quick remedial lesson in biology. Male fetuses, she explained, are bathed in testosterone in the womb; that signals the reproductive organs to do the guy thing. There is another hormonal spike shortly after birth. Boy babies also tend to be larger (both their brains and bodies) and somewhat fussier than girls and are more vulnerable to illness. For the most part, however, at least in the beginning, the behavior and interests of the two sexes are nearly indistinguishable. Both go gaga over the same toys: until they're about a year old, they are equally attracted to dolls; and until they're around three, they show the same interest in actual babies. In other words, regardless of how we dress them or decorate their rooms, when they are tiny, children do not know from pink and blue.

Then the whole concept of labeling kicks in—sometime between the ages of two and three they realize that there is this thing called "boy" and this thing called "girl" and something important differentiates them. But whatever, they wonder, could that be? There is a legendary story about a four-year-old boy named Jeremy, the son of a psychology professor at Cornell, who wore his favorite barrettes to school one day. "You're a *girl*," one of his classmates said accusingly, but the boy stood firm. No, he explained, he was a boy because he had a penis and testicles. The other child continued to taunt him. Finally, exasperated, Jeremy pulled down his pants to prove his point. His tormentor merely shrugged. "*Everyone* has a penis," he said. "Only girls wear barrettes." (Jeremy, incidentally, is probably well into his forties by now and, I imagine, wishes people would stop repeating this anecdote.)

The point is, the whole penis-vagina thing does not hold quite the same cachet among the wee ones as it does among us. Yet if toting the standard equipment is not what makes you male or female, exactly what does?

Well, *duh*, it's barrettes.

At least that's what kids think: it is your clothing, hairstyle, toy choice, favorite color. Slippery stuff, that. You can see how perilously easy it would be to err: if you wore pink or your mom cut your hair too short, you might inadvertently switch sex. It could happen: until around age five kids don't fully realize that their own identities (not to mention their anatomies) are fixed. Before that, as far as they're concerned, you could grow up to be either a mommy or a daddy. And they don't understand that other people's sex stays the same despite superficial changes— that a man who puts on a dress is still a man—until as late as age seven. "In general, the concept of permanence is hard for children to grasp," Eliot said. "The prefrontal cortex of the brain is what looks to the future, and that's the slowest part to develop. Another example would be death: young children have a very hard time understanding that a pet or a person they love who has died is gone forever. They may listen to what you say and seem to get it, but secretly they believe it can change."

It makes sense, then, that to ensure you will stay the sex you were born you'd adhere rigidly to the rules as you see them and hope for the best. That's why four-year-olds, who are in what is called "the inflexible stage," become the self-appointed chiefs of the gender police. Suddenly the magnetic lure of the Disney Princesses became more clear to me: developmentally speaking, they were genius, dovetailing with the precise moment that girls need to *prove* they are girls, when they will latch onto the most exaggerated images their culture offers in order to stridently shore up their femininity.

Initially, as a parent, I found this came as a bit of a relief. The pod princess that had taken over my daughter's body did not represent a personal failure on my part; it was entirely unrelated to anything I did or did not do, wear, or say. I couldn't even blame it on her preschool classmates. Her extremism, it turns out, was natural, something kids will and, apparently, should go through. At the same time, that left me in a quandary: Did that mean my battle to minimize the pink and the pretty had been misguided? Worse than that, was it actually harmful? I flashed on a trip to the grocery store—the O.K. Corral of our Disney Princess showdowns. Daisy had pointed to a Cinderella sippy cup. "There's that princess you don't like, Mama!" she had shouted.

"Mmm-hmm," I'd said noncommittally.

"Why don't you like her, Mama?" she had asked. "Don't you like her blue dress?"

I'd had to admit I did.

She had thought about that. "Then don't you like her face?"

"Her face is all right," I'd said, though I was not thrilled to have my Japanese-Jewish child in thrall to those Teutonic features. (And what the heck are those blue things covering her ears?) "It's just, honey, Cinderella doesn't really *do* anything."

Over the next forty-five minutes, we would run through that conversation, verbatim, approximately thirty-seven million times, as Daisy pointed out Cinderella Band-Aids, Cinderella paper cups, Cinderella cereal boxes, Cinderella pens, Cinderella crayons, and Cinderella notebooks—all cleverly displayed at the eye level of a three-year-old trapped in a shopping cart—as well as a bouquet of Cinderella Mylar balloons bobbing over the checkout line (any day now, I had muttered to myself, they'll come out with Cinderella tampons). The repetition had been excessive, even for a preschooler. At the time I'd wondered what it was about my answer that confounded her. Now, in retrospect, I fretted: what if, instead of helping her realize "Aha! Cinderella is a symbol of the patriarchal oppression of all women, another example of corporate mind control, and power to the people!" my daughter had been thinking "Mommy doesn't want me to be a girl?" By forbidding her immersion in Princess products, had I unintentionally communicated that being female (to the extent that Daisy was able to understand it) was a bad thing? Wasn't there something else she could cling to, some other way she could assert her femininity, besides dousing herself in Sleeping Beauty perfume? In one kindergarten class I read about, for instance, boys hopped to the front of the room to get their milk at snack time; during art, girls skipped to the shelf where paper was kept. Hopping made you a boy, skipping a girl. Anyone who got it "wrong" was subject to ridicule. That may sound absurd, but really, is it any more random than declaring that only girls can wear skirts?

But the Big Kahuna of sex differences, according to Eliot, is toy choice. Boys push cars, girls push strollers. You even see it in primates. In a 2002 study, researchers gave two stereotypically masculine toys (a police car and a ball), two stereotypically feminine toys (a doll and a cooking pot), and two neutral toys (a picture book and a stuffed animal) to forty-four male and forty-four female vervet monkeys. The vervets had never seen the items before and were (obviously) unaware of their connotations. The results? Though males and females were similarly drawn to the neutral items, the males gravitated toward the boy toys, while the females went for the doll and—grrr!—the cooking pot. A fluke? Maybe, but six years later, that finding was replicated by a second group of researchers studying rhesus monkeys. Meanwhile, among us humans, girls who are born with a genetic disorder that causes them to produce high levels of male hormones are more physically active than other girls and favor traditional "boy" toys.

Listening to Eliot, I began to think that the toy makers might be right in gender coding their wares. This was not just business, it was not just marketers' manipulation. I mean, if boys will be boys and girls will be girls—even among *monkeys*, for heaven's sake—there is no point in further discussion, is there? Pop will reveal Popself any day now by becoming obsessed with either Bob the Builder or Barbie (or their Swedish equivalents). And X is fated to remain in the realm of fiction.

That may be where most parents intuitively land, if less ambivalently than I, but it is not the whole story. Toy choice turns out to be one of the largest differences between the sexes over the entire life span, bigger than anything except the preference (among most of us) for the other sex as romantic partners. But its timing and intensity shore up every assumption and stereotype we adults hold: little boys naturally like backhoes, ergo men won't ask for directions. That blinds us to the larger truth of how deeply those inborn biases are reinforced by a child's environment.

Eliot's own research is in something called "neuroplasticity," the idea that our inborn tendencies and traits, gender-based or otherwise, are shaped by our experience. A child's brain, she explained, changes on a molecular level when she learns to walk, learns to talk, stores a memory, laughs, cries. Every interaction, every activity, strengthens some neural circuits at the expense of others—and the younger the child, the greater the effect. So though kids may be the most rigid about gender during the princess years, their brains are also at their most malleable, the most open to long-term influence on the abilities and roles that go with their sex. In other words, Eliot said, nurture *becomes* nature. "Think about language. Babies are born ready to absorb the sounds and grammar and intonation of *any* language, but then the brain wires itself up to only perceive and produce a *specific* language. After puberty, it's possible to learn another language, but it's far more difficult. I think of gender differences similarly: the ones that exist become amplified by the two different cultures that boys and girls are immersed in from birth. That contributes to the way their emotional and cognitive circuits get wired."

The environment in which children are raised affects their behaviors as well as their aptitudes. Boys from more egalitarian homes, for example, are more nurturing toward babies than other boys are and more flexible about toy choice. Meanwhile, in a study of more than five thousand three-year-olds, girls with older brothers had stronger spatial skills than both other girls *and* boys with older sisters; boys with older sisters were also less rough in their play than their peers. (The sibling effect worked only one way, incidentally—the younger sibling had no impact whatsoever on the older's gendered behavior, nor, interestingly, did opposite-sex twins exert such influence on each other.) Similarly—and notably for parents—in 2005, researchers found that mathematically inclined girls whose fathers believed females aren't "wired" for the subject were less interested in pursuing it. Even the tragic case of David/Brenda—the boy with the botched circumcision who killed himself after being raised as a girl—is no proof that biology trumps culture. David was nearly two when his sex was surgically reassigned as female, old enough, according to Eliot, for his brain to have absorbed a great deal about his gender; he also had an identical twin who remained male, a constant reminder of what might have been. What's more, a 2005 review of similar cases found that only seventeen of seventy-seven boys whose sex was reassigned chose to revert to male. The other sixty lived out their lives contentedly as women.

Hormones, genes, and chromosomes, then, aren't quite as powerful as we tend to believe. And that has implications for how we raise and educate our children. "If you believe it's all immutable, then what is the harm in plunking girls in a pink ghetto or letting boys get by without doing art or singing or all the things they used to like to do before they got associated with girls?" Eliot asked. "But if you believe these disparities in adults are shaped by development and experience . . ." She paused a moment. "Of course, this assumes you see a value in bringing out the full spectrum of emotional and cognitive abilities in any individual."

∽

On a blisteringly hot morning in Phoenix, Arizona, I stood behind a one-way mirror, the kind cops on TV use when they're watching an interrogation. But the "suspects" on the other side of the glass were not criminals: they were just a passel of preschoolers getting ready for "outside time." A little boy with freckles and a sandy Dennis the Menace cowlick came right up to his reflection, pressed his face against it, and stuck out his tongue. The woman I was with laughed. "They're used to us coming and watching," she explained, "so they figure someone is probably back here."

Released onto the playground, the children dashed around the spongy surface, splitting off from one another like amoebas, forming and re-forming their groups. The pattern in their chaos eventually became clear—girls and boys might alight next to each other but soon whirled away, back to their own kind.

And that's nothing special, right? Girls play with girls; boys play with boys. You would see it at any preschool anywhere. It was nothing special: yet to the woman I had come here to meet, Carol Martin, a professor of child development at Arizona State University and one of the country's foremost experts on gender development, it meant everything. Martin and her colleague Richard Fabes co-direct the Sanford Harmony Program, a multimillion-dollar privately funded research initiative, aimed (for now) at preschoolers, kindergarteners, and middle schoolers. Its goal, over time, is to improve how boys and girls think of and treat the other sex in the classroom, on the playground, and beyond: to keep their small behavioral and cognitive differences from turning into unbreachable gaps.

Martin, who has a shock of white hair and preternaturally blue eyes, has spent three decades looking at how kids develop ideas about masculinity and femininity, as well as the long-term implications of those beliefs. In addition to the Sanford program, she has been conducting research on "tomboys." Among her findings: a third of girls aged seven to eleven that she surveyed identified themselves with the term. Yet in previous studies up to three-quarters of adult women claimed that they had been "tomboys" as kids. That interested me: presumably, most of them were mis-remembering their past, but why? Why would recalling themselves as less conventionally feminine be so appealing? Maybe because tomboys are resisters; they're thought of as independent, adventurous, brave—characteristics that women may prize more as adults than they did as girls. Perhaps in hindsight they feel more trapped by the trappings of girlhood than they did at the time, more conflicted about its costs. Or maybe, like me, they're merely comparing their experience with what they see around them today—the explosion of pink froth—and thinking "Well, I was never like *that*."

Martin and I left the preschool, which was on the Arizona State campus, and strolled over to the social science building to join Fabes, several other faculty members, and a group of graduate students in a conference room. This team had spent hours watching preschoolers in action, painstakingly tagging their behaviors: solo play, parallel play, same-sex play, cross-sex play (that is, one boy and one girl), mixed-sex play. Fabes flipped open a laptop and, as an example, began projecting a video clip against the wall. The classroom I had just left came into view, but with different kids. A group of boys huddled around a table talking and playing (it was unclear exactly with what), while a gaggle of girls worked together to build a fort of blocks. Fade to black. In a second clip, a boy and a girl stood next to each other, watering plants.

"That's a missed opportunity," Fabes commented, pointing at the screen. "I don't understand why teachers don't see this."

I looked at him blankly. It seemed like a good thing to me: a boy and a girl playing happily together. What was the problem? "They're not playing together," he corrected. "They're playing *next* to each other. That's not the same thing. People see girls and boys playing side by side and consider that interaction, but it's not."

Typically, it is girls who initiate the church-and-state separation of childhood, pulling away at around age two and a half from boys who are too rough or rowdy. Shortly after that, the boys reciprocate, avoiding girls even more scrupulously than the girls did them. By the end of the first year of preschool, children spend most of their time, when they can choose, playing with others of their sex. When they do have cross-sex friendships, they tend not to cop to them in public—the relationships go underground. As much as the story of X would like us to think otherwise, that self-segregation, like toy choice, is universal, crossing all cultures—it appears, Martin said, to be innate. The threat of cooties continues, with boys and girls inhabiting their own worlds, through elementary school until middle school, when children realize there might be something to this opposite-sex business after all.

Every cliché I have staunchly refuted plays out in childhood single-sex groups: girls cluster in pairs or trios, chat with one another more than boys do, are more intimate and cooperative in their play, and are more likely to promote group harmony. They play closer to teachers and are more likely than boys to choose toys and activities structured by adults. Boys, on the other hand, play in packs. Their games are more active, rougher, more competitive, and more hierarchical than girls'. They try to play as far as possible from adults' peering eyes.

Martin and Fabes make clear that they are not pushing for 1970s X-style neutrality. They do not want to discourage or even necessarily diminish segregated play. "We just want to offset its limitations," Martin explained. "A little girl who only plays with girls and learns the gender behavior and interaction of little girls . . . well, what they do together is limited. Same with little boys." Single-sex peer groups reinforce kids' biases, and over time, as Lise Eliot pointed out, that changes their brains, potentially defining both their abilities and possibilities. By age four, girls—who have a small inherent advantage in verbal and social skills—have outstripped boys in those areas. Around the same time, boys, who have a slight natural edge in spatial skills, begin pulling ahead on that front.

This separation of cultures, as anyone who was ever a child will recall, also contributes to an us-versus-them mentality between males and females. That not only provides endless material for third-rate stand-up comics but, Fabes and Martin believe, undermines our intimate relationships. Years of same-sex play leave kids less able to relate to the other sex—and can set the stage for hostile attitudes and interactions in adolescence and adulthood. "This is a public health issue," Fabes proclaimed. "It becomes detrimental to relationships, to psychological health and well-being, when boys and girls don't learn how to talk to one another. That divergence of behavior and communication skills in childhood becomes the building blocks for later issues. Part of the reason we have the divorce rates we do, domestic violence, dating violence, stalking behaviors, sexual harassment, is lack of ability to communicate between men and women."

Eliminating divorce or domestic violence may be an ambitious mandate for a preschool curriculum, but it's not without basis: young children who have friends of the other sex have a more positive transition into dating as teenagers and sustain their romantic relationships better. But how does one go about changing behavior that is not merely entrenched but, apparently, inborn? Sometimes, Martin explained, it is easier than one might imagine. Take the case of the boy and girl watering the plants: an alert teacher just needs to mention how the kids are helping each other. "When teachers comment on mixed-sex or crossed-sex play, the likelihood it will happen increases. When they stop commenting, it stops happening. So they need to reinforce it." Although the curriculum is still in its earliest phases of development, Martin said, it will focus on creating "a higher sense of unity" as a classroom rather than as girls and boys—by choosing a group mascot together, for example. Teachers will be advised not to divide children by gender when lining them up to go outside; there might be "buddy days" or other cooperative learning opportunities during which boys and girls work together. Teachers can integrate discussions of similarities into classroom activities ("Lots of kids like pizza: some are girls and some are boys"). There will also be a series of lessons about exclusion and inclusion involving "Z," a genderless cartoon alien who is trying to figure out our world. Kids may still largely stick with their own sex, Martin acknowledged, and that's fine, but maybe they will play more together as well.

Consciously encouraging cross-sex play clearly runs counter to toy marketers' goals. It also defies a hot trend in education reform: using brain research to justify single-sex classrooms in public schools. Proponents such as Leonard Sax, the author of *Why Gender Matters* and president of the National Association for Single Sex Public Education, claim that the differences between boys and girls are so profound, so determinative, so immutable that coeducation actually does kids a disservice. Among the assertions: boys hear less well than girls (and thus need louder teachers), see action better, and are most alert when taught while standing up in a chilly room. Girls, by contrast, like it hot—their classrooms should be around 75 degrees and decorated in warm hues—prefer sitting in a circle, and excel at seeing colors and nuances. Even if all that were true (a dubious assumption: multiple studies have, for instance, shown that sex-based hearing and vision differences are so negligible as to be irrelevant), presumably, segregation would only deepen those divides, increasing the distance between boys and girls and making them strangers to each other.

At any rate, gender is a pretty weak predictor of a child's potential gifts or challenges; the differences within each sex in any given realm (including math and verbal skills) tend to be far greater than the ones between them. Jay Giedd, the chief of brain imaging at the Child Psychiatry Branch of the National Institute of Mental Health, told *The New York Times* that assigning kids to classrooms based on gender differences would be like assigning them to locker rooms based on height: since males tend to be bigger, you'd send the tallest 50 percent of kids to the boys' side and the shortest 50 percent to the girls'. You might end up with a better-than-random outcome, but not by much: there are simply too many exceptions to the rule. Nonetheless, the number of single-sex public schools and classrooms has skyrocketed since the mid-1990s, due largely to the influence of Sax and his colleagues. That made me rethink Lise Eliot's comment about her work: the presumption that we, as a society, want to bring out the full potential in all of our children. What parent would disagree with that? Yet we are often reluctant to examine assumptions and actions that amplify gender differences—even if that means we create a self-fulfilling prophecy.

I am not against single-sex schools in the private sphere (as long as they don't justify their existence through half-baked "brain research"), but I would much rather have Daisy and her classmates, male and female, take part in something like the Sanford program. I hope Martin and Fabes are right and their work can, down the line, improve relationships between the sexes, both in the workplace and in the home (at least, as Fabes joked, "we can guarantee none of our research subjects will divorce in the next five years"). I hope it encourages kids to work together more effectively regardless of differences within or between the sexes—teaching them to appreciate the bumps in the playing field rather than trying to level it entirely. But it will be years before they know for sure, before the curriculum is fully in place, before they figure out how to evaluate its long-term efficacy.

I left Phoenix feeling less concerned that Daisy had suddenly gone femme on me—that now seemed both unavoidable and healthy. At the same time, if early experiences with mixed-sex play have a lifelong positive impact on kids' behavior, aptitudes, and relationships, the segmentation of every possible childhood item by sex was more troubling than I had initially imagined—and for a whole new slew of reasons. I felt better educated as I headed home, better grounded in theory, but no closer to understanding how to put it into practice while raising a daughter: where was the point that exploration of femininity turned to exploitation of it, the line between frivolous fun and JonBenét? Maybe to stake out that middle ground, I needed to check out the extreme.

```
      ***********************

College Hill Library (WPL)
03/30/16  10:02AM
Patron Name: ENGEL, BRIDGET A

Queen Clarion's secret /
3302000719369          Date Due: 04/20/16

The longest ride /
3302000704767          Date Due: 04/20/16

Cinderella ate my daughter : dispatches
3302000492496          Date Due: 04/20/16

Item total: 3

Overdue fees are $ .20 a day per item.

Renew materials by calling
303-404-5710

For account information, call
303-658-2601
(Please have your library card and PIN)
```

Chapter Five

Sparkle, Sweetie!

*a*t six in the morning on a summer Saturday in Austin, Texas, Taralyn Eschberger was getting ready to sparkle. She was perched on a chair in the Hill Country Ballroom of a Radisson hotel, her blue eyes still bleary with sleep as a makeup artist fussed around her, plucking sponge rollers from her hair, teasing and combing out the curls, preparing to augment them with a cascading hairpiece whose strawberry blond shade precisely matched Taralyn's own. Next, to bring out her features, came blush, candy pink lipstick, cerulean eye shadow, black liner and mascara; then press-on nails that simulated a French manicure. The makeup artist held up a hand mirror, and Taralyn nodded, satisfied. A little bronzer on her legs to even out her spray tan (which keeps her from looking washed out under harsh stage lights), and she would be ready to compete for the $2,000 Ultimate Supreme prize at the Universal Royalty Texas State Beauty Pageant.

Did I mention that Taralyn was five years old?

Taralyn's mom, Traci, a former dancer turned medical sales rep, watched from a few feet away, smiling. She could well have been a beauty queen herself: tall and slim, with highlighted blond hair, enviably perky breasts, gleaming white teeth, and, even at this hour of the morning, her own makeup meticulously in place. She showed me the dress Taralyn would wear in the pageant, a two-piece off-the-shoulder turquoise number with a crystallized Swarovski rhinestone-encrusted bodice, a frothy, multitiered tutu skirt, and a detachable choker necklace. Serious contenders like the Eschbergers can pay up to $3,000 a pop for these hand-sewn "cupcake dresses," though since the seamstress who made this one "just *loves* Taralyn" and uses the girl as a model, Traci got it at cost. Even so, the $16,000 Taralyn had won so far during her year in competition wouldn't nearly cover her expenses: the dance coach, the makeup artist, the home tanning equipment, the head shots, the extravagant frocks and swimwear, not to mention the entry fees—which can run as high as $1,000—as well as travel, accommodations, and meals for the thirty pageants she'd attended in Florida, Tennessee, Kentucky, and Texas. With that level of investment, Traci said, you had better bring your best game: you had better be prepared. You had better pay attention to every detail, and every detail had better be perfect. In addition to hair and makeup, girls in the tooth-losing phase famously wear "flippers"—custom-made dental prosthetics that cover any gaps to create a flawless smile. Taralyn had one but rarely used it. "When the judges are sitting further away from the stage, it does make their smile look bigger," Traci said. "But it doesn't look natural. It doesn't look like her. I like her cute little smile."

Taralyn hopped off the chair, presented herself for Traci's approval. "You look just like a princess!" the older woman exclaimed, and her daughter grinned. I recalled museum portraits I had seen of eighteenth-century European princesses—little girls in low-cut gowns, their hair piled high, their cheeks and lips rouged red—that were used to attract potential husbands, typically middle-aged men, who could strengthen the girls' families' political or financial positions. So, yes, I thought, I suppose she does look like a princess.

Any sane mother would find the pageant world appalling, right? They would feel queasy, as I did, at overhearing a woman advise her six-year-old that "one of the judges is a man, so be sure you wink at him!" or a father telling a TV reporter that he enjoys getting a sneak peek at what his four-year-old will look like when she's sixteen. It would be easy pickin's for me to attack parents who tart up their daughters in hopes of winning a few hundred bucks and a gilded plastic trophy; who train them to shake their tail feathers on command, to blow kisses at the judges and coyly twirl their index fingers into their dimpled cheeks.

But really, what would be the point? That story has been told, to great success and profit. *Toddlers & Tiaras*, which each week follows families through a different pageant, has been a megahit for TLC, and the more evil and clueless the "momsters" it covers, the better. Traci herself was once featured on the show, grabbing Taralyn's arm and reprimanding her for flubbing a routine. ("They filmed two days of positive footage," Traci told me, "then that was what they chose to air. We were stupid to fall for it. We were dumb.") MTV, *The Tyra Banks Show*, *Good Morning America*, *Nightline*, and even England's august BBC have all featured the "controversy" over baby beauty queens. The formula each of those followed was as clever as it was foolproof: a parade of preschoolers tricked out like Las Vegas showgirls was followed by commentary from psychologists who (with good reason) link self-objectification and sexualization to the host of ills previously mentioned—eating disorders, depression, low self-esteem, impaired academic performance. The moms defend their actions, the psychologists rebut, the moms get the last word, the girls take the stage again, and the piece is over. The shows purport to be exposés, but in truth they expose nothing, change nothing, challenge nothing. What they do is give viewers license, under the pretext of disapproval, to be titillated by the spectacle, to indulge in guilty-pleasure voyeurism. They also reassure parents of their own comparative superiority by smugly ignoring the harder questions: even if you agree that pageant moms are over the line in their sexualization of little girls—*way* over the line—where, exactly, is that line, and who draws it and how? What might those little princesses reveal about how the rest of us, we supposedly more enlightened parents, raise our own daughters?

తిందా

A spangled blue curtain hung behind the stage of the Radisson's ballroom. A row of glittering tiaras and banner-draped trophies—some up to five feet high—stood in front of it. A table off to one side was laden with smaller trophies, giant teddy bears, and "goodie bags" stuffed with candy and toys. Every contestant at a Universal pageant walks away with a prize; for that privilege, they pay a mandatory $295 general entry fee (which includes the

Formal Wear competition), a $125 DVD fee, a $15-per-person admission fee, plus optional fees of $50 to $100 each for additional events such as the swimsuit competition, facial beauty, "Mini Supremes" (which carries a $200 cash prize), talent, and hair/makeup. It was easy to see how child pageants, which are the fastest-growing segment of the pageant market, have become a reported multibillion-dollar industry.

Universal Royalty had already been featured three times on *Toddlers & Tiaras*. It is the country's largest "high-glitz" child pageant system, according to its owner, Annette Hill, a former child beauty queen herself, whose two grown daughters were also pageant vets. A tall African-American woman dressed simply in a black sheath, her hair swept into a French twist, Miss Annette, as she is known, was also the pageant's mistress of ceremonies: she stood behind a lectern introducing contestants in each category, from infants on up. Her nonstop stage patter included the children's names, their favorite foods (pizza for the older kids; "a big plate of mashed bananas" for the babies), TV shows (*"Hannah Montana*, of course"), hobbies ("swimming, talking on the phone, and shopping and shopping and shopping!"), as well as a detailed description of each outfit. The girls strutted across the stage in turn, pausing to wave at the judges or to pose with their chin on folded hands, jiggling their heads like baby dolls newly come to life. Surprisingly, few were classically pretty and several were on the chunky side—stripped of their glitz, I would never have pegged them for pageant queens. But beauty was not exactly what they were being judged on. It was more about how well they performed pageant conventions—the walk, the stage presence, the nonstop smile, the nymphet moves—and, of course, the flashy outfits and gaudy makeup. Judges and parents referred to this as "the total package."

Taralyn was one of the front-runners in the pageant's sweet spot, the four- to six-year-old division, in which competition was fiercest. Her chief rival, Eden Wood, was a chubby-cheeked, tow-headed four-year-old from Taylor, Arkansas (population 566), who had been on the pageant circuit since age one. Eden's mother, Mickie (who, like many of the moms, was once a contestant herself), was notorious for her on-the-spot, uninhibited coaching. Most of the girls' mothers used hand signals, similar to the kind you would see at high-end dog shows, to remind their daughters of where they were supposed to walk, when to stop, when to spin. But Mickie planted herself a few yards behind the judges, out of their sight lines but well within her daughter's, and performed Eden's routine exuberantly right along with the girl. Mickie was a big, busty woman, but she could still shake it. It was a mesmerizing sight—together mother and daughter bent their arms at the elbow, turned up their palms, and twirled. Together they blew kisses over their shoulders at the judges, together they vamped and waved, together they leaned forward and shimmied. Their movements were so synchronized that it seemed as if they were attached by an invisible string, marionette and puppeteer. Periodically Mickie punctuated their dance with encouraging shouts of "E. E.!" and "Go, baby!" and "Get it, girl!" Miss Annette, meanwhile, noted that Eden's ambition was "to rule the world."

Pageant parents are surely not the only ones who could be accused of living through their children. Think about gymnastics, ice skating, ballet, competitive cheerleading, acting, soccer, spelling bees, concerto contests, math meets. A number of those, while requiring more specialized skills, can be as potentially objectifying of girls as pageants. And for each, I suspect, you'd hear the same justifications as the ones I heard from every single pageant mom I spoke with, almost as if they had memorized a script:

Pageants build a child's confidence, give her a kind of poise that will someday be useful in job interviews and professional presentations. Their daughters do plenty of things that have nothing to do with beauty or body (Eden Wood drives a miniature pink 4×4 all-terrain vehicle back in Arkansas). Pageants are about old-fashioned Hollywood-style glamour, not sexualization—if you think a five-year-old looks sexy, then *you* are the sick one. What's more, their girls *choose* to compete: "If she didn't want to do this, there's no way I could make her," I was repeatedly assured, and "The second she says she doesn't want to do it, we'll stop." Hearing that reminded me of the classic marketers' defense: "We just gave the girls what they wanted." But once again the questions arose: Where does desire end and coercion begin? When does "get to" become "have to"? I'm not sure parents who are that deeply invested in their children's success are able to tell. And if love, however subtly, seems conditional on performance—whether on the playing field, in the classroom, or onstage—how can a child truly say no?

"Did you see how she watched her mother?" Traci Eschberger asked when Eden's routine was over.

I nodded. "It was amazing," I replied, still in awe of the display.

Traci smiled tightly—that was not the response she was going for. "Eden has been doing this for years," she explained, "and she *still* has to watch her mother for every move? Taralyn never had to do that."

Case in point: when Taralyn hit the stage, Traci offered her no direction, though she did stand where her daughter could see her and occasionally called out, "Sparkle, sweetie!" which, as it happens, is precisely what Shirley Temple's mother used to say before the cameras rolled. Taralyn sauntered across the stage, threw the requisite kisses, then, in a move all her own, skipped along the front edge, pointing to each judge in turn and winking. She was so light on her feet, she almost floated. It was clear she had inherited her mother's grace and athleticism. I mentioned this to Traci, who nodded, pleased, then added, "You can't force that. She loves to perform. She *wants* to be onstage."

After a break, the swimsuit competition began. Taralyn's father, Todd, an affable redhead in a maroon polo shirt, entered the ballroom with their nine-year-old son, Tallon, also a strawberry blond and, like Taralyn, a handsome kid. Or he would have been, if circumstances had been different. Tallon was born with severe mental and physical disabilities: his brain, for reasons that were never determined, had not developed past infancy, leaving him unable to hear, talk, walk, or even sit up on his own. He was gripping an electronic plastic Simon game, its lights flashing in random patterns that users are supposed to memorize and replicate. Although he couldn't play, he seemed fascinated by the blinking colors. Todd parked Tallon's wheelchair on an aisle and took a seat next to him, stroking the boy's arm as he watched the girls onstage. Occasionally, Tallon banged his toy too loudly against his wheelchair tray; Todd gently extracted it, then handed it back a few minutes later. His patience never wavered, nor did Traci's. Their devotion to their son was both rock-solid and devoid of self-pity. I might question what they were doing to their daughter, but I admired how they cared for their son.

After Tallon was born, his doctors had advised the Eschbergers against having any more children. They didn't listen. "I said, 'You know what?'" Traci recalled. "'We have to have faith that we'll have a normal, happy child.' And now I think God is blessing us on the other end of the spectrum because Taralyn's very bright and talented. So we have both ends. We have one child who will not, unfortunately, be able to do a whole lot. But we're just thankful he's still with us."

I glanced from Tallon to Taralyn, with her wide smile and supple body. Her brother's health crises had been hard on her. That's part of why the family had been so gung ho about the pageants. "I feel guilty because she lost the first two years of her life because of Tallon," Traci told me. "At that point, we couldn't leave the house. It was that debilitating." Pageants became a way for Taralyn to escape, a "special time" when the focus was solely on her. Often, she and her mother would go to competitions alone and enjoy a bit of girl bonding. "We cherish these weekends," Traci said. "We really do. We get to stay at the hotel, and Taralyn gets to go swimming and jump on the bed."

Of course, that "special time" did not have to involve dressing up like Pretty Baby. Still, I could sympathize with the pride—the relief—the Eschbergers must feel whenever Taralyn is crowned, when she is publicly celebrated not only for her normalcy but for her miraculous perfection. I could only imagine how difficult the family's path has been, the lifelong burden Taralyn will carry: the mixture of resentment and protectiveness, love and guilt. She did deserve something of her own, a place to be free, to be a child—maybe even, for a moment, to feel that she, or at least her life, is perfect. And isn't that, at its core, what the princess fantasy is about for all of us? "Princess" is how we tell little girls that they are special, precious. "Princess" is how we express our aspirations, hopes, and dreams for them. "Princess" is the wish that we could protect them from pain, that they would never know sorrow, that they will live happily ever after ensconced in lace and innocence.

I had seen several television shows featuring the Eschbergers, but none had mentioned Tallon. I suspect that would have complicated the story, elicited sympathy from the disapproving audience, humanized the parents—thrown shades of gray into a narrative that is best seen in black and white. I'm not letting the Eschbergers (or parents like them) off the hook, but it is so easy to portray the freak-show aspects of these families. No question, they have taken the obsession with girls' looks to an appalling extreme; but, one could argue, the difference between them and the rest of us may be more one of degree than of kind. "Ordinary" parents might balk at the $3,000 dress or the spray tan, but guess what? In 2007, we spent a whopping $11.5 billion on clothing for our seven- to fourteen-year-olds, up from $10.5 billion in 2004. Close to half of six- to nine-year-old girls regularly use lipstick or gloss, presumably with parental approval; the percentage of eight- to twelve-year-olds who regularly use mascara and eyeliner doubled between 2008 and 2010, to 18 and 15 percent, respectively. "Tween" girls now spend more than $40 million a *month* on beauty products. No wonder Nair, the depilatory maker, in 2007 released Nair Pretty, a fruit-scented line designed to make ten-year-olds conscious of their "unwanted" body hair. And who, according to the industry tracking group NPD, most inspires girls' purchases? Their moms. As a headline on the cheeky feminist Web site Jezebel.com asked, "How Many 8-Year-Olds Have to Get Bikini Waxes Before We Can All Agree the Terrorists Have Won?"

ᏫᎢᏀᏂᎩ

Watching the pageant contestants promenade onstage, I thought about a suburban shopping mall I had visited some months earlier to check out a store called Club Libby Lu. Aimed at the VIP (Very Important Princess) ages four to twelve—again, a span whose extremes, it seems, should have little in common—it was conceived of by Mary Drolet, a Chicago-area mother and former executive at Claire's (she later sold out to Saks for $12 million). Walking into a link of the chain, I had to tip my tiara to her: Libby Lu's design was flawless, from the logo (a crown-topped heart) to the colors (pink, pink, pink, purple, and more pink) to the display shelves scaled to the size of a ten-year-old (though most of the shoppers I saw were closer to six). The decals on the walls and dressing rooms—I LOVE YOUR HAIR, HIP CHICK, SPOILED—were written in what they called "girlfriend language." The young salesclerks at this "special secret club for superfabulous girls" were called "club counselors." The malls themselves were chosen based on a secret formula called the GPI, or "Girl Power Index," which, in an Orwellian bit of doublespeak, predicts potential profitability.

Inside, I browsed through midriff-baring tops with ROCK STAR scrawled across them in sequins, cheerleader outfits, feather-covered princess phones, pillows emblazoned with the word BLING in rhinestones. I moseyed over to the "Style Studio," where a seven-year-old girl was being transformed into a "Priceless Princess" through a "Libby Du" makeover. Her hair was teased into an elaborate updo, crowned with a tiara, and liberally sprayed with glitter. Blue eye shadow was stroked across her lids, followed by a dusting of blush and watermelon pink lip gloss. *Hello, Taralyn!* Libby Lu also offered birthday parties at which, after their makeovers, girls could ramp up the tunes and strut a catwalk pretending to be Pussycat Dolls or supermodels. So, okay, they weren't competing for money (however, the makeovers *cost* as much as $35 per child), and they probably were not doing it every weekend—though kids do go to an awful lot of birthday parties, and they are often all the same—but still, how different was the message?

When Libby Lu started, the typical customer was about ten, but over the next few years that age gradually drifted downward, so that the girls I saw making their own cosmetics at the Sparkle Spa station were closer to Taralyn's age. Marketers call that KGOY—Kids Getting Older Younger. The idea, similar to the rejection of Barbie for Bratz by six-year-olds, is that toys and trends start with older children, but younger ones, trying to be like their big brothers and sisters, quickly adopt them. That immediately taints them for the original audience. And so the cycle goes. That's why the cherry-flavored Bonne Bell Lip Smackers that I got as my first "real" makeup at age twelve are now targeted at four- to six-year-olds (who collect flavors by the dozens). I have often idly wondered, since those same KGOY theorists claim that adults stay *younger* older—fifty is the new thirty!—whether our children will eventually surpass us in age. Or perhaps we will all meet at a mutually agreed upon ideal, a forever twenty-one.

But I don't want my daughter to be twenty-one when she is twelve. I don't think *she* will want to be twenty-one when she is twelve, not really. As it is, girls are going through puberty progressively earlier. The age of onset of menstruation has dropped from seventeen at the beginning of the twentieth century to barely twelve today; pediatricians no longer consider it exceptional for an eight-year-old to develop breasts. That means ten-year-old girls frequently resemble sexually mature women—sexually mature women who have been encouraged, in an unprecedented way, to play at being hot since early childhood. Yet, although they are physically more advanced, the pace of girls' psychological and emotional development has remained unchanged; they only look, and act, older on the outside. In his thoughtful book *The Triple Bind*, Stephen Hinshaw, the chair of the Department of Psychol-

ogy at the University of California, Berkeley, warns that imposing any developmental task on children before they are ready can
cause irreparable, long-term harm. Consider the trend toward
academically accelerated preschool: at best, young children who
are drilled on letters and numbers show no later advantage compared with those in play-based programs. In some cases, by high
school their outcomes are *worse*. That inappropriately early pressure seems to destroy the interest and joy in learning that would
naturally develop a few years later. Girls pushed to be sexy too
soon can't really understand what they're doing. And that, Hinshaw argues, is the point: they do not—and may never—learn to
connect their performance to erotic feelings or intimacy. They
learn how to act desirable but not how to desire, undermining
rather than promoting healthy sexuality.

It would seem, then, that parents should be working harder
than ever to protect their daughters' childhoods, to prevent them
from playing Sesame Street Walker. And most parents you would
talk to, whatever their policy on child-friendly eye shadow for
three-year-olds, would say that is exactly what they are trying to
do. But I can't help recalling an article describing the ways pageant moms rationalize their behavior. Two strategies particularly
caught my eye. The first was "denial of injury"—the idea that the
children are not harmed by the experience and may actually benefit. The second was "denial of responsibility": they may personally disapprove of pageants, but their four-year-olds *so* wanted
to compete that they had no choice but to comply. Rejigger that
wording a bit, substitute "Disney Princess 21-piece play makeup
set" or "mani-pedi birthday party" or "Rock & Republic Jeans,"
and it sounds like a conversation you would hear on any suburban
playground.

I don't mean to imply that shielding one's daughter from

sexually charged toys, clothing, music, and images is easy. They are, after all, standard fare in the aisles of the big-box stores. Even Walmart's size 4–6X Sassy Vampiress Halloween getup with its tight pink-and-black bustier top (for what bust, I ask you?) hardly raises an eyebrow. One exception: in 2010, a video went viral featuring a group of eight- and nine-year-old competitors in a national contest—dressed in outfits that would make a stripper blush—bumping and pumping to Beyoncé's "Single Ladies (Put a Ring on It)." The routine sparked public outcry, was berated on CNN and FOX News, and truly, it was a gift to the world's wired pedos. But I sympathized (sort of) with the girls' parents, who went on *Good Morning America* to defend them: the choreography had been lifted from a scene in *Alvin and the Chipmunks 2*, in which gratuitously tarted-up "Chipettes" shook their furry booties to the same tune while Al and his bros leered. No one had objected to *that*. The girls were only mimicking what they had seen in a family film (which, by the by, has raked in more than $440 million worldwide).

I am hardly one to judge other mothers' choices: my own behavior has been hypocritical, inconsistent, even reactionary. There was the time when Daisy was four and we were walking through the Los Angeles airport on the way to visit her paternal grandma. Daisy's eye fell on a display of Ty Girlz dolls, made by the same company that brought you Beanie Babies, best known for the faux pas of creating dolls based on Malia and Sasha Obama without permission (which the company was forced to rename). Ty Girlz are like a plush version of Bratz, for the fashion-forward preschooler. They have names such as "Oo-LaLa Olivia," "Classy Carla," and "Sizzlin' Sue." But they're cuddly. And apparently they exude some invisible gamma ray that hypnotizes small girls. "Mama!" Daisy cried, dashing over to the wire rack of dolls that had been placed in front of a newsstand. "Can I have one of those?" I took in the Angelina Jolie lips, the heavily shadowed eyelids, the microscopic skirts, the huge hair—and I kept right on walking.

"No," I said.

"But maybe for my birthday?" she tried.

Something in me snapped. "No!" I said, more firmly than was strictly necessary. "Not for your birthday, not for Chanukah, not for anything. You will never, *ever* get one of those dolls!"

"But *why not?*" she pressed.

I wanted to yell, *"BECAUSE THEY'RE SLUTTY, THAT'S WHY!"* But I didn't, because Lord knows I did not want to have to explain what "slutty" meant. Instead I relied on the default parenting phrase, a prim "Because they're inappropriate."

"But *why* are they unappropriate?"

Suddenly I was furious. Why should I even have been put into a position where I had to have this conversation with my four-year-old? I felt as though Ty Girlz had me over a barrel, a barrel to whose slats I would have to become increasingly accustomed. I didn't want to tell her why I objected to the dolls, because the explanation itself was as "unappropriate" as the product. And, yes, it could have been an opportunity for yet another lesson, but I was sick and tired of being confronted by these endless "teachable moments." It was beginning to dawn on me that I had been caught in a cunningly laid trap: I was attempting to offer Daisy more choices—a broader view of her possibilities, of her femininity—by repeatedly saying no to her every request. What were the odds *that* was going to work? Even the forbidden-fruit argument I so often hear seemed a scam: it still forced me to buy something I did not even want her to know about in the hope that it would quench her desire rather than stoke it, that she would, as Disney's

Andy Mooney had said, "pass through the phase" rather than internalize it (earning his company a tidy profit in the meanwhile).

So I found myself ping-ponging through girl land. I gave in on Polly Pocket with her endless itty-bitty rubber clothes, but not to the Pollywheels Race to the Mall racetrack set ("The first car to reach the boutique captures a shopping bag!"). Yes to Groovy Girls (which, like Pollys, have gotten markedly skinnier and more fashion-conscious since they were introduced), but absolutely no way to Ty Girlz. And Barbie? Oh, Barbie, Barbie, Barbie. The fifty-year-old vector of all body-image complaints. She, too, has been the catalyst of many a toy store meltdown—mine, not my daughter's. I am not proud of the incident at Target when, while I was off searching for cleanser, Steven told Daisy she could have a cheesy blue Fairytopia Barbie with crappy plastic wings. I demanded that he take it away from her. She started to cry. So I gave it back.

"You're confusing her," Steven said.

I did the mature thing: I blamed him.

"Look, I'm sorry I started this," he replied. "But you need to decide where you stand on this stuff and stick to it."

He was right, so I took the doll away again. I promised I would get her a *well-made* Barbie instead, perhaps a Cleopatra Barbie I had seen on eBay, which, at the very least, was not white or blond and had something to offer besides high-heeled feet. As if the ankh pendant and peculiar tan made it all okay.

"Never mind, Mama," she sobbed. "I don't need it." Then I started to cry, too, and bought her the damned Barbie.

No wonder my kid is confused. So am I.

By noon, the four- to six-year-old competition was over, and crowning would not begin until eight that evening. Taralyn, still full of energy, continued to perform her routines in a corner, just for her own pleasure, then, obligingly, several more times for the TV crews who descended on her. "I haven't seen this many reporters outside of some kind of presidential press conference," Traci joked.

It was true: there were moments that day when it seemed as though there were more press than contestants. And the cameras all focused on Taralyn and Eden, though they were far from the only girls here. I wandered over to where Jamara Burmeister, age seven, was preparing for her first statewide contest, in the six- to seven-year-old division. Jamara was the only girl under eleven dressed in a floor-length gown: its full, Cinderella-style skirt was rose and white, decorated with bows and accessorized with elbow-length gloves and a strand of pearls. Her hair was swept up, a few tendrils escaping. She looked comparatively dignified, more like a flower girl than a high-glitz competitor. Which meant, essentially, that she was doomed.

"We didn't know," explained Jamara's mother, Tammi. "We'd never done this before."

Their only pageant experience was back home in south Texas, where contestants were more natural and, unlike in Universal pageants, were evaluated in part by how they handled interview questions both onstage and in unrehearsed private meetings with the judges.

It was Jamara's father who had originally pushed to put her into pageants, after seeing an episode of *Toddlers & Tiaras*. "He saw those girls and thought, 'Jamara could do that,'" Tammi said. "Because she's, well . . ." She paused and smiled. "Every parent thinks their child is beautiful. But Jamara has got 'it,' you know?"

Jamara entered her town pageant earlier this year and won handily. "She was so enthusiastic," Tammi said, "we decided to try this. It's her thing, and we're going to run with it."

Pageant families come from all walks of life. There are those, like the parents of JonBenét Ramsey, who are white and affluent, who spend thousands of dollars on dance classes, voice coaches, gowns, wigs, head shots. Eden Wood's mother, Mickie, said she has spent about $70,000 on her daughter's pageant career. Most of the folks competing in Austin, though, were of more modest means. Jamara, who like many contestants was Latina, raised money for her gown and entry fees by going door-to-door among the businesses in her small town asking for sponsorship. As Tammi adjusted the girl's skirt and fussed with her hair, she told me that she and her husband could not afford the competition on their own. They run an answering service and, last year, in addition to their own five children, took in three more, those of an employee with a drug problem, to keep them out of the foster care system. "We prayed about it a lot," she said of that decision. "It was the right thing to do."

Again I found myself looking at a pageant mom through a different, more compassionate lens. As with Traci, there was something else going on here. It seemed that, for a variety of reasons—a disabled child, the hope of upward mobility, an escape route from small-town life—these little girls had become the repository of their family's ambitions. That made a certain kind of sense. Historically, girls' bodies have often embodied families' upwardly mobile dreams: flawless complexions, straight teeth, narrow waists—all have served as symbols of parental aspirations.

A few days ago, I might have been appalled to see a seven-year-old decked out like Jamara, but after six hours of immersion in the world of pageants, my standards had begun to shift. I was starting to see the girls as their parents did—as engaging in a little healthy fun, merely playing an elaborate version of dress-up. Yet even pageants had not always promoted the Lolita look. Back in the 1960s, when children's competitions began, all a contestant needed to enter was a party frock, a pair of Mary Janes, and a satin hair bow. The rest was introduced over time, as prize money escalated, competition intensified, and both contestants and pageants needed to distinguish themselves. "I thought it was bizarre, too, when we started," Traci Eschberger had told me. "I didn't think I'd ever do it. I do think all that makeup makes them look older. But we wash it off as soon as the pageant ends. As long as she's having fun and it's not hurting her."

Maybe that's what happens to us in the "real" world, too. Our tolerance for hypersexualization rises without our realizing it. Moxie Girlz seem subdued after our exposure to Bratz. We get used to seeing twelve-year-olds in lip gloss, low-slung jeans, and crop tops that say BAD GIRL, and soon the same outfit seems unremarkable on an eight-year-old. A woman who did not get her first manicure until she was twenty-five finds herself throwing a "primping" birthday party for her seven-year-old at a nail salon in Brooklyn. Parents in San Francisco send kids whose ages are still in the single digits to a spa summer camp where they "de-stress" by creating their own makeup and moisturizer (as if third-graders are in danger of developing wrinkles?). It is easy to become impervious to shock, to adjust to each new normal. Also, as mentioned earlier, even brief exposure to stereotypes—in advertisements, television shows, and the like—unconsciously increases women's and girls' acceptance of them. At one point, looking around the ballroom, I actually caught myself thinking, Hell, my daughter could do this, too.

By nine that night, an hour into the crowning ceremony, the girls were exhausted. One four-year-old lay splayed across three chairs, arms akimbo, asleep, still wearing her cupcake gown, snoring sweetly, small bubbles of spit gathering at the corner of her mouth. The rest of the girls had become a blur of sequins, fake tans, and big hair. I could hardly tell one from another. According to Miss Annette, Taralyn and Eden were in a dead heat for the top prize. "The judges are looking at personality," she said. "They're looking at facial beauty. They're looking at expressions, the overall appearance of the dress, the modeling ability. So it's a very, very hard competition, very stressful."

When the lesser awards for the four- and five-year-olds were announced, Taralyn cleaned up, winning trophies for most beautiful, most photogenic, best swimsuit, and best personality. But it was Eden who took the division crown. I assumed that was a loss, but Traci's smile as she clapped for her daughter's rival looked too real. She explained that if you win the division, which carries no cash prize, you're done: out of the running for everything else. So this result was actually a good thing, what they wanted.

Jamara, meanwhile, did not win a single trophy in her division. Her parents didn't know that should give them hope for the bigger prizes until I told them. A few minutes later, she took the crown for Little Miss Sweetheart. No cash came with the title, but she and her family seemed pleased. "I don't feel bad that she didn't win something bigger," said her father, Jason, who had dressed in a suit and tie for the occasion. "I don't want her to alter herself like these other girls. I just want her to feel comfortable with her looks and feel good about her natural beauty. That's what's important to us."

"This was definitely out of our league," added Tammi, Jamara's mother. "It's not what we're used to. It wouldn't have occurred to me to buy one of those tutus. But we're just starting out. It was a learning experience. Next time we'll know. And we'll be back."

Across the room, Taralyn sat on the floor near her mother, surrounded by her trophies. She had dumped out the contents of her goodie bag and was busily gobbling up the candy and twisting the Play-Doh into pretend rings and bracelets. She did not much seem to care about what was happening onstage, though when the Grand Talent winner was about to be announced she squeezed her eyes shut and gritted her teeth in anticipation. When the name called was not hers, she relaxed. "Yes!" she said happily, then went back to playing. She was still in it.

Finally, all the sets of "ice crystal rhinestone" crowns, gilt trophies, and monogrammed sashes had been handed out except one, as had all the smaller cash prizes for the "Mini Supremes." Miss Annette milked the final, suspenseful moment like a pro. "And the winner of the Universal Royalty Texas State Pageant Overall Grand Supreme and a two-*thousand*-dollar cash prize is . . ." She waved the money, twenty crisp hundred-dollar bills which, as is typical in pageants, had been spread out and stapled into a double-decker fan. "Miss . . ." Another wave of the cash. *"TARALYN ES-CHBERGER!!!"* Taralyn let out a war whoop as Todd hoisted her aloft and Traci leapt to her feet, clapping wildly. The girl ran to the stage, accepted the fan of money, then displayed it to the crowd, remembering first to place one foot at a ninety degree angle from the other (a position called "Pretty Feet") and paste her best beauty queen smile on her face. TV cameras rolled and flashbulbs popped: in child pageants, the money shot *is* the money shot.

The evening's other winners joined Taralyn onstage for a

photo session. Partway through, she stifled a yawn—it was nearly ten o'clock, long past her bedtime—but before anyone noticed, she put that trouper smile right back on, pulled back her shoulders, and . . . sparkled.

Maybe someday Taralyn will wash off her pageant mask forever, rebel against it. Maybe she won't. Maybe she will even put her own child into pageants, either because she loved the experience or because she is trying to recapture the attention and adoration she received on nights like this. Maybe the affirmation of her beauty will indeed build her confidence—given how important girls, *all* girls, learn beauty is, why wouldn't it?—or maybe being judged as if she were an object will eventually undermine it. Maybe one day Taralyn will come to believe she is loved only for her beauty, loved only if she can *stay* beautiful—thin and unblemished, with the right breasts and teeth—if she can be perfect, if she does not let her parents down. One prominent former child beauty queen, nineteen-year-old Brooke Breedwell, who at age five was featured in the BBC documentary "Painted Babies," has attributed her poise as an adult to her pageant experience. She has also said that pageants damaged her relationship with her mother and instilled a crippling need to be perfect at anything she tries. Who knows whether the same will be true for Taralyn?

As the stagehands struck the set, they offered bouquets of helium balloons to the children who were straggling out. Taralyn was ecstatic with hers. She was only five, after all. Two thousand dollars meant nothing to her, but twenty balloons—now, *that* was a prize. "I could have just gone down to the party store and saved a lot of money," her father, Todd, said to me, and smiled.

We both watched as Taralyn zoomed across the room with her balloons, laughing. Just like an ordinary five-year-old. Just a little girl having fun.

Chapter Six

Guns and (Briar) Roses

*M*ama, can I have this for Chanukah?" I was
standing in Mr. Mopp's, our charmingly
dilapidated neighborhood toy shop, looking for a birthday present for a friend's toddler. Although Daisy was
barely five at the time, I could not, for the life of me, remember what bestirred the three-year-old heart. The
changes kids go through are so quick, so intense, and
you are so bloody exhausted when they're happening.
It feels as though you'll never forget, but you always
do. All I could recall about three was that it was the
age when kids supposedly stop shoving pennies up
their noses. So how to celebrate that blessed milestone,
the safety of small parts: A Playmobil set, perhaps?
Marbles? I admit I felt a certain pressure: the child in

question was a princess-loving female, but her mother (and all of the other moms who would be at the party) knew how I felt about that. They would be watching, skeptical and bemused, to see if I could come up with a viable alternative.

While I mulled over the options, Daisy hit the dress-up rack and promptly became mesmerized by a pair of purple plastic mules festooned with faux ostrich feathers accompanied by a string of cheap, glittery beads that wouldn't hold together for five seconds. Tawdry *and* badly made—what a bargain! She pretty much expected the "no" she got when she showed me that one. A few minutes later, though, she was back, brandishing something else: a die-cast silver cap gun with a shiny pink grip and matching vinyl holster cunningly embellished with a cowgirl on a horse.

How many ways could that toy blow the modern mommy's mind? But rather than being appalled, I found myself sinking into reverie. I have two older brothers, and as a girl I had loved playing with their hand-me-down pistols: the feel of the grip in my hand, the shiny muzzle, the satisfying snap when the hammer released, the acrid sulfur smell rising from a roll of red caps, the thrilling possibility of burning a finger (did that ever really happen?). I was not a violent kid. Nor am I a violent adult: I road-tripped from rural Ohio to New York City in the 1980s to march against nuclear proliferation. I took to the streets in San Francisco during the first invasion of Iraq. (At the time of the second, Daisy's nap time conflicted with the protests. Priorities change . . .) In fact, I am already against the *next* war. In other words, playing with guns did not make me a sociopath. On the other hand, there was no industry trying to convince me that violence was the cornerstone of my femininity, no pressure to define myself by my bullets.

Daisy already owned a cowgirl hat, woven of straw and trimmed in red. I had bought it when she was around four years old, because I thought it was adorable—and because I hoped it might offset the princess stuff.

"But what do cowgirls *do*, Mama?" she asked when I placed it on her head.

I was at a bit of a loss. Among my peers, cowboy play had ridden off into the sunset when we realized that the Indians were not necessarily the bad guys. So what was left? Judging by TV shows about the Wild West, such as David Milch's *Deadwood*, the answer was cussing, whoring, and getting stinking drunk.

"Um," I said, reaching for another option, "I guess they keep track of all the cows?"

So much for the romance of the Old West. She never wore the hat again.

But a gun. Should I let her have a *gun*?

Thinking quickly, I told her we were not there to buy a present for *her*, but if she wanted, she could put the gun on her birthday list. Then, when we got home, I asked Steven what he thought. He shook his head. "I don't see any reason to have war toys in the house," he said.

But, I pressed, didn't you love your guns as a child?

"Sure," he admitted. "But that was a different time."

I also polled my friends. "No way," said the one with five children. Then she paused. "Well, if one of the girls wanted one it would be okay, that would be defying stereotypes. But not the boys. *Never* the boys." This from a woman whose house was awash with light sabers, Transformers, and swords.

"Do you also refuse the girls makeup and Barbies but let the boys have them?" I asked.

At this point she began to get annoyed, so I let the subject drop.

And honestly, let's be realistic. Playing with a toy gun—even yelling "Bang! Bang! You're dead"—was not going to turn my kid (or hers) into Hannibal Lecter. In addition to my beloved pistols, I watched stupefying amounts of Tom and Jerry and Road Runner cartoons (probably while hopped up on Froot Loops followed by a Pixy Stix chaser), though, admittedly, I found them as excruciating as I do the recent craze for Larry David–style "cringe humor."

The truth is, there is virtually no research on the impact of violent images or play on girls. For whatever reason—biological, environmental, developmental—girls are not as drawn to bashing one another as boys are. Their aggression tends to be more interpersonal than physical. It is worth considering, though, that adults tend to ignore behavior that doesn't fit our beliefs about gender and seize upon that which does. So when boys point their fingers like pistols, we chalk it up to nature; when girls do it (and I have seen Daisy draw her "hand guns" on friends a number of times), it goes unnoticed. Either way, violent play is not by definition bad or harmful for kids. Any child shrink worth her sand table will tell you it can help them learn about impulse control, work out the difference between fantasy and reality, cope with fear. But there is a catch: according to Diane Levin, a professor of education and coauthor of *The War Play Dilemma*, violent play is useful only if it *is* truly play, if kids control the narratives, if they are using their imaginations to create the story lines, props, outcomes. That is what has changed since my own cap gun days, she explained. Beginning in the 1980s, children's television advertising was deregulated; the number of commercials instantly doubled—you could run the same cereal ad three times in a row if you wanted. Programs themselves essentially became vehicles to sell toys. My Little Pony. Rainbow Brite. Care Bears. Girls were flooded with a resurgence of sweet and pretty. Boys were deluged with action figures: Masters of the Universe, Teenage

Mutant Ninja Turtles, Power Rangers. In surveys of parents and teachers across the country, Levin found that, rather than engaging in creative play, children began imitating what they saw on-screen, reenacting rote scripts with licensed products. Whether in Portland, Maine, or Portland, Oregon, their play became homogenized. Nor was there evidence that their stories were evolving, that they were making the kind of inner meaning out of their dramas that would provide psychological resolution, as they once had.

So to an extent, then, my husband was right: times had indeed changed. As for guns that are not "really" guns, Levin told me, "We're fooling ourselves if we think those are better. When you give kids a light saber, you know exactly what they are going to do with it, and every kid who has one will do the exact same thing. There is no creativity there." Like princess play, then, boys' gunplay may resonate with parents' own childhood memories, but, given the marketing culture in which they are immersed, their relationship to those toys and images, as well as the impact on them, may be different.

I will leave the world of boys for someone else to explore, but it is clear that children of both sexes crave larger-than-life heroes. They need fantasy. They also, it seems, need a certain amount of violent play. I'm not talking Resident Evil 4, where within minutes gamers confront a female corpse pinned to a wall with a pitchfork through her face, but something that allows them to triumph in their own way over this thing we call death, to work out their day-to-day frustrations; to feel large, powerful, and safe. Because as much as we want to believe that children are innocent, by the time they enter the dog-eat-dog jungle of preschool, they have realized that everyone is capable of senseless cruelty and spite. Even their parents. Even themselves. The Big Bad Wolf is out there, baby, and Mom and Dad may not be able to stop him.

Which brings me back to fairy tales. After World War II, Allied commanders banned publication of the Grimm brothers' stories in Germany, believing that their bloodlust had contributed to the Nazi atrocities. For the same reason, they fell out of favor among American parents. Take the brothers' "Snow White": at the end the wicked queen is invited to her stepdaughter's wedding, where—surprise!—she is forced into a pair of red-hot iron shoes and made to dance until she dies. Like I need my five-year-old to have that image in her head?

The thing is, though, if you believe the psychologist Bruno Bettelheim, we avoid the Grimms' grimness at our peril. His classic book *The Uses of Enchantment* argues that the brothers' gore is not only central to the tales' appeal, it's crucial to kids' emotional development. (An earlier intellectual rock star, John Locke, disagreed; he deemed the fairy tales too gruesome for little ears, but then again, he also thought the offspring of the poor should be put to work at age three.) According to Bettelheim, fairy tales and *only* fairy tales—as opposed to myths or legends—tap into children's unconscious preoccupations with such knotty issues as sibling rivalry or the fear of an omnivorous mother. In their tiny minds, a fearsome giant may be transformed into the school bully, a menacing wolf into a neighbor's pit bull. Fairy tales demonstrate that hardship may be inevitable, but those who stand fast emerge victorious. What's more, he wrote, the solutions to life's struggles that fairy tales suggest are subtle, impressionistic, and therefore more useful than either the spoon-fed pap that passes for kiddie "literature" these days or the overly concrete images of television (and now the Internet). He goes so far as to say that without exposure to fairy tales a child will be emotionally stunted, unable to create a meaningful life.

I guess *Knuffle Bunny Too* won't do.

Nor, apparently, will the stacks of revisionist, modern-day princess books I had checked out of the library. Anyway, most of them seem to equate "pro-girl" with "anti-boy," which does not strike me as an improvement. Take *The Paper Bag Princess*, a staple of kindergarten classrooms everywhere. The heroine outwits a dragon that has kidnapped her prince, but not before the beast's fiery breath frizzles her hair and destroys her dress, forcing her to don a paper bag. The ungrateful prince then rejects her, telling her to come back when she is "dressed like a real princess." She summarily dumps him and skips off into the sunset happily ever after, alone.

To me, that is *Thelma & Louise* all over again. Step out of line, and you end up solo or, worse, sailing crazily over a cliff to your doom. I may want my girl to do and be whatever she dreams of as an adult, but I also hope she will find her Prince (or Princess) Charming and make me a grandma. I do not want her to be a fish without a bicycle; I want her to be a fish with another fish. Preferably, a fish who loves and respects her and also does the dishes, his share of the laundry, and half the child care. Yet the typical "feminist alternative" to the marry-the-prince ending either portrays men as simpletons or implies that the roles traditionally ascribed to women are worthless. Thus you get *Princess Smartypants*, in which our heroine, uninterested in marriage, bestows a chaste smooch on the prince who has won her hand in a contest sponsored by her father, the king; the prince promptly turns into a frog, and she is freed to live contentedly with her pets. To me, that's not progress; it's payback.

Unquestionably, the Grimms routinely bumped off mothers, equated beauty with virtue, and pitted women against one another in a battle over husbands. Understandably, parents' first impulse is to keep the stories' grisliness far, far away from their children. But what if Bettelheim was right? What if their horrors do help our kids to explore their fears safely, to answer the Big Questions of existence? Should we deny them that wealth in favor of a $50 "official" Cinderella gown? Maybe I had been hasty in dismissing fairy tales as a bastion of passive heroines and Prince Charming hype. Uncle Walt may have most successfully reinterpreted the tales for our era, but why should he get the final say? Maybe I needed to revisit the traditional stories myself.

What do you know: I began with a (toy) gun to my head and found that when I stared down the barrel, I was once again looking smack into the eyes of Cinderella.

〰️

Calling the Grimms' fairy tales the "originals" is as absurd as conferring that designation on Disney's. The brothers culled their stories from a rich, distinctly adult oral storytelling tradition, then edited, embellished, and heavily sanitized them. Did you seriously think the prince merely *kissed* the comatose Sleeping Beauty? That Rapunzel and her beau whiled away their time in that phallic tower holding hands? Before the Grimms gussied them up for the nursery, both girls were in a family way—each pregnant with *twins*!—well before the Happily Ever After kicked in. Fairy tales have been called the porn of their day: bawdy, raucous, full of premarital shenanigans and double entendre. They were also rife with incest or the threat of it. The Grimms took that out, too. The brothers' delicacy, however, did not extend to violence: on the contrary, they ratcheted up the bloody bits, believing they would scare children out of bad behavior.

As for Cinderella (whom the Grimms called "Aschenputtel," a name which, understandably, did not catch on)? There are at least five hundred versions of that story told around the world. The Chinese Yeh-Shen, whose story was recorded in A.D. 850, gets her mojo from the carcass of a dead fish. The Japanese Hachikazuki spends years with a flowerpot wedged on her head. The Russian Cinderella is saved by a magic cow; in Brazil she is born with an enchanted snake curled around her neck. There are Cinderellas in African tribes and Native American ones. Her slippers are made of glass, fur, or gold, and sometimes there is no footwear at all. But the basic plotline never wavers: a beautiful, kind girl is brought low by a parent's untimely death, then humiliated by her new guardian; she is transformed through some act of bippity-boppity-boo so that her exterior sparkles as brightly as her heart; she loses an item of clothing while fleeing a love-besotted noble-man who relentlessly tracks her down; there is the big reveal of her true identity—bummer for the evil relatives!—and she lives happily ever after with the man of her dreams. Apparently we, like our preschoolers, are suckers for that arc. Even today, Cinderella stories are guaranteed box-office hits: *Pretty Woman, Ever After, Maid in Manhattan, Ella Enchanted, Princess Diaries* (I *and* II)—even *Enchanted*, which gently spoofed the genre. Something so enduring, so universal must have—well—*something*, right? Perhaps I had judged this particular princess too harshly.

There is no pumpkin in the Grimms' "Aschenputtel," no foot-men, not even a fairy godmother. Disney cribbed those from "Cendrillon," a seventeenth-century French version by Charles Perrault. Instead, Jacob and Wilhelm's heroine plants a hazel branch on her dead mother's grave, waters it with her tears, and watches it grow into an enchanted tree. Whenever she wishes for something—such as, oh, a gown for the ball—a dove perched among the leaves tosses it down to her. I liked that: her mother's love was so powerful that it transcended death. Admittedly, the story still sucks for stepmoms. If it is any comfort, psychologists say that splitting the mother into two characters—one good and one evil—serves a developmental purpose: it helps kids work through their inevitable resentment against Mom without directly copping to it. To which my stepmother friends respond: "Whatever."

That aside, making the mother the source of the magic interested me. One of the things I had found most disturbing about the Disney Princesses was that somehow the wand had been transferred to the girl. The heroines of the stories had never before been magic—not even in the studio's own movies. It was not enough that the writers had whacked all the mothers and made their surrogates loathsome; now they had given the boot to the fairy godmother as well—the sole remaining symbol of adult female guidance and protection. It was almost sinister, the implication that women had no place in girls' development. And it certainly reflected the current marketing mentality—cut out the middleman (or, in this case, woman), and sell directly to the child. I often wonder what the long-term results of that change will be: rather than raising a generation of Cinderellas, we may actually be cultivating a legion of stepsisters—spoiled, self-centered materialists, superficially charming but without the depth or means for authentic transformation.

I say: let's bring back that tree!

But the biggest surprise of "Aschenputtel" is that it's not about landing the prince. It is about the girl herself: her strength, her perseverance, her cleverness. It is a story, really, about her evolution from child to woman. It is Cinderella herself who plants the magic tree and requests the finery for the ball (which is celebrated over the course of three days). She walks to the party each night rather than traveling by enchanted coach. She leaves not because she has some arbitrarily imposed curfew but because she has danced enough. Then she escapes both the pursuing prince and her own father by hiding in a dovecote or nimbly scaling a tree. When the prince finally comes a-calling, shoe in hand, Cinderella greets him dressed in her sooty rags. He may be looking for the beauty with the dainty foot, but, as Joan Gould, the author of *Spinning Straw into Gold*, notes, she demands that he witness the woman she has been, dirt and all, not just the one she will become. So while he provides the occasion for her transformation, he is not the one responsible for it—she can only do that herself.

Not bad for a pair of medieval chauvinists. Except for this: as usual, the stepsisters try on the tiny golden slipper before Cinderella does; in order to jam their big fat clodhoppers into it, one slices off her heel and the other her toe. Some fancy academic might see that as a metaphor, a warning to girls against contorting themselves to fit unattainable standards of beauty, but, truly, it is just gross. And the Grimms seem to relish it, describing how the sisters grit their teeth, how the blood "spurts" from the shoe, staining their white stockings. Even Cinderella, seemingly so gracious, proves distressingly vengeful in the end. She invites the stepsisters to join her wedding party, but as they enter the church, one on either side of her, doves (again, perhaps, representing her mother) perched on the bride's shoulders peck out their eyes. That's right: Peck. Out. Their. Eyes. Imagine *those* wedding photos.

Still, I thought, remembering Bettelheim, I would not want to permanently scar my kid by denying her the blinding of the stepsisters. Maybe I could work up to it, start with something easier, like, I don't know, "Rumpelstiltskin." My memory of that story was a little vague, something about a gnome spinning a roomful of straw into gold and flying away on a spoon. How bad could that be?

A few days after the gun incident, I decided to give it a try. I hauled out my annotated Grimms, a 462-page tome with a navy-and-gold filigree cover. Daisy was, well, enchanted. We flipped through, examining its nineteenth- and early-twentieth-century illustrations (Bettelheim, who believed that pictures corrupt the power of the text, would have disapproved). Then I started reading.

"Once upon a time . . ." I began.

At the sound of those ageless words, Daisy snuggled close. I kept going: "there lived a miller who was very poor, but had a beautiful daughter." Okay, I thought, as the story moved forward, maybe the girl is treated like chattel by her dad and is supposed to be delighted to marry the greedy king who initially imprisoned and threatened to kill her if she did not make him rich, but at least there's no gushing blood. And the girl is resourceful, tricking the gnome and saving her baby. She even has a vaudevillian's sense of dramatic timing, stringing her tormentor along, pretending she does not know who he is until . . .

"Could your name possibly be, *Rumpelstiltskin?*"

Daisy's eyes shone as I continued. "The little man screamed and in his rage he stamped his right foot so hard that it went into the ground right up to his waist. Then in his fury he seized his left foot with both hands . . ."

My eye skipped ahead but it was too late: " . . . and tore himself asunder," I finished lamely.

Yikes! What happened to the spoon?

"He did what, Mommy?" Daisy asked, confused.

"Well," I said, "he was so mad, he ripped himself in half."

"Oh," she said, nodding.

Then: "Read another!" she commanded.

What to do? I considered ditching the Grimms for Hans Christian Andersen, maybe trying the original "The Little Mermaid." I have already grumbled about Disney's Ariel, who gives up her *voice* to get a guy. What kind of message is that? I ask you. I suddenly recalled, though, that Ariel got off easy compared with her precursor. In the Andersen version, the sea witch does not painlessly extract the mermaid's voice. Oh, no. She grabs a big old knife and hacks out the poor creature's tongue. Once the girl has her land legs, every step feels like "walking on knife blades so sharp the blood must flow," yet she dances for the prince on command, never hinting at the agony it causes her. As in the Disney film, the prince seems to return her love but then heaves her over for someone else, a princess he wrongly believes has saved his life. In this version, however, he never discovers the truth; he marries the other woman, explaining to the mermaid that he knows she would want him to be happy. Then the lout asks her to hold up the train of his bride's gown during the shipboard ceremony—and *she does it*, knowing all along that his marriage to another means her demise. Late that night, the mermaid's sisters appear; they have shorn their hair and traded it to the sea witch for a magic dagger. All the little mermaid has to do is stab the prince in his heartless heart; his blood on her legs will fuse them back into a fish tail and she will survive. But she can't do it. Instead, she flings herself overboard and disintegrates into sea foam. The only nod to happily-ever-after is that she eventually becomes a "daughter of the air" who, after three hundred years of good deeds, *might* earn an immortal soul. There may be valuable lessons in all of this—don't change for a guy; don't let him treat you like dirt; you deserve to be loved for what is special, magical, unique about you. But jeez, what a buzz kill.

So "The Little Mermaid" was out. But Daisy was still sitting next to me, looking expectant. Okay, Bruno, I thought. It's now or never. I took a deep breath and turned to "Cinderella."

Daisy listened intently for a while, then rolled onto her back and began kicking her legs in the air.

"Do you want me to stop, honey?" I said hopefully.

"No," she said firmly.

So I read it, the whole thing, without censorship, explanation, or any inflection to influence her reaction. Just as Bettelheim said I should. Then I asked what she thought.

"Eh," she said, waggling her hand.

"You didn't like it?"

"It was creepy," she said, wrinkling her nose. "The eye part. Yuck."

"Would you ever want to hear it again?"

She thought about that for a moment. "No," she said, then jumped off the couch and skipped away, chanting "Roo coo coo! Roo coo coo! Blood is dripping from the shoe!" and laughing.

Later, I would search out lesser-known traditional fairy tales about spunky, ingenious girls. I was surprised to find how many there were—at least as many as stories that celebrated the bravery of boys or men, perhaps more. Yet none was problem-free: In "The Robber Bridegroom," the heroine shrewdly foiled her fiancé's plot to murder her—after she secretly watched him tear off another young woman's clothes, hack her body into pieces, and salt it. In "Fitcher's Bird" a feisty girl saved her sisters from an evil wizard who had kidnapped them—by reassembling their limbs, which he had severed so that their "blood ran down all over the floor." In "Furrypelts," a Cinderella variant, a princess fearlessly took control of her destiny, fleeing her castle upon discovering she would be forced into marriage—to her father. "The Six Swans," in which a princess took a seven-year vow of silence to save her cursed brothers, became a favorite with Daisy even though the evil mother-in-law took advantage of the heroine's muteness by stealing each of her three babies upon their births, smearing chicken's blood on the princess's unspeaking mouth, then telling her son that the girl had eaten them (Mom-in-Law also tries to convince the castle cook to make the infants into a stew and feed them to their father). I loved Diane Wolkstein's adaptation of "The Glass Mountain," which amped up the princess's role in her own fate, but Daisy rejected it (as would Dr. Bruno, I reckon). She was partial to an Algonquin Indian legend—admittedly not an official fairy tale—about a young bride who saved herself and her husband from cannibal demons, but . . . cannibals? I put the kibosh on that. No matter how macabre the stories got, though, Daisy did not flinch. None gave her the kind of nightmares that the movie version of *Chitty Chitty Bang Bang* had.

Score one for Bettelheim.

Compared with Stephenie Meyer, the Grimms come off like Andrea Dworkin. Meyer, a Mormon homemaker turned novelist, is the author of the most successful fairy tale in recent memory: the *Twilight* saga. Initially imagined in a "vivid dream," the four-book series had, at this writing, sold more than 100 million copies worldwide, while films based on the first two had grossed more than a billion dollars. No wonder it has been compared to crack for teenage girls.

Twilight follows the ethereally named Bella Swan, who, at age sixteen, moves in with her father in the Pacific Northwest so

Mom can tag behind her new hubby on the minor-league baseball circuit. On the first day of school, Bella meets the prince of her new hometown's royalty: the hypnotically handsome, brilliant, mysterious, wealthy—did I say handsome?—Edward, who at first seems repelled by her. But no, she has merely confused uncontrollable attraction with open disgust: Edward, it turns out, is a "vegetarian" vampire (that is, he does not feed on humans) who finds the scent of Bella's blood intoxicating. Being near him puts her in mortal danger, yet she is powerless to resist. As is he. The two fall in love, and for some 2,444 pages (or about 483 minutes of film) pursue their chaste, star-crossed romance, which is further complicated by Jacob Black, a hunky werewolf, also in love with Bella, whose pack members despise vampires.

But it is Bella, not the supernaturals she falls in with, who is the true horror show here, at least as a female role model. She lives solely for her man; when he leaves her in *New Moon*, the series' second installment—something about needing to protect her from him, which sounds like the vamp version of "It's not you, babe, it's *me*"—she is willing to die for him as well. Realizing that she conjures Edward's image at times of extreme danger, Bella flings herself off a cliff into a stormy sea and nearly drowns: "I thought briefly of the clichés, about how you're supposed to see your life flash before your eyes. I was so much luckier. Who wanted to see a rerun, anyway? I saw *him*, and I had no will to fight. . . . Why would I fight when I was so happy where I was?"

Oh yeah, I want my daughter to be *that* girl.

Even before the self-destructiveness kicks in, Bella has little to recommend her. Scratch that: absolutely *nothing* to recommend her. She is neither smart, interesting, kind, graceful, nor even pretty—more Ugly Duckling than Bella Swan. She is in perpetual need of rescue. She pines for an emotionally unavailable guy who simultaneously vows to protect her and warns that his love for her might make him kill her. She repeatedly reminds him that he is too good for her, and, except for the little business about his being undead, it is hard to disagree. Edward's (and Jacob's) attraction to Bella—at least in the books—is inexplicable.

There has been much hand-wringing over why today's girls would go for such claptrap. Colette Dowling, whose best seller *The Cinderella Complex* explored women's unconscious resistance to independence, has suggested that perhaps girls still feel "some fear they can't really take care of themselves." The social critic Laura Miller mused on *Salon* that "some things, it seems, are even harder to kill than vampires"—specifically, the dream of being rescued by a dreamy-looking, powerful man who instantly perceives how special you are: who will support you, adore you, and cushion you from life's hardships. Yet why should that fantasy be dead or even surprising? We have drilled our daughters in it from the time they wore diapers—diapers decorated with Disney Princesses.

Bella may be a Cinderella; however, she is no Aschenputtel. Her story comes squarely from the Disney tradition, in which the plotline has shifted from the heroine's transformation to the prince's courageous battle to possess her; she, rather than he, is reduced to a narrative device. And that—Bella's overweening blandness—as much as the guilty-pleasure rescue fantasy, may explain the series' appeal: *Twilight*'s heroine is so insipid, so ordinary, so clumsy, so Not Hot.

Isn't that great?

Think about it: what a relief that must be for girls who feel constant pressure to be physically, socially, and academically perfect! Bella does not spend two hours with a flatiron, ace her calculus test, score the winning goal in her lacrosse match, then record a hit song. Bella does not spout acidly witty dialogue. Bella does not wear $200 jeans on her effortlessly slim hips. Even in the Hollywood incarnation, as played by Kristen Stewart, she is relatively plain, modestly attired, and excruciatingly awkward. Yet Edward, the most desirable dude in the room, loves her— now, *that* is a fairy tale. The fact that he refuses to consummate their relationship may make him all the more attractive to post-pubescent girls weary of the mandate to be sexy and please boys. (The couple does consummate their relationship once in book four, on their wedding night, but readers are not privy to the moment.) So, yes, Edward, the dangerous, emotionally withhold-ing male, is a parent's worst nightmare. Yes, Bella's perspective on intimacy is warped. Yes, the series glamorizes dating abuse. Yes, reading the books makes me grind my teeth until my jaw pops. And yet ˙ . . *Twilight* may have given girls something they needed: a way to explore their nascent sexuality on their own terms, to feel desire rather than perform it. Sure, I prefer *Buffy the Vampire Slayer*, whose tough-but-vulnerable heroine meets the challenges of romance and sex head-on, but I understand the im-pulse. *Twilight* lets a girl feel heat without needing to look hot. In that way, its popularity seems less problematic than what girls see every day in magazines and on screens big and small: the example set by real-life, flesh-and-blood celebrity "princesses" as they attempt to transform from girl to woman.

Chapter Seven

Wholesome to Whoresome:
The Other *Disney Princesses*

*t*he photograph captures its subject in that liminal space between girlhood and womanhood. She sits naked, seemingly perched on an unseen bed, a satin sheet clasped to her chest as if caught by surprise. Her hair is tousled, her lipstick slightly mussed. Has she just woken up? If so, was she alone? She gazes at the viewer over one shoulder, her languorous eyes just a touch defiant.

In many ways, it is an artful portrait: the contrast between pale skin and dark hair; the sculptural folds of the sheet; the vulnerability of her emerging sexuality; the shock of her scarlet lips. Maybe if the girl had been older—say, eighteen rather than fifteen—or if she hadn't spent the previous two years positioning herself as the world's most responsible role model for eight-year-olds (a Faustian, if lucrative, bargain), it might all have been perceived differently. But she wasn't. And she had. The girl, of course, was Miley Cyrus, also known as Hannah Montana. Until the publication of that photo in the June 2008 issue of *Vanity Fair*, she had represented all that was good and pure and squeaky clean about Disney's intentions toward our daughters: the promise, begun in the Princess years, that if parents stuck with the brand—letting girls progress naturally from Cinderella to the Disney Channel divas with their TV shows, movie spin-offs, and music downloads—our daughters could enjoy pop culture without becoming pop tarts. Remember the in-house survey at Disney in which moms associated Princess with the word "safe"? That is how we're meant to perceive the entire brand, from toddler to tween. Safe. Innocent. Protective. Sheltering. So when that image blazed across the Internet, parents felt not only furious but betrayed. "Miley Cyrus is younger than my daughter!" railed one daddy blogger. A second wrote, "Holy Hell! What on earth were her parents thinking?" A mom fumed, "She is a *child* for God's sake," and another, referring to the Everest of available Hannah Montana gear, wryly quipped, "Bonfire anyone?"

Poor little rich girl! Miley was quoted in the accompanying article as saying she thought her seminudity was "really artsy. It wasn't in a skanky way," then later had to backpedal hard, releasing a formal mea culpa to her fans. "I took part in a photo shoot that was supposed to be 'artistic' and now, seeing the photographs and reading the story, I feel so embarrassed. I never intended for any of this to happen." Still there was speculation: how premeditated was this "slip"? Was she apologizing all the way to the bank? Were Miley and her master-"minder" father, the country singer Billy Ray Cyrus, consciously trying to nudge the singer's image, to prepare her for the next step of her career? In the *VF* profile, the writer Bruce Handy asked, "How do you grow up in public, both as a person and as a commodity?"

I reread that sentence several times as I scrutinized the notorious photo. Handy might more specifically have wondered how you grow up in public as a *woman* and a commodity, what Miley's attempts and missteps would mean not only for her but for her millions of worshipful fans. By the time girls are five, after all, the human Disney Princess du jour is meant to supplant the animated ones in their hearts. Miley. Lindsay. Hilary. Even, once upon a time, Britney (who launched her career in 1993 as a Mouseketeer on *The All-New Mickey Mouse Club*). All were products of the Disney machine. Each girl's rise became fodder for another media fairy tale, another magical rags-to-riches transformation to which ordinary girls could aspire. But some two hundred years after the Grimm brothers first published their stories, had that trajectory become any more liberating? The nineteenth-century Cinderella, Sleeping Beauty, and Snow White served as metaphors, symbols of girls' coming-of-age, awakening to womanhood. The contemporary princesses do as well, and though the end point may be different—marrying the handsome prince has been replaced by cutting a hit single—the narrative arc is equally predictable. In their own way their dilemmas, too, illuminate the ones all girls of their era face, whether publicly or privately, as they grow up to be women—and commodities.

The year 2000 was a banner year for monarchy. At least at Disney. Because, just as Andy Mooney was having his "could've had a V8" moment at the Phoenix ice show, realizing that the hundreds of girls who were using their *imaginations* to dress as Cinderella could instead be buying *official licensed products*, Anne Sweeney, then president of the Disney Channel Worldwide, was preparing a coronation of her own. Up until that point, the network broadcast mainly classic cartoons for the toddler set as well as films like *Pollyanna* that harkened back to the golden age before Walt himself was (supposedly) cryopreserved. Like Mooney, Sweeney, who had a ten-year-old son, saw a marketing vacuum that begged to be filled: the "underserved" 29 million or so kids who were hovering between Mickey Mouse and MTV. The trick was to find shows that appealed both to tweens and to the parents who still monitored their viewing habits. Nickelodeon had hit the mark a few years earlier with the charming *Clarissa Explains It All*, proving in the process that a female lead could play to both sexes (previous conventional television wisdom had held that while girls would watch a male protagonist without complaint, the reverse was untrue, so hanging a show on a female star would instantly halve your market share). Sweeney, too, saw potential in a perky, semiempowered female character, though—again like Mooney—I'm not sure she realized how monumental that decision would come to be. At any rate, she gave the green light to *Lizzie McGuire*, a sitcom starring the then-twelve-year-old Hilary Duff, which portrayed the frothy fun and foibles of a just-like-you-but-cuter middle school girl.

Lizzie premiered as a weekly show on the Disney Channel in January 2002; it was an instant smash and overnight launched Duff as Disney's first multiplatform "mogurl." Within a year, *Lizzie* was airing daily. There were a series of spin-off *Lizzie* books, a *Lizzie* clothing line, and a *Lizzie* sound track (which went platinum). Duff's face graced Happy Meals, dolls, games, room decor, jewelry. *The Lizzie McGuire Movie*, released in 2003, debuted at number two its opening weekend and grossed nearly $50 million in the United States. Its sound track also went platinum. Duff quit the franchise soon after the film's release, when Disney refused to meet her price on a new contract. She has subsequently attempted, with mixed success, to re-create that empire on her own. For its part, Disney simply replicated *Lizzie*'s formula with a new "property," former Cosby kid Raven-Symoné: filming sixty-five episodes of her equally inoffensive show, *That's So Raven*, in rapid succession—before the star could age—then airing them at leisure (not to mention ad nauseam). There was the now-familiar tsunami of merchandise. The hit movies included *The Cheetah Girls*, based on a series of books about four high schoolers who start a band (Raven starred as the lead singer, Galleria, a word that, as it happens, means "shopping mall"). As Disney Channel's first original musical, *The Cheetah Girls* not only launched its own ginormous juggernaut but laid the groundwork for the eventual monolith *High School Musical*.

Then came Hannah. For those of you who may have spent the last decade on planet Romulus, *Hannah Montana* is a sitcom about a girl with a secret: Miley Stewart (played by Miley Cyrus, who took on the role at age thirteen) is an ordinary teen by day, but by night she becomes—a POP STAR! Only her best friends know the truth; everyone else is miraculously fooled by the Barbie-blond wig she wears onstage. Apparently, in Miley Stewart's world—unlike Miley Cyrus's—there are no paparazzi with telephoto lenses camped outside celebrities' homes, no journalists asking annoying questions, no Internet gossips analyzing their every move or circulating incriminating cell phone pics (one nosey parker reporter does catch up to her in the Hannah Montana movie, only to be won over by her cornpone charm). Miley Stewart's father and minder/manager is played by Billy Ray Cyrus, who—wait for it—is Miley *Cyrus*'s real-life father and minder/manager! (He's also the mullet-haired impresario behind the song "Achy Breaky Heart.") *Hannah Montana* debuted in March 2006; as of this writing, it boasted a reported 200 million viewers globally. The album *Hannah Montana 2/Meet Miley Cyrus* spent twelve consecutive weeks in *Billboard*'s top five, the first double album to do so since Stevie Wonder's *Songs in the Key of Life* in 1977. Tickets for Miley/Hannah's 2007 seventy-city Best of Both Worlds Tour sold out within minutes; some were later scalped for thousands of dollars. The limited-release 3-D film of the event earned the highest per screen box-office average *ever* and went on to gross $70 million; a year later, *Hannah Montana: The Movie* pulled in more than $155 million worldwide. The amount of stuff with Hannah/Miley's face on it rivals that of all the animated princesses combined. Toys "R" Us even sells Hannah Montana hand sanitizer. According to *Portfolio* magazine, Cyrus is on track to be worth $1 billion by her eighteenth birthday (eat her dust, Duff).

Hannah's appeal is obvious: she is the fresh-faced girl next door with just enough gumption to make her interesting to kids but not so much as to be threatening to parents. Fans love her wardrobe and bouncy girl-power-lite lyrics; and, for the most part, the songs don't make adults' ears bleed. Hannah is by no means perfect: the show filters its sunny lessons (usually some version of "be yourself") through the lens of celebrity, subtly suggesting that famousness itself is the greatest possible achievement—even as it denies that is the case. Clarissa and Lizzie were comparatively real—or at least real-esque—teens, closer to the ones that graced the small screen back in the day when you had to stand up to change the channel. In that bygone era, Marcia Brady was ashamed to have her boyfriend see her in braces. These days, Hannah Montana, hired as the face of an international campaign for acne cream, is horrified to discover a zit has been Photoshopped onto her billboard-sized forehead. Both characters eventually learn that "looks aren't everything," yet the package that lesson is wrapped in could not be more different (and, for the record, Hannah/Miley, who has her own clothing line at Walmart, notably hedges on that moral, telling her best friend, "Looks are *important*, but they're not everything").

But maybe in a celebrity-saturated world, that is mere quibbling. Better Hannah Montana than the Pussycat Dolls, aimed at the same demographic, who gyrate to lyrics such as "Don't cha wish your girlfriend was a freak like me." Hannah, like the animated princesses, is, more or less, blandly unobjectionable. Her chirpy, if insipid, wholesomeness acts as an assurance to parents—just like playing princess—that our little girls are still little girls. Until, that is, they are not.

❧

The thing is, as Maurice Chevalier once chortled, little girls grow bigger every day. Child stars have always been pesky that way, and how to handle their inevitable maturation has been a perpetual challenge for the entertainment industry. Even Shirley Temple had to grow up: by the time she had reached age eleven, Fox had terminated her studio contract, effectively putting her out to pasture. Although she subsequently made a few small films, she never reclaimed her childhood success and, to her credit, gracefully exited the business by age twenty-one. Around the same time, MGM forced the sixteen-year-old Judy Garland to bind her breasts for her role as little Dorothy Gale in *The Wizard of Oz* (the blue gingham pattern on her dress was also chosen to obscure her womanly figure). In the early 1960s, Annette Funicello, who famously "blossomed" during her stint as an original Disney Mouseketeer, defied Mr. Disney by donning a navel-baring swimsuit in the "Beach Party" movies; though she was twenty-one at the time, her rebellion sparked a scandal.

It may be all well and good for today's pop princesses to play the G-rated role model at fourteen or fifteen, but by sixteen it no longer feels so sweet: adulthood looms. How can those self-proclaimed paragons prove to the world that they are grown? How can they leave their Snow White reputations behind? What guidance can they offer to their carefully cultivated legions of idolizing prepubescent fans? The answer has become so familiar that it seems almost written into the script. They cast off their values by casting off their clothes. Hilary Duff appeared almost in the buff on the cover of *Maxim* magazine (as did *Clarissa's* Melissa Joan Hart—who, by then better known for *Sabrina*, was touted by the lad mag as "your favorite witch without a stitch"). So many photos of the scantily clad Vanessa Hudgens, *High School Musical's* "good girl," have circulated on the Internet that she has been accused of posting them herself to earn some adult street cred. In the video for her breakout hit, "Dirrty," Christina Aguilera, another former Mouseketeer, stepped into a boxing ring clad in a bra, red thong, and ass-baring chaps: "Shake a little somethin' (on the floor) I need that, uh, to get me off," she sang to a roaring crowd, feigning (I hope) masturbation and, later, simulating intercourse with half-naked greased-up men. *I Know Who Killed Me*, a film starring the postadolescent Lindsay Lohan, whom the critic Roger Ebert had once compared to Jodie

Foster, was declared by the *New York Post* to be "a sleazy, inept and worthless piece of torture porn." Lohan, who admitted to drug use in *Vanity Fair* (note to child stars: do not let yourself be profiled by that magazine), has also taken several spins through the revolving door of rehab and cannot seem to keep track of either her panties or her court-mandated alcohol-monitoring bracelet. In the summer of 2010, she was sentenced to a brief, highly publicized jail term after violating probation for a DUI.

But the winner for most spectacular slide from squeaky to skanky has got to be Britney Spears. It is hard to believe now, but the singer's original audience was as young as—maybe younger than—Miley Cyrus's. Six-year-olds adored the singer the way they would a favorite babysitter, the one who lets you brush her hair. Britney was a relatively mature seventeen when she shimmied onto the scene in 1998, and her success was arguably the template for all the contradictory, mixed, or bait-and-switch messages that have since defined mainstream girls' culture: flaunt your sexuality but don't feel it, use it for power but not for pleasure. From the start, Britney tried to have it both ways, selling sex *and* candy. In her breakthrough video, " . . . Baby One More Time" (the ellipses a stand-in for the words "Hit Me"), she wore a short Catholic schoolgirl's skirt, knee socks, and a white blouse tied to reveal her midriff and unbuttoned to show a black bra. A year later, she confessed, "Oops! . . . I did it again!" while writhing on her back under the video camera's leering eye. It is tempting to say that Britney in her prime was just another iteration of Madonna, challenging expectations, messing with assumptions, self-consciously exploiting herself before the culture could do it for her: *commenting on* rather than *participating in* girls' sexualization. She encouraged that connection by infamously tongue-wrestling the older performer onstage—Britney dressed as a bride, Madonna as a groom—while performing "Like a Virgin," at the 2003 MTV Video Awards. But in the end, the comparison fails. I have to admit that I am not a huge Madonna fan. Although I'm happy to hit the dance floor for "Lucky Star," I was never convinced that she was so revolutionary, that she ever really "empowered" anyone but herself. A lot of women who spent their teen years wearing their bras on the outside of their shirts may disagree, but whether you got into her groove or not, Madonna never denied what she was doing—quite the opposite. From the start, with her BOY TOY belt and dangling crucifix, it was she who called the shots: she was self-created, explicit both about her intent and about the contradictions of women's sexuality that she explored. She was also an actual adult—age twenty-five when her first album was released—and she was not aggressively courting second-graders as fans. When she skipped through Venice singing "Like a Virgin," it was darned clear she was not one.

Britney, on the other hand, publicly insisted on her chastity (at least for a while). She was not only a loud-and-proud virgin, urging other girls to follow her example, but acted willfully clueless about the disconnect between her words and deeds. So although in 1999, while still seventeen, she appeared on the cover of *Rolling Stone* in short shorts and a black push-up bra, clutching a stuffed Teletubby, inside the magazine she declared in all earnestness, "I don't want to be part of someone's Lolita thing. It kind of freaks me out." People are so pervy, she would sigh, it wasn't *her* fault if they got the wrong idea. Later, in an *Esquire* interview illustrated by a photo in which she posed naked save for microscopic undies and several artfully placed strands of pearls, she commented, "Look, if you want me to be some kind of sex thing, that's not me." She did it again! How can she be blamed—she just can't help herself! She has no idea what she's doing! She may radiate sex, but how, at her tender age, could she be responsible for that? It was her stubborn disingenuousness—her winking detachment from her actions and impact—that eroticized Britney's (not so) innocence and, unintentionally or not, that of the millions of elementary school–aged girls who slavishly followed her. When they bared their midriffs—or performed sexually charged dance moves or wore "sassy" costumes—they were not in on the joke.

Eventually, though, Britney got older and needed to evolve; when she dropped the act and became consciously rather than "accidentally" sexy, the public turned on her, and the knowing naïf was branded a slut. How were fans supposed to understand that? Suddenly Britney's fairy tale was transformed into a cautionary tale: woe to girls who step over the ever-shifting invisible line between virgin and whore (or as one group of middle school ex-fans referred to Britney, "slore," an elision of "slut" and "whore"). Over the course of five years, the singer married and divorced, shacked up with a guy whose previous girlfriend was eight months pregnant with his child, bounced through rehab, shaved her head, stopped wearing panties in public (what is *with* that?), had two sons, lost them in a custody battle, and finally was hauled from her house on a gurney and diagnosed with bipolar disorder. Given the schizoid comments she had been spewing since high school, was that such a shock? I'm not saying that every girl who teeters on the tightrope between child and woman risks ending up institutionalized, but, again like Cinderella in her time, Britney embodies the predicament of ordinary girls writ large. They, too, struggle with the expectation to look sexy but not feel sexual, to provoke desire in others without experiencing it themselves. Our daughters may not be faced with the decision of whether to strip for *Maxim*, but they will have to figure out how to become sexual beings without being objectified or stigmatized. That is not easy when self-respect has become a marketing gimmick, a way for female pop stars to bide their time before serving up their sexuality as a product for public consumption.

⟨∞⟩

Miley Cyrus grinned down from giant banners flanking the entrance to the Oracle Arena in Oakland, California. MILEY CYRUS: ONLY AT WALMART! they announced. Beneath them, fans lined up five-deep hoping to catch a glimpse of their idol live as she strode from her tour bus in the parking lot to her backstage dressing room. It was the fall of 2009, and this was the second stop on Miley's forty-five-city Wonder World Tour, her first since her spate of miniscandals. The crowd—mostly in the six- to nine-year-old range with a smattering of ten- to twelve-year-olds and a few stray teens—seemed unfazed by her media spankings. They waved homemade cardboard signs with Miley's or Hannah's picture pasted on them, surrounded by hand-drawn flowers, puff-painted hearts, or feathers. MILEY, YOU ROCK THE HOUSE! one read. HANNAH MONTANA SONGS ARE THE BEST! claimed another.

A year ago, my own daughter had come here for a "Disney on Ice" show, invited by a friend who was celebrating her birthday. The party guests had dressed as Cinderella, Belle, Ariel (though Daisy, perhaps due to months of maternal propaganda, chose Pocahontas, the only child to do so in a crowd of thousands). The mob of girls here tonight, including the ones just a year or two older than the ice show crowd, were also dressed up as Disney Princesses, though the nature of the costumes had changed: they wore miniskirts bare-legged with high-heeled boots, topped off by pink-and-black buffalo-checked fedoras; zebra-print shirts with sparkling bodices that would have highlighted their cleavages had they had any. Several little girls swung by in white furry boots and low-rise black pleather "jeggings" (a combo of jeans and leggings). A stretch Hummer pulled up to disgorge a group of what I am guessing were second-graders in black minis with chains slung low across the hips and pink fingerless gloves.

I doubt that the six-year-old with the crimped hair and fuchsia mini would describe what she was wearing as sexy. To her it was just fun, attention-getting; she is the real-life, genuine version of the Britney Spears *Rolling Stone* cover. Disney's Andy Mooney had told me that Princess (and so, presumably, by extension, Hannah & Co.) was "aspirational"; I was not so sure I would want my daughter aspiring to this. Pink-and-pretty had been marketed to parents of preschoolers as evidence of their innocence, a harmless, even natural, way to identify as a girl. Now, for their older sisters, the pitch was changing: looking hot or at least hot-esque—at concerts, on Halloween, after school, in your dance routines—was the way to express femininity, to "be true, be you." Two slightly older girls walked by, gum cracking, hips swaying, eyelids darkened with thick liner. They wore identical skintight microminis, black camisoles, and boots, again with bare legs. One had flung a pink neon feather boa around her neck, the other a chartreuse one. They seemed about twelve, so I figured they were old enough for the look. Then I recalled the beauty pageant I had attended, how quickly I had become accustomed to five-year-olds with spray tans, teased hair, and lipstick, and I reconsidered: when, exactly, had a twelve-year-old Stripperella ceased to shock?

When Miley finally appeared, the crowd crushed forward, screaming at a frequency attainable only by young girls and

Wagnerian sopranos. Next to me, a little girl in a Hello Kitty T-shirt and pink cowboy boots jumped up and down, nearly out of control. "I can't see, I can't see!" she hollered. Miley, dressed in her preshow outfit of black cargo pants with a tank top and oversized shades, crinkled her nose endearingly and waved at the crowd. Her smile seemed genuine as she stopped to pose for photos and sign a few hurried autographs. Even after she was well out of sight the fans continued to shriek, just for the joy of it. A ten-year-old with a SECRET STAR shirt and multicolored barrettes stared in disbelief at the picture of Miley she'd snapped on her cell phone. "I'm sending this to everyone on my contact list *right now*!!" she announced. It was, admittedly, sort of heartening to see girls swoon for a female star rather than for the latest Backstreet/Hanson/Jonas pretty boy.

Inside, real-time text messages sent by the audience scrolled by on screens surrounding the stage. "WE LOVE YOU MILEY!" "I LOVE YOU!" "MY 5-YEAR-OLD'S FIRST CONCERT. SHE LOVES YOU!" When the lights finally dimmed, the crowd hollered again, frantically waving light sticks. Smoke-machine fog rolled across the stage, clearing to reveal what appeared to be a giant chrysalis, surrounded by whirling dancers. A figure stepped out, head covered by a drab shawl. Suddenly flames exploded, lasers bounced across the stage, the figure threw off the shawl, and . . . it was Miley, her brown hair flowing, her cargo pants and tank top replaced by black leather hot pants and a low-cut leather vest. She burst into a song titled "Breakout." "It feels so good to let go-o-o!" she sang.

This was a very different girl from the one who, some two years earlier, on the eve of her fifteenth birthday, had confided to Oprah Winfrey that "I look way young, and that's the way it's more comfortable to me"; the one who had said that she chooses clothing that "will get a thumbs-up from girls and their parents";

the one whom, only a year before, Barbara Walters had introduced as "any parent's antidote to the common crop of teen train wrecks." Back then, Miley had earnestly told Walters why she was different from Britney, Jamie Lynn (Britney's sister, the star of Nickelodeon's *Zoey 101*, who became pregnant out of wedlock at age sixteen), Lindsay, and the Olsen twins: "Some people don't have a family to fall back on and faith." She, by implication, was a girl whom parents could trust not to treat clean values as a stepping-stone to something else—she was *sincere*.

The *Vanity Fair* photos hit the Web less than three months later.

Even those who were inclined to cut Miley some slack, to chalk that incident up to a momentary lapse in judgment, began to wonder in the summer of 2009, when she debuted her new single, "Party in the U.S.A.," on the Teen Choice Awards (whose audience is made up largely of preteen girls). She strutted out of a trailer in booty shorts and a sparkly tank slit up the sides to expose her bra. As she sang, she stepped offstage, onto an ice cream cart topped with a pole, the kind that would typically be used as an umbrella stand; then, hanging on with one hand, she dropped into a squat, her knees splayed, her back arched. The move was, to say the least, at odds with the image of the family-friendly pop star she portrayed on TV.

Once again, controversy broke out: What kind of sticky-sweet treat was this flavor of the moment selling? Miley claimed the crouch was insignificant, not to mention personally approved by her father. Bloggers called the umbrella stand "a stripper pole with training wheels" and accused Billy Ray of pimping his sixteen-year-old child rather than doing his paternal duty by protecting her. Around that time, Miley was also photographed in *Elle* magazine lying on a table wearing a short skirt and thigh-high black boots. In both cases, she once again apologized to her fans, though she was beginning to come off as the child-star version of Richard Nixon. More and more, the "mistakes" were seen as part of the plan. It was Miley's turn to cast off the role model mantle, along with the worshipful audience who had believed it was real.

By the time I saw Miley in concert, she had agreed, after some tense negotiation, to stay at the Disney Channel for a final season of *Hannah Montana*. But the Mouse House was already moving her out. There is always a new girl in the wings, someone who promises never to disappoint by shucking her principles along with her clothes. For the moment, both Selena Gomez and Demi Lovato—show business veterans who met on the set of *Barney and Friends* in 2002—were being promoted as the Anti-Mileys (Bridgit Mendler, the star of the show *Good Luck Charlie*, is another contender). Selena, who also appeared on *Hannah Montana*, had since 2007 played a girl with magical powers on the Disney Channel's *Sabrina* knockoff, *Wizards of Waverly Place*. Demi's more recent "zit-com," *Sonny with a Chance*, is a more overt *Hannah Montana* rip-off: she plays a small-town girl who lands a role on a TV show and has to adjust to her newfound stardom. As of this writing, Selena seems to be breaking bigger: her first solo album, *Kiss & Tell*, debuted at number nine on the charts. In addition to a *Wizards* made-for-TV movie, she co-starred in the 2010 release *Ramona and Beezus*, and her likeness has been plastered on some 30 million packages of Sara Lee baked goods.

Wizards is, all things considered, a pretty entertaining show. Gomez has the best comic timing of any Disney girl to date: at the very least, her repertoire of reactions extends beyond eye-bugging. The character she plays is strong, smart, and, aside from the hocus-pocus, surprisingly real: she does not seem to be all about being pretty, nor does she always make the right choices.

It goes without saying that Gomez herself comes off as down to earth and adorable. That is her job. A *Wall Street Journal* profile gushed that her every-teen dressing room was decorated "with a bright floral rug, a shag blanket thrown across a sofa and a few scattered bookshelves." A quick Google search of news items generated right around the time of her album's release portrays her as a UNICEF ambassador to Ghana, a dog lover, and someone who "gives back to her community" (bestowing a thousand dollars' worth of supplies on her elementary school alma mater courtesy of OfficeMax). Although she is actually a year older than Miley, she looks younger, and she assured the *Journal* reporter that she is "in no rush to be twenty-five." Sound familiar?

Historical memory for pop culture tends to be short, especially where children's idols are concerned. The parents of today's six-year-olds have only a hazy recall of Hilary Duff's or Britney Spears's or even Lindsay Lohan's stints as "good-girl" icons. So it is easy to convince them that *this* girl is unlike those others, that *this* time it honestly will be different. I want to believe it myself— I like Selena. But I wonder: her virginity has already been made a selling point—like Miley before her, she wears a "true love waits" ring, meaning she has vowed to remain "pure" until marriage, presumably to a Justin Bieber clone on a white horse. I suspect that you cannot commodify a girl's virginity without, eventually, commodifying what comes after. Regardless, how realistic—how *desirable*—is that Disney version of girls' sexuality, either for Selena or for her fans?

Let me be clear here: I object—strenuously—to the sexualization of girls but not necessarily to girls having sex. I expect and want my daughter to have a healthy, joyous erotic life before marriage. Long, long, *long* before marriage. I do, however, want her to understand why she's doing it: not for someone else's enjoyment, not to keep a boyfriend from leaving, not because everyone else is. I want her to do it for herself. I want her to explore and understand her body's responses, her own pleasure, her own desire. I want her to be able to express her needs in a relationship, to say no when she needs to, to value reciprocity, and to experience true intimacy. The virgin/whore cycle of the pop princesses, like so much of the girlie-girl culture, pushes in the opposite direction, encouraging girls to view self-objectification as a feminine rite of passage.

The debate over whether Miley's (or Britney's or Vanessa's or someday, mark my words, Selena's) photo spreads are "too seductive" or "too suggestive" for her age is beside the point. Of course they are. They have to be. What other choice do these girls have? What choices are they given? I would like to see the *Hannah Montana* episode in which Miley Stewart confronts the real truth about what it means to be a girl growing up in the privilege and the confines of the spotlight's glare. What would that look like? A lot, I would bet, like Miley Cyrus's actual microscopically dissected life. Ultimately, it was not the *Vanity Fair* shoot or the stripper stunt or the hooker heels that crossed the line: it was the fetishizing of Miley's wholesomeness, the inevitable trajectory from accidentally to accidentally-on-purpose to simply on-purpose sexy. Why isn't it until that final leap, when a girl actively acknowledges and participates in what is happening, that parents of young fans cry foul?

Back at the Oracle Arena, Miley paced the runway; flipped her mane; got jiggy with the boys in the band; lay down on her back, legs tucked under, jamming on an air guitar. She donned a harness and went airborne while performing her hit "Fly on the Wall." She soared again on a candy apple red Harley during a cover of Joan Jett's classic "I Love Rock and Roll." During the entire ninety-minute set, however, she sang only two *Hannah Montana* songs (one of which was conspicuously steamed up), and through multiple costume changes she never went near a blond wig. This was emphatically a *Miley* show, but many of the grade school fans there that night, not to mention their moms, had failed to get that memo—and they were not happy about it. The little girl sitting next to me, who, judging by her missing teeth, was about seven, watched the spectacle, her ponytail bobbing with the rhythm of each song. But eventually she seemed to grow impatient, possibly overwhelmed by the thumping bass.

"Where's Hannah?" she asked her mother. The older woman glanced at the stage where Miley was getting busy, grinding her pelvis against a backup guitarist with lank hair and an untucked plaid shirt. Then she turned back to her child.

"I don't know, honey," she said, shaking her head. "I guess she's not here."

Chapter Eight

It's All About the Cape

*O*ne of Daisy's classmates, Ava, is five years old. She is five years old, and she is fat. She was a fat infant. She was a fat toddler. It is pretty clear that she'll stay a fat little girl and she'll likely be a fat teenager. Fat—that is to say, having a body mass index above what is considered medically healthy—is her natural state, the way she is built. She is a big girl with a big appetite. And that, her mother, Holly, knows, could make Ava's life difficult. Holly worries that her daughter will spend her girlhood locked in a losing battle against her size, sinking into self-loathing when she fails. She wonders daily how she can help her daughter to eat healthfully, be more physically active, but also feel good about the body she's got. She and her husband work with Ava's pediatrician on portion control, on how to distract their perpetually hungry daughter from reaching for seconds or thirds. Sometimes, though, Holly admitted, she fights the urge to just snatch the food right out of the child's mouth. The weight would be an issue if Ava were a boy, too, but for a girl, one who is already enamored of Hannah and Selena and all things teenagerly, Holly said she feels as if "there is a train heading straight for us.

"It must be so nice not having to worry about this," she sighed as we sat in her kitchen, our two girls upstairs in Ava's room playing Calico Critters. I shook my head, told Holly she was mistaken: rare is the mother—whether her girl is thin, fat, or somewhere in between—who does not worry about her daughter's body image. The standards of female beauty are so punishing that even should a girl miraculously fit them, she may still believe she falls short. As mothers, we may not want our daughters to feel compelled to conform to that ideal, but what to do with a child who, either physically or temperamentally, cannot—or does not want to? What is the alternative to thin, pretty, and hot (regardless of other qualities) as the source of feminine power and identity?

Holly herself is tall and slim. She has never had to work at that, which is not to say she doesn't have her own issues about weight and food. Growing up, she would walk away from friends when the topic turned to pounds, and she refused to step on a scale. "It was so important to me *not* to think about it," she said, "which means, of course, that it did have a hold on me. But I lived in my head. The truth is, I hardly had a perception of myself as having a body. Ava is a really embodied person."

Ava also happens to be a little ray of sunshine, one of the most delightful, happy, intuitive children I have ever met. But lately, the occasional cloud has skittered across her bright eyes. She is beginning to recognize that there is something about her that is different from other children, and whatever that something is, it matters. Take the boy on the school playground who taunted her for being "fat." Ava marched home and wrote him a note saying she had not appreciated the comment. She presented him with it the next morning. "I was so impressed," Holly said. "I thought, 'Oh, please, hold on to that ability for your whole life. Because you probably *will* need it.'"

There have been other incidents, too, and so far, Ava has stood her ground. I marveled that these kindergartners already knew that being fat was *shameful*, not a characteristic so much as a matter of character. I mean, of course they did, right? I had read the studies that said nearly half of girls in first through third grades want to be thinner; that 81 percent of ten-year-old girls were afraid of getting fat; that half of nine-year-old girls surveyed were already dieting; and that by seven Canadian girls of normal weight believed they were too heavy. I had even heard glimmers of fatphobia from my own daughter, while playing Old Maid (a politically incorrect game in any event): Daisy did not so much as twitch an eyebrow when she picked the twinkling-eyed spinster with the blue sunbonnet—my girl has a poker face that would rival the gambler Annie Duke's—but she groaned whenever she drew the Fat Lady. When I asked her why, she rolled her eyes and whispered, "Mom, she's *fat*."

Where did that come from? I never, *ever* comment on my own body size in front of her and certainly don't mention hers. Did she learn it from her classmates? Absorb it from the movies and books that routinely portray fat people as stupid, greedy, or sinister (when was the last time you saw a chubby Disney Princess, animated or human)? Could revulsion toward overweight people be natural? After all, the Bible warns against gluttony, and the ancient Greeks preached (though did not always follow) a doctrine of moderation. Or, as with the assumption that girls are born loving pink, have we so thoroughly internalized our response to fat that we've forgotten it was not always thus? Plump women may today be portrayed as unattractive and loved only by their cats, but pinups of mid-nineteenth-century stage stars show bosomy ladies with bodacious thighs and ham-hock arms. In that era, it was slender women who were considered suspect—desiccated and asexual—especially once they had hit middle age. Those not blessed with embonpoint would mask their deficiency under layers of bustles and ruffles. Children were considered sickly unless they were stuffed like Thanksgiving turkeys. Ava would have been held up as the model daughter and Holly as the perfect mother.

According to the historian Peter Stearns's book *Fat History*, public sentiment began shifting toward the svelte in the 1890s, when overweight was first linked to chronic disease. Fat did not take on a moral dimension, however, until the cause was taken up by Christian ministers, who railed against the increasing sedentariness of the postindustrial middle class. The timing of that trend was fortuitous: their previous target—rising materialism—was proving unpopular. Weight, Stearns writes, was a perfect substitute, not only replacing conspicuous consumption but legitimizing it: as long as you exercised restraint over eating, you could freely indulge your appetite for luxury. Initially, fat was equally demonized in both sexes, but by the 1920s, the focus had narrowed primarily to women and girls. Since then, one could argue, the more extreme our consumer culture has become, the more hostile we have grown toward even slight overweight in women. Not just concerned, not just disapproving, but *repelled*. And all the while, our own scales tip ever heavier.

"Maybe in ten years, by the time Ava is a teenager, the pendulum will have swung," Holly said, hopefully. "Then again, you have Kate Moss going around saying 'Nothing tastes as good as skinny feels.'"

Now, this is where I should step in to give advice to Holly, to you, to *myself* about how to combat the outrageous expectations foisted onto our daughters, to ensure, whether they are thin, fat, or anywhere in between, that they grow up with a positive and healthy body image: how to insulate them from eating disorders or simply garden-variety hatred of their butts. And believe me, after twenty years of writing and talking about girls, I know what to say: I have delivered the script hundreds of times at colleges and high schools, in churches and temples, to parent groups, teachers, Girl Scout leaders. So, for the record, here is what you are Officially Supposed To Do: stress what your daughter's body can *do* over how it is decorated. Praise her for her accomplishments over her looks. Make sure Dad is on board—a father's loving regard and interest in a girl, as the first man in her life, is crucial. Involve her in team sports: a flotilla of research shows that participation lowers teen pregnancy rates, raises self-esteem, improves grades, probably cures the common cold. Volunteerism can give girls greater perspective and purpose, reducing body obsession. Media literacy can raise consciousness about marketers' manipulations.

I would have rattled off those solutions with the greatest confidence and authority—before I had a daughter of my own. Because the truth is, regardless of what we say, from the get-go everything else, everyone else, in our culture tells girls that their weight and looks matter—a lot. Though appearance *shouldn't* dictate how they are treated by others—let alone their self-worth—it does. Talent? Effort? Intelligence? All are wonderful, yet by middle school, how a girl feels about her appearance—particularly whether she is thin enough, pretty enough, and hot enough—has become the single most important determinant of her self-esteem (which, by the way, makes self-esteem itself a trickier concept than most people realize; it is not an inherent good but must be derived from appropriate sources). If Princesses, Moxies, and Mileys are not responsible for that, exactly, Lord knows they reinforce it. Even as I wish it were otherwise—even as I *fight* for it to be otherwise—I, too, know in my heart that how girls look does make a difference in how the world perceives them, and the more progress they make in other areas, the more that seems to be true.

And true for longer. Take an article I recently saw in *More* magazine: "Stars Who Make over 40 Look Fab." The publication runs pieces like this all the time, and I can never decide whether they make me feel better or worse about my own (I'll just say it) middle age. Though I applaud its rebel yell that women can remain attractive as we get o-l-d-e-r, I also feel a creeping despair—like, dang, now I *have* to be. I was secretly looking forward to letting it all go to hell at a certain point. But more than that, the mag did not even mention that every single one of the women they were holding up as role models had dyed away their gray; most had frozen time with Botox; others had moved on to a full complement of fillers, tucks, and lifts. Is that now so presumed, once princess ascends to queen, that it goes without saying? These were not great-looking older women. They were great-looking women who both can't afford to get old and *can* afford not to. These days postforty women in the spotlight who go au naturel are considered courageous if not downright foolhardy. That perception is gradually trickling down to the rest of us. It is a nasty bind, as psychologists (and former models) Vivian Diller and Jill Muir-Sukenick write in *Face It*, a guide for women on coping with changing appearance: "Should women simply grow old naturally, since their looks don't define them, or should they fight the signs of aging, since beauty and youth are their currency and power?" Whether we like it or not, whichever we choose is a statement, one that earlier generations were not forced to make. What's more, in another twist on KGOY, women are asking that question at ever-younger ages. Most of the 9.3 million women who underwent cosmetic procedures in 2008 were between thirty-five and fifty; nearly another quarter were between nineteen and thirty-four. That trend has created a market for a new picture book, *My Beautiful Mommy*, in which a little girl does everything she can "to help Mommy achieve her beautiful results."

And Mommy had best get ready to return the favor, because just as the imperative to look good has extended further up the age spectrum, it is also creeping further down. Nearly 43,000 children under age eighteen (mostly girls, of course) surgically altered their appearance in 2008—over twice as many as a decade earlier. That does not include the tens of thousands who scheduled chemical peels, dermabrasion, or laser hair removal. Or (and someone please explain *this* to me) the 12,000 injections of Botox administered in 2009 to children ages thirteen to nineteen, presumably to prevent rather than remove wrinkles. So—stick with me here—that means girls are now simultaneously getting older younger *and* staying younger older. It also explains why the identical midriff-baring crop top is sold to eight-year-olds, eighteen-year-olds, and forty-eight-year-olds. The phases of our lives have become strangely blurred, as girls try to look like adult women and adult women primp and preen and work out like crazy in order to look like girls. Once again we are in fairy-tale territory, but instead of the jealous queen, it is the MILF who is gazing in the Magic Mirror, competing with her daughter to be Fairest of Them All.

A century ago, female self-improvement did not presume a

stint under the scalpel, hours at the gym, or even a trip to the cosmetics counter. In her indispensable book *The Body Project*, the historian Joan Jacobs Brumberg wrote that for girls growing up before World War I, becoming a better person meant being *less* self-involved: helping others, focusing on schoolwork, becoming better read, cultivating empathy. To bring home the point, she compared New Year's resolutions of girls at the end of the nineteenth century with those at the end of the twentieth. Here's what a young woman of yore wrote:

"Resolved: to think before speaking. To work seriously. To be self-restrained in conversations and actions. Not to let my thoughts wander. To be dignified. Interest myself more in others."

And the contemporary girl:

"I will try to make myself better in any way I possibly can. . . . I will lose weight, get new lenses, already got new haircut, good makeup, new clothes and accessories."

As in the American Girl books, it seems that though the nineteenth-century girl may have lived in a more repressive era—before women could vote, when girls' sights were set solely on marriage and motherhood—her sense of self-worth was enviably internal, a matter of deed over dress. Whatever other constraints she felt, her femininity was not defined by the pursuit of physical perfection; it was about character. I wonder why we adult women, with all our economic, political, and personal freedoms, have let this happen to our daughters.

When I was reporting *Schoolgirls*, a book for which I followed students at two different middle schools through eighth grade, I noticed my own habit, after a few days' absence, of greeting my young subjects by commenting on some aspect of their appearance: their earrings, a new shirt, their hairstyles. I decided, as an experiment, to stop cold turkey, to find another way to connect:

asking how a play rehearsal was going or what they were reading in English class. Anything. It felt surprisingly forced: physical compliments grease the conversational wheels among women and girls. After the book's publication, I would speak about that experience, encouraging my audience to give it a try themselves for a few days. They would nod their heads; then, after a beat, someone would ask uncomfortably, "You mean we shouldn't say *anything* about their looks?" How about this, I would counter: try not commenting on your *own* looks—on the size of your thighs or the tightness of your jeans. At least not in front of your daughter. Girls receive enough messages every day reducing them to their appearance without women they love delivering them, too.

Like Holly—like all of the women I know—I want to raise a girl who has a reasonable perspective on her body regardless of her shape, who does not plunge into a shame spiral whenever she looks at herself sideways in a mirror. Someone, in other words, who is not like me. My high school memories include hiding laxatives in my school locker, breaking sticks of sugar-free gum in half and calling that lunch. The hopeless feeling that accompanied my self-imposed starvation remains more vivid to me than anything else from that time. Although my body and I have reached if not peace, at least a state of détente, "fat" remains how I experience anger, dissatisfaction, disappointment. I feel "fat" if I can't master a task at work. I feel "fat" if I can't please those I love. "Fat" is how I blame myself for my failures. "Fat" is how I express my anxieties. A psychologist once told me, "Fat is not a feeling." If only it were that simple. As for so many women, the pathology of self-loathing is permanently ingrained in me. I can give in to it, I can modify it, I can react against it with practiced self-acceptance, but I cannot eradicate it. It frustrates me to consider what else I might have done with the years of mental energy I have wasted on this single, senseless issue.

Given all of that, I wonder how I could expect—or even *hope*—to raise a daughter who is both less invested in and more confident about her appearance than I was, even if it is slightly (or wildly) imperfect, as, of course, it will be. Certainly, I do my best, and I follow all the expert advice I have mentioned above, but I don't have an intuitive—a gut, if you will—feeling for whether or not I am on the right track. Not the way I do with ensuring that she is well mannered or values kindness, creativity, intellect. I am hardly the only mother who wrestles with this: I recalled the conversation I'd had about the Disney Princesses with the mothers of Daisy's preschool classmates. One of them felt the answer was to shower her daughter with compliments about her looks as a kind of inoculation: she wanted to impress upon her girl that, regardless of what anyone might say, she was beautiful. Besides, the woman said, if you *never* tell your daughter she is pretty, rather than realizing that appearance is unimportant, she may suspect you think she's ugly. Maybe. Yet *over*-emphasizing a girl's looks is clearly hazardous—and that overemphasis is pervasive. How to find the sweet spot?

I took the quandary to Catherine Steiner-Adair, the director of eating disorders education and prevention at the Klarman Eating Disorders Center at McLean Hospital in Massachusetts. "Well," she said, when I called her, "'You're beautiful' is not something you want to say over and over to your daughter, because it's not something that you want her to think is so important.

"That said," she continued, "there are times when it *is* important to say it: when she's messy or sweaty, when she's *not* dressed up, so that she gets a sense that there is something naturally beautiful about her as a person. And it's also important to connect beauty and love. To say, 'I love you so much. Everything about you is beautiful to me—*you* are beautiful to me.' That way you're not just objectifying her body."

I appreciated that advice, the way it redefined beauty as something that was both internal and eternal. I passed it along to Holly, who was somewhat less impressed. "I actually think it's fine to reserve 'beautiful' for when she's dressed up or has a new haircut or has done something special," she said. "What's important to me in a day-to-day way is to unhook looks from size, not to link the two for her—or, because of her, for me." Take the challenge of buying Ava's clothes—nix on jeans or those cute little Boden dresses—which will only intensify as she gets older and more aware of Abercrombie and Hot Topic. "Pretty to me is not the point," Holly said. "I think Ava is pretty. I think she's lovely. And I hope she'll think so, too. But she's always going to be a big girl—unless she starts dieting in an unhealthy way."

I ached for Holly and her daughter, for the complicated position they were in. Yet I realized that along with that concern and love I did feel a certain . . . relief. Because, as Holly said, my own daughter *is* thin. True, she may still someday struggle, but I don't have to worry that she will be teased about her size on the first day of summer camp. I wish appearance did not matter so much, that it did not confer so much power. But given that it does, I find that I am grateful for hers. Does that make me a hypocrite?

Women. Beauty. Power. Body. The ideas and images remain so muddled, so contradictory; how to disentangle them for our girls? By the end of kindergarten, Daisy had, blessedly, exited the Disney Princess phase. "The princesses are just, like"—she struck a "lovely Carol Merrill" pose and simpered—"'I'm so pretty, Handsome Prince, won't you rescue me?'" Later she added, "All Sleeping Beauty ever does is sleep."

I admit to feeling a smidge of guilt (along with pride) at that pronouncement, because it was a reasonable approximation of what I had been drilling into her head for three years—but then again, if Disney could try to brainwash my child, I suppose I could, too. At any rate, I waited anxiously for what might come next: would I be moaning over *Monster High*? Were we bound for Tinker Bell's Pixie Hollow, a realm of moralistic nice girl/mean girl dynamics? Would I have to decide whether to empty my wallet for that full-on American Girl rig (I had been sorely tempted by a newly introduced historical doll, a Russian-Jewish girl from the early twentieth century, whose accessories included a $68 "Sabbath set")? Instead, she surprised me: for her sixth birthday, she asked for a Wonder Woman costume.

Finally, a stage I could get with! I was even willing to up the ante: why stop at Wonder Woman? I trolled eBay for action figures of Hawkgirl and Big Barda (a superheroine from the 1970s who defends her milquetoast husband). I scored a PVC-free Supergirl lunch box. I searched YouTube for snippets of the short-lived animated *Spider-Woman* TV series from 1980. Yes, it gave me pause that the lunch box was pink, that, given her druthers, Big Barda preferred housewifery to crime fighting, and that all of the superheroines have the proportions of Kim Kardashian— more mammary than muscle. It disappointed me, though did not surprise, when Daisy declined a friend's offer of a Wonder Woman from his bobblehead collection: the head was too big for the body, she explained to me later, and the face was, well, kind of butch (my word, not hers). On the other extreme, she was so appalled by Hawkgirl's excessive assets that she never took the toy out of the box. And one day while drawing Supergirl, who wears a miniskirt and a crop top, she mused, "Sometimes girl superheroes show their belly buttons. I don't know why." So I hadn't exactly succeeded in finding a strong feminine image that wasn't idealized or sexualized, but how far was I willing to push it? Maybe the message that power does not play without the pretty will mess her up in ten years, but right now, I needed something to say yes to; like so many moms, I was willing to compromise to find some mutually acceptable middle ground.

Besides, I figured there were intriguing possibilities in this new phase. Little girls may have more real-life role models than they used to, more examples of how to be in the world, but they have precious few larger-than-life heroes, especially in the all-important realm of fantasy, where they spend so much of their free time. It's true, as we've seen, that the research on gender and play indicates (with the big blinking caveats that there are vast variations within, as opposed to between, the sexes and that nature is heavily influenced by nurture) that little boys are more readily drawn to competitive, rough-and-tumble games, while little girls (again, big blinking caveat, see above) strive for group harmony over individual dominance. But all that aside, let's face it, the options for girls have not exactly been compelling. Who can even remember Batgirl's secret identity? (She was Barbara Gordon, the commissioner's daughter—or, in some versions, his niece.) And, with all due respect, Wonder Woman's invisible airplane is . . . how to put this delicately—*lame* compared with the gleam of a Batmobile. Still, I think superhero play, when it is not overdetermined by the *Justice League* script, has something specific to offer girls, something beyond an outlet for aggression or even the satisfaction (similar to Bettelheim's claims for fairy tales) of gaining control in an arbitrary world.

I went through a brief Wonder Woman phase myself in the

early 1970s. Even then I could not have told you much about the character's backstory, but I didn't care: all I knew was that I had an excuse to fasten a towel around my neck with a clothespin and climb onto the roof of a friend's garage. The distance to the next building was slightly longer than my leggy child's stride, yet I took a deep breath and leapt—screaming "Wonder Woman! Wonder Woman!"—my towel cape streaming behind me. In that moment of flight, soaring between the two rooftops, I felt—no, I *knew* I was—invincible; the sensation was equal parts exhilarating and frightening. What might I dare to do next? What else was possible?

As a writer, I have revisited that memory in my work more often than any other. It was so different from my typical, earthbound play, and the emotions it elicited were so unfamiliar—feelings of freedom, of power. And isn't that ultimately the superhero's task: coming to grips with the gifts and challenges of power—accepting it, demanding it, wielding it wisely, grappling with moral choices about the nature of might and goodness? Those themes, so rarely explored in the culture of little girls, would seem particularly relevant given the complexities women can still face as leaders. Consider a 2007 survey of 1,231 executives in the United States and Europe, ominously subtitled *Damned if You Do, Doomed if You Don't*. Conducted by Catalyst, a nonprofit organization dedicated to the advancement of women in business, it found that female managers who behave consistently with gender stereotypes—prioritizing "work relationships" and expressing "concern for other people's perspectives"—were liked but considered to be ineffective. Those who were seen as behaving in a more "male" fashion, on the other hand—who "act assertively, focus on work task, display ambition"—were seen as competent but roundly disliked. I was tempted, initially, to dismiss that as a generational issue, something that would take care of itself as old-timers aged out of the workforce. Except that, according to a 2008 J. Walter Thompson report, "Millennial Women Face Gender Issues," 40 percent of men in their *twenties* still say they would prefer a male over a female boss. Nor, when you think about it, have the wildly different connotations of Super*man* and Super*woman* changed over time: the former is mysterious, admirable; the latter is hectic, harried, a woman who does too much and none of it well. That is not something I would want for myself or my girl. Besides, really, how many of us would like to be referred to as the Woman of Steel?

I was mulling over those disparities one sunny Saturday morning as Daisy and I strolled along Berkeley's Fourth Street on our way to our favorite breakfast joint, passing boutiques that sold handcrafted Japanese paper, diaphanous Stevie Nicks–inspired frocks, wooden toys imported from Europe. This was a few weeks before the 2008 Democratic primaries. Daisy spied a bumper sticker plastered on a mailbox: a yellow caricature of Hillary Clinton leering out from a black background. Big block letters proclaimed THE WICKED WITCH OF THE EAST IS ALIVE AND LIVING IN NEW YORK.

"Look, Mama," Daisy said, excitedly. "That's Hillary. What does it say?" What should I have told her? It's not that I thought that Senator Clinton was a victim—she often gave as good as she got. So it was not the attack that disturbed me so much as the form it took, the default position of incessant, even gleeful misogyny toward an unapologetically assertive (even aggressive) high-achieving woman. Contemplating the months of LIFE'S A BITCH, DON'T VOTE FOR ONE T-shirts, the silver-plated thighs of the Hillary nutcrackers (Woman of Steel!), the comparison to the bunny-boiling Alex Forrest of *Fatal Attraction*, I had often wondered whether Clinton was a symbol of how far we'd come as women or how far we had to go. Was she proof to my girl that "you can do anything" or of the hell that will rain down on you if you try? Was she a Wonder Woman or more like the hundred-plus super-heroines listed on the Web site womeninrefrigerators.com—so named because they had all been depowered, raped, driven insane, or chopped up and stuffed in a refrigerator? Damned if you do, doomed if you don't indeed.

Nothing so horrific happened to then-Senator Clinton (though Republican presidential candidate John McCain did respond, "Excellent question!" to someone at a campaign event who asked, "How do we beat the bitch?"); still, analysis of her actual policies was dwarfed by chatter—among both Republicans and Democrats, men as well as women—about the senator's hair, the pitch of her voice, the thickness of her ankles, her "likability," her relative femininity. Rush Limbaugh declared that Americans didn't want to watch a woman grow old in the White House. The journalist Christopher Hitchens called her an "aging and resentful female." Writing in the anthology *Thirty Ways of Looking at Hillary*, the novelist Susanna Moore wished that Clinton were more sensuous. And then there was the *real* debate: over her pantsuits. In a typical swipe, *The Washington Post*'s Robin Givhan wrote, "The mind . . . strays from more pressing concerns to ponder the sartorial: How many pantsuits does Hillary Clinton have in her closet?" There may have been a host of legitimate reasons to support Barack Obama over Clinton, but among them seemed to be that she was not young, pretty, slim, or stylish enough to represent the nation.

That was certainly not the case for the inexperienced-but-babelicious Sarah Palin, whom McCain chose as his running mate. Never mind that as governor of Alaska, she used her position to pursue personal vendettas, hired cronies to fill vacant posts, and fired officials who crossed her. Or that in an interview with CBS news anchor Katie Couric, she was unable to name a single periodical she read regularly to stay informed. Or that, when asked by CNBC, she could not describe the job of the vice president. Palin had been dubbed "America's Hottest Governor," and that propelled her forward. In the weeks after her nomination, top Internet searches involving her name included "Sarah Palin *Vogue*," "Sarah Palin bikini," and "Sarah Palin naked." As with Clinton, the former beauty queen's appearance—her clothing, glasses, and hairstyles (not to mention how much they cost)—seemed as relevant to her leadership potential as her policies. How were girls supposed to interpret that?

I know it is not the 1950s. It's not even the 1970s. Women are university presidents, governors, surgeons, titans of industry—even if not in the numbers one would wish or expect. Yet though we tell little girls "You can be anything you want to be," we know, from life experience, that that is still not quite true. At least not without a price. It's not as if when Daisy was three and announced that she wanted to be a firefighter I chimed in with "Honey, that's great, but last week I read an article about a woman at a firehouse in Austin, Texas, who came to work after a big promotion to find that her male coworkers had smeared her locker with human excrement." Still, as my daughter waited expectantly for me to read that bumper sticker, I did wonder how much to tell her—and when—about the tensions that persist around women and power.

Not surprisingly, friends have given Daisy a library full of "girl-positive" picture books designed to address this very issue. But, as with the "feminist" princess tales, I find I rarely pull them out—not only because they seem a tad spinachy but because they often undermine their own cause. Take *Elenita*, a magic realist tale about a Mexican girl who wants to be a glassblower. Her father says she can't do it: she is too little, and besides, the trade is forbidden to women. The lesson, naturally, is that with a little ingenuity girls can be glassblowers or stevedores or [fill in the blank]. Nice. Still, I found myself hesitating over the "girls can't" section. Daisy had never heard that "girls can't be" or "girls can't do," whether glassblowers, firefighters, or baseball players. Why should I plant the idea in her head only to knock it down? Even my treasured *Free to Be You and Me*, rather than teaching Daisy that William deserves a doll and mommies are people, merely confused her. "What's a sissy?" she asked me as we listened to "Dudley Pippin." And, later, during a sketch in which one newborn baby (voiced by Mel Brooks) is trying to convince another (Marlo Thomas) that *he* is the girl, "Why did that baby just say that girls can't keep secrets?" Overt discrimination and stereotyping may be less pervasive than when I was a child, but how can I explain—and gird her against—the subtler kinds that remain?

Daisy's birthday falls in the middle of summer. So from the end of July all the way through Labor Day, she happily zipped around the backyard swinging her lasso of truth and repelling bullets with her golden bracelets, upholding the forces of justice. Then school started, and within a few weeks I found her Wonder Woman gear balled up behind her dress-up bin. I asked what had happened, and she shrugged.

"None of the other girls want to play superheroes," she said.

They don't? I asked. Really?

"Not for very long, anyway," she hedged. "Mostly they just want to play *princess*." She looked dolefully up at me.

Suddenly I recalled the other part of the superhero story— that the gift of power elevates but also isolates. That's fine if you are a comic book character, not so much if you are a six-year-old girl. Now, I don't know if what she said was entirely true—her female classmates were hardly a bunch of pink-bots—but it didn't matter: that was her perception. This is the kind of thing all the books about raising smart, strong girls fail to mention. Frequently, after I have given a lecture on the topic myself, someone has commented, "My daughter *does* speak up and stand up for herself, and she *doesn't* wear trampy clothes or caked-on makeup. And do you know what she gets called? A bitch." To which I nod sympathetically and say, "If you don't toe the line, whether you are a girl or an adult woman, you do risk being punished. But you have to believe she will ultimately be better off." Now I realized what cold comfort that was. No one wants her child to be the sacrificial lamb to a cause. No one wants her daughter to feel excluded by her peers, to be ostracized for having the wrong clothes, hair, or pop preferences. No one wants her daughter to be caricatured on a bumper sticker. If Holly's daughter, Ava, did not fit the feminine ideal by chance, my daughter seemed to be rejecting it by choice. That was what I had wanted, right? For her to share my values, accept my wisdom? Yet I wondered where it would lead her.

In their insightful book *Packaging Girlhood*, Sharon Lamb and Lyn Mikel Brown write that the culture ultimately offers a girl two models for female identity. She can be "for the boys"—dress for them, perform sexually for them, play the supportive friend or girlfriend. Or she can be "one of the boys," an outspoken, feisty girl who hangs with the guys and doesn't take shit. The latter starts out as the kindergarten girl who is "independent and can think for herself." That would be my daughter. The trouble is, Brown and Lamb say, being "one of the boys" is as restrictive as the other option, in part because it discourages friendship with other girls: a girl who is "one of the boys" separates herself from her female peers, puts them down, is ashamed or scornful of anything associated with conventional femininity.

I was already seeing inklings of that attitude from Daisy. In kindergarten, her best friends were all male; she was sometimes the only girl at a birthday party. That was fine, but she also turned down a playdate with a female classmate, dismissing her as "too pinkie-pink." While looking for sandals online, she rejected pair after pair as too pretty/flowery/pink/girlie. She finally found some flip-flops to her liking in the boys' section (with a supersecret maze embedded in the outsole!). I appreciated the critique of the footwear industry, but her disdain made me uneasy: I thought back to our conversation several years before in the grocery store, when I had tried to explain my aversion to Cinderella. Had my worst fears during that episode come to pass? Rather than becoming more conscious of manipulation, had she instead learned that the things associated with girls—and by extension being a girl itself—were bad? Was the long-term impact of pinkness—all those one-off Scrabble boards and skateboards—to divide girls against themselves? Certainly, I didn't want her to think that all things snips 'n' snails—like, gulp, superheroes?—were *superior*. It was one thing to reject the image of girlhood being sold to her, another to reject girls who might embrace it. All I had wanted was to offer her a sense of worth as a girl that was not contingent on the cut of her clothes, a femininity grounded in something other than the bathroom mirror. Still, I had wanted her to stay allied with other girls. There had to be something like that out there, right?

⚭

For a moment, back in the early 1990s—before Britney, before Miley, before Princess and Bratz—it looked as if there might be. It is hard to recall now, but the idea of linking the word "girl" with "power" seemed minimally implausible and to most a contradiction in terms. Yet, launched by the punk-influenced Riot Grrrl movement (which replaced "girl" with a growling *grrrl*), "Girl Power" became a dare, a taunt, a primal scream: it was the word "slut" scrawled across the belly of a fleshy, shaved-headed young woman in a miniskirt and combat boots who was passing out hand-printed copies of her 'zine about incest. Set to a beat by bands like Bikini Kill (whose songs included "Suck My Left One"), the movement went alt-rock mainstream with Hole, whose frontwoman, Courtney Love, pioneered the "kinderwhore" look: ripped baby-doll dresses with fishnets, tiny plastic barrettes in badly dyed hair, overdone smeared makeup. The Riot Grrrls rejected market-driven images of femininity. Their cri de coeur, "Revolution Girl Style Now!" was all about female solidarity, self-reliance, and do-it-yourself media. They were not always pretty. They were not always palatable. They were also not for actual *girls*: although as a thirty-year-old I dug the movement, as a mom—call me old-fashioned—I would not especially want my first-grader "reappropriating" the word "cunt."

Enter the Spice Girls. With one impossibly infectious 1996 hit, "Wannabe" (you remember: "If you wanna be my lover, you gotta get with my friends"), they plucked the rrrrage right out of "Grrrl Power," rendering it apolitically appealing to the tweenybopper set and, more important, to their parents. Their opportunistic philosophy—most of the Pre–Fab Five had never met before auditioning for the band—was "about a positive attitude to life, getting what you want, and sticking by your friends." Who could argue with that? The Spices also offered girls a range of identities that nonetheless let them feel part of the group, a perfect developmental fit with the band's demographic. I recall endless conversations in which my nieces discussed which Spice they were—Sporty, Scary, Baby, Posh, or Ginger—then which Spice I was, then which Spice every female they had ever met might be, including their eighty-year-old grandmother (Old Spice, of course). It was tedious, but if not exactly grrrlishly subversive—where was Chubby Spice? Brainy Spice? Bi-Curious Spice?—it did not seem exactly *offensive*. At least, I figured, they weren't obsessed with the Backstreet Boys. This was a good ten years before *Hannah Montana* debuted, and I appreciated seeing them scream their heads off over other girls, rocking out to music that was made for them and about them. It was actually kind of exciting: the Spices were all about the girlfriends, Girlfriend. At least, that's what they claimed.

Around the time the Spice Girls broke, something called "girlie feminism" was also on the rise: far less threatening than Riot Grrrls, it held that women's traditional roles and skills (whether scrubbing floors, nurturing relationships, or knitting) had intrinsic value; that sexual equality need not require gender neutrality; that painting your nails and wearing a PORN STAR T-shirt were, if not radical acts, at least a woman's right, a viable form of self-expression and personal pleasure. That is, if done by the right people for the right reasons with the right soupçon of irony. The arguments were provocative but difficult to control. Just as they had with Riot Grrrls, Spice Girls skimmed off the easily consumable surface of girlie feminism—cute clothes! makeup!—and tossed its transgressive core. Rather than "empowering," then, the Spice World battle cry, "Strength and courage and a Wonderbra!" became increasingly confusing, especially to fans who weren't old enough to know what a Wonderbra actually was. By 1998, when Ginger Spice ditched her so-called forever friends, "girl power" had devolved into little more than an empty slogan on a shrunken pink T-shirt. The phrase may have started the decade representing one irony, but it ended by expressing quite another. Those extra *r*'s in Riot Grrrl, which had heralded a rejection of consumerized femininity, were replaced by the now-ubiquitous *z* (as in Ty Girlz, Moxie Girlz, Bratz Girlz, Baby Phat Girlz, Glitter Girlz, Clique Girlz, "Disney Girlz Rock"), which embraced it. *Z* did not seek to expand choices, break down barriers, address injustice. *Z* signaled "empowerment" as the power to shop, old-school stereotypes recast as the source of liberation rather than an impediment to it.

Disney Princesses, Miley Cyrus, child-friendly makeup, the proliferation of pink, are all outgrowths of that marketing sleight of hand. And, since the Riot Grrrls dispersed, no homegrown culture has risen up to challenge them. Mothers, meanwhile, want (really, really want, as the Spice Girls might sing) so desperately to guide their daughters to an authentic, unconflicted balance of feminism and femininity, one that will sustain rather than constrain them. Witness, for instance, the success of two "advice manuals" for girls published in 2008: *The Daring Book for Girls* and *The Girls' Book: How to Be the Best at Everything* (as well as their endless sequels, such as *The Double-Daring Book for Girls* and *How to Be the Best at Everything Again*). Both volumes were spin-offs of *The Dangerous Book for Boys*, a gilt-embossed paean to old-school adventure whose tantalizing chapters on building a go-cart and making secret ink from (presumably your own) pee induced nostalgia among fathers—typically the ones purchasing the book—for their own huckleberry childhoods, those halcyon days before cable, Wii, Facebook, and cell phones. The girls' books, however, do something entirely different. Rather than harking back to—heaven forbid!—bygone days, they evoke nostalgia for a time that has yet to be, a girlhood that we mothers may wish we'd had but did not, one that we hope will nourish our daughters and prepare them to be the kind of women we're not sure we were fully able to become.

The Girls' Book, published by Scholastic, is solidly in the *z* camp: that extra X chromosome, it implies, stands for Xcessorize, and "having it all" comes with a hefty credit card debt. The book may advise readers on "how to cross Niagara Falls on a tight-rope," but its more realistic fare includes how to "act like a ce-lebrity," "make your own luxury bubble bath," and "give yourself a perfect manicure." I'm not above seeking a little pick-me-up at the cosmetic counter myself, mind you, but I am not nine years old. Even so, in some ways, I mourn what has been taken from me by the rise of this girlz-with-a-*z* culture—when I was pregnant, I imagined occasionally playing "manicure" with my daughter as my mom had with me; I had a bag of old (probably bacteria-infested) lipsticks and eye shadows that I planned to bequeath to her for dress-up play. But by the time Daisy was three, I had tossed them all and become a hard-liner on all questions of nail polish and makeup. That was for grown-ups, I would tell her, not for little girls. Period. I know my response was extreme, possibly excessively so. But there was so much more out there than when I was a girl that urged her to define herself from the outside in, to believe identity was for sale; adding to all that, even in a small way, felt too much like collusion.

The Daring Book for Girls, by contrast, makes the case for a separate-but-equal girls' culture of play—one that, like its male counterpart, deserves resurrection and preservation. Any for-mer girl (read: current mom) would find its chapters on jacks, hand-clap games, and that staple of Girl Scout campfires, the sit-upon—*the sit-upon!!!!*—pretty much irresistible. I know I did. This might be more of what the 1990s "girlie feminists"—the ones revaluing cooking and crafts—had in mind: a feminism that expects parity with boys and men, yet does not strive to be like them or see their conventional roles and behavior as more desirable. As a nod to the fact that today's girls will not, like their forebears, live their lives in a "separate sphere" from men—as well as acknowledgment that "different" can quickly be tagged as "lesser"—the book also provides tutorials on "How to Negotiate a Salary" and "Finance: Interest, Stocks and Bonds." Useful skills, but ones that will probably appeal primarily to mothers. Girls themselves, I would wager, will see them as the equivalent of a granola bar in the Halloween bag.

Daring Girls was the closest thing I had seen to what I was looking for: a concept of girlhood as a community, a vision that was dynamic and character-building rather than decorative. At the same time, most of what was in the book seemed so arbitrary I wondered whether it truly upheld tradition or just created yet another trap. Segmenting play by sex, remember, may be good for sales but not necessarily for kids' development. So you tell me which of these activities (pulled at random from the boys' and girls' books) seems feminine and which masculine: Building a Campfire; Making Cloth Fireproof; Fourteen Games of Tag; Five Pen-and-Paper Games; Snowballs; Cloud Formations (answers: girls, boys, girls, boys, girls, boys). Why can't girls make crystals or juggle (those are in the boys' book)? Why can't boys construct a lemon-powered clock or learn Five Karate Moves (those are in the girls' book)? Perhaps more pointedly: what about the boy who, à la *How to Be the Best at Everything*, wants to "put together the best dance routine"? Now, *that* would be "dangerous."

Maybe the wisest course of action would be to rip off the

covers of all of the books and let children choose for themselves the activities they find feminine or masculine or just plain fun. That could even help with the kind of casual, naturally occurring interaction the Sanford program's Carol Martin and Rick Fabes are trying to foster between boys and girls. I think Daisy would enjoy such a project (once she can read). And I would, too.

As the school year went on, she rebounded from her disappointment and returned to superhero play, albeit mostly when she was by herself. She also added a new character to her repertoire named Wildcat: technically, he was a male superhero; she had feminized him with Batgirl ears and socks on her hands. I was not sure how I felt about that. I know that if I could imbue her with a superpower, it would be the ability to withstand the pressures of the culture around her, to be her own woman despite the potential costs: I would give her the courage of her convictions, the power to be the hero of her own story without ambivalence or fear, to embrace her gifts regardless of her body's size or shape—even if I have not been fully able to embrace mine.

Meanwhile, I did a little digging about Wonder Woman. It turns out her real name was Diana, daughter of Hera, queen of the Amazons. That makes her, of all things . . . a princess.

Chapter Nine

Just Between You, Me, and My 622 BFFs

i think it was the pig snout that put me over the line.
I was trying to meet some girls on the Internet, to chat with them in real time about how they presented themselves on social networking sites and virtual worlds—increasingly popular fantasy landscapes in which users interact with one another through avatars. How did their online selves reflect, reinforce, or differ from who they were offline? What role did this new world have in shaping their identities, their femininity? I had started by hopping onto an award-winning educational site called Whyville, whose 5 million "citizens," largely young teens, could play games, buy "virtual goods," and chat electronically with one

another. There is no need to "friend" a person in a virtual world, so it is easy to observe (as well as talk to) complete strangers.

In order to go onto the site, I had to create an avatar—a word that once denoted the human incarnation of a Hindu deity. I put a lot of thought into what she (because I decided to remain a she) should look like. I ended up giving her—or was it myself?—a whimsical, spiky purple 'do, glasses, a goofy grin, and, just for the heck of it, a pig snout for a nose. When I took that bad self "in world," however, I found a land of girls with big hair and chunky highlights; full, glossy pouts; thickly lined doe eyes; and skimpy, fashion-forward outfits. Girls, in other words, who'd styled themselves like a line of hot, trendy dolls. Was that how they saw themselves? How they wished they looked? How they aspired to look? How they thought they should look? A cartoon bubble popped up above the head of a girl named "Sweetiepi," whose avatar was staring directly at me. It said she was "whispering" with another girl, named OMGBrooke. I got the uneasy feeling they were discussing my snout.

෴

Back in the midnineties, the concern among parents and educators was that girls were not going online at the same rate as boys. A digital divide was looming, and it threatened to leave girls stranded on the wrong side of economic opportunity. That notion turned out to be *sooooo* twentieth century. These days, 35 million kids ages three to eighteen—80 percent of kindergartners alone—are online, though by the time you read this those numbers will surely be higher. A solid half of those users are female.

Girls spend the same amount of time as boys on the Internet, but their activities differ. Predictably, more boys are gamers. They are also more likely to produce videos to post on their online profiles or sites such as YouTube. Girls, meanwhile, are out front in communication: more girls than boys blog, instant message, text, create Web pages, and join virtual worlds and social networking sites.

I skimmed that information with mounting disapproval: kids seemed to be going online so young—maybe too young. Then I remembered that Daisy had been on the Internet, tooling around the Nick Jr. site, since she was three years old. I suspect, in fact, that she first associated the word "mouse" not with a rodent but with a piece of computer hardware. I have watched with equal parts curiosity and anxiety as she has navigated with preternatural skill through the site's games. Her obsession with the Dora pages seemed harmless enough, but what would she do next? What would she *see* next?

This was a place in my reporting, I realized, where, to gain deeper insight, I had to leave the littlest girls behind for their older sisters. For one thing, older girls can read, something that instantly expands the online experience. Beyond that, the sites for little girls were all mind-numbingly the same. The virtual worlds of BarbieGirls, Be-Bratz, Ty Girlz, Moxiegirlz were all extensions of their offline counterparts. Each featured similar games girls could play to "earn" points with which to engage in their favorite activity: shopping. They could visit virtual malls to buy stylin' fashions for their avatars or a flat-screen TV for their virtual cribs. They could indulge in makeovers at the spa or purchase pets to pamper. They could also hone their ambitions for the future by playing at rock star or celebrity or . . . rock star or celebrity. On the New Dora's "Dora

Links," for instance, the "mysteries and adventure" in which girls can engage include changing the length of their avatar's hair, eye color, earrings, and necklace and getting "ready for a benefit concert."

The Disney Princesses site could well be crowned the dullest of them all: a user can enter the "enchanting" world of her favorite princess and, in each one, play a version of the *identical game*: Cinderella/Belle/Sleeping Beauty/Ariel is on her way to an important parade/fair/birthday party/tea party but— *Oh no!* She forgot to pick out an outfit and now doesn't have time! Can she count on *you* to do it for her by clicking on one of several predetermined choices? None of this is a surprise, and I am tempted to gloss right over it. Yet more and more of children's time is spent online. Doll sales have declined by nearly 20 percent since 2005. Girls are casting them aside in favor of online play, which offers even fewer opportunities to go off script. It chilled me to read, in the market research group NPD's report on this trend, a quote from a nine-year-old Barbie.com fan who said, "I don't think I'm good at making up imaginary things; I didn't know what to do with dolls." So it is at least worth mentioning that, even more than the original toys, these sites funnel our daughters toward very specific definitions of both girlhood and play.

Sites for the youngest children are protected by the Children's Online Privacy Protection Act (COPPA), which requires "verifiable parental consent" at registration and restricts the amount of personal information—addresses, phone numbers, sex, preferences in music—corporate marketers can collect from children. Chatting is typically limited and inappropriate behavior punished by suspension or expulsion. Once children turn thirteen, however, all bets are off. They are legally considered adults online, free to join any site that is not X-rated (though since the age of users on those sites is rarely verified, they could join those as well). You would be hard pressed these days to find an eighth-grader without a Facebook account. Meanwhile, 3.7 million teens log on to a virtual world each month. Today's platforms will probably be obsolete by the time Daisy is a teenager (if not by next year), but regardless of whatever Web site or matrix or brain implant arises to take their place, my questions remain the same: How will the Internet shape my daughter's understanding of herself? Will its vastness—its infinite nooks and crannies—intensify the contradictions of girlhood or provide opportunities for refuge? Will she lose control of her identity or gain new insight into it? And how can I, as a mom, sort out the legitimate from the sensationalist in the headlines about predators, anonymous bullying by peers, easy-access porn? (Try Googling "schoolgirls.com" or, as an eight-year-old daughter of a friend of mine innocently did, "cute girls.")

I am no Luddite. I am well aware of what an incredible, creative tool the Internet can be, offering split-second access to a diversity of perspectives and information that previously seemed unimaginable. But I have heard it said that we adults are immigrants to this land of technology; our kids are natives. They use it differently than we do. They experience it differently, without our old-world accents or values. Much as the mall was for a previous generation, the Internet has become a place where they experiment with identity, friendship, and flirtation. The fact that none of it is real does not make it any less revealing.

Erin, who is fourteen, has been online since she was in third grade. "I used to love doing the painting pages on the Dragon Tales site," she said, laughing. "I did them until I was much too old."

Erin and three of her friends were sitting in her family's Albany, California, living room. Her mother had set out an array of healthy snacks for us—hummus with carrots, fresh strawberries—but the girls shunned those for a bucket of shamrock-shaped, green frosted sugar cookies bought at the grocery store in celebration of Saint Patrick's Day. Each one here today had been online since she was seven or eight. Each carried her cell phone as if it were a fifth limb. Each owned an iPod touch. Each used computers daily, often in the privacy of her bedroom. Naturally, they all had Facebook accounts, which, judging from my communication with them, they checked numerous times during the school day. They'd had some amazing experiences online: one of the girls, Katie, fourteen, who had been adopted as an infant, told me she had found her birth mother on Facebook. So she'd friended her. "It was an open adoption, so I always knew her name," Katie explained, "but she'd never visited or anything. She was only seventeen when I was born." The two ended up meeting in person some months later, when the woman passed through San Francisco. "It was cool," Katie said, though she had no plans to see the woman again. The casual way she related the story confused me. Finding your birth mother with a few clicks—on Facebook, of all things—would seem momentous, yet Katie was treating it like it was no big deal. Maybe she was just playing it cool, but I wondered whether the unlimited possibility for connection had somehow devalued its worth.

Each of these girls had more than 400 friends on the networking site—one, Felicia, had 622—which was so unremarkable that I almost didn't note it. But really? Six hundred twenty-two friends? There were only about 250 students in her entire grade at school. One of my favorite books as a child was Joan Walsh Anglund's *A Friend Is Someone Who Likes You.* These days, a better title might be *A Friend Is Someone You Have Actually Met in Person.* There is no way Felicia could know all those people offline, though she claimed to have at least *met* each of them. Even so, 622 people can witness everything she writes, every picture she posts. Six hundred twenty-two people can pass that information on to *their* 622 friends. Six hundred twenty-two people are watching her, judging her, at least in theory, every hour of every day. How does that influence a child's development?

Apparently, quite a bit. In short order—a matter of a few years—social networking and virtual worlds have transformed how young people, male as well as female, conceptualize both their selves and their relationships. According to Adriana Manago, a researcher at the Children's Digital Media Center in Los Angeles who studies college students' behavior on MySpace and Facebook, young people's real-life identities are becoming ever more externally driven, sculpted in response to feedback from network "friends." Obviously, teens have always tested out new selves among their peers, but back in the dark ages (say, in the year 2000), any negative response was fleeting and limited to a small group of people they actually knew. Now their thoughts, photos, tastes, and activities are laid out for immediate approval or rejection by hundreds of people, many of whom are relative strangers. The self, Manago said, becomes a brand, something to be marketed to others rather than developed from within. Instead of intimates with whom you interact for the sake of the exchange, friends become your consumers, an audience for whom you perform.

The impact, back in the offline world, appears to be an up-tick in narcissistic tendencies among young adults. In the largest study of its kind, a group of psychologists found that the scores of the 16,475 college students who took the Narcissistic Personality Inventory between 1982 and 2006 have risen by 30 percent. A full two-thirds of today's young adults rank above average; excessive self-involvement is associated with difficulty in maintaining romantic relationships, dishonesty, and lack of empathy. And, it turns out, empathy, too, seems in measurably shorter supply: an analysis of seventy-two studies performed on almost 14,000 college students between 1979 and 2009 showed a drop in that trait, with the sharpest decline occurring since 2000. Social media may not have instigated that trend, but by encouraging self-promotion over self-awareness, they could easily accelerate it.

I don't mean to demonize new technology. I enjoy Facebook myself. Because of it, I am in touch with old friends and relatives who are scattered around the globe. It has also served as a handy vehicle to promote my work, to alert the readers among my "friends" that I have published something new. Yet I am also aware of the ways Facebook and the microblogging site Twitter subtly shifted my self-perception. Online, I carefully consider how any comments or photos I post will shape the persona I have cultivated; offline, I have caught myself processing my experience as it occurs, packaging life as I live it. As I loll in the front yard with Daisy or stand in line at the supermarket or read in bed, part of my consciousness splits off, viewing the scene from the outside and imagining how to distill it into a status update or a Tweet. Apparently, teenagers are not the only ones at risk of turning the self into a performance, though since their identities are less formed, one assumes the potential impact will be more profound.

Girls, especially, are already so accustomed to disconnecting from their inner experience, observing themselves as others might. Unlike earlier generations, though, their imagined audience is all too real: online, every girl becomes a mini-Miley complete with her own adoring fan base that she is bound to maintain. In fact, if you try to choose the screen name "Miley" in a virtual world, you will be told no dice, though you can be Miley1819 or higher, if you would like. According to Manago, girls attract the most positive feedback when they post provocative photos or create hot avatars—as long as they don't go too far. Just as with real celebs, then, girls online engage in perpetual, public negotiation between appearing "beautiful, sexy, yet innocent" (which they reportedly want) and coming off as "a slut" in front of hundreds of people (which they do not). Perhaps that high-wire act, as much as anything, reveals the lie of girls' popular culture: if the sexualization and attention to appearance truly "empowered" girls, they would emerge from childhood with more freedom and control over their sexuality. Instead, they seem to have less: they have learned that sexiness confers power—unless you use it (or are perceived as using it). The fastest way to take a girl down remains, as ever, to attack her looks or sexual behavior: Ugly. Fat. Slut. Whore. Those are the teen girl equivalent of kryptonite.

Erin and her friends have their own ideas about how to strike the right balance. Jessica, fourteen, explained, "I never put up a picture *just* of me. That's slutty."

I asked how merely posting a solo shot of herself could qualify as "slutty." "Well," she responded, "it's self-centered, though, which is kind of the same thing."

She pulled up the profile of one of her classmates to show me what she meant. The other girls crowded around the screen. How strange, I thought; I don't know this girl and never will, but here I was rifling through her photos, reading what other people thought of them. One snapshot showed her leaning forward in a bikini top; in another, she posed with one shoulder thrust coyly toward the viewer. "Look at her," said Felicia, disgusted. "She's dyed her hair *blond*. Badly. And look at that." She pointed to a close-up shot of the girl mugging for the camera with a boy. "He is in her bed! Her *bed*!"

Felicia did not stint on comments about other girls, even though she herself had been branded a slut in eighth grade by classmates who were jealous of the boy she was dating. Also, she has large breasts, which had developed early, and, really, isn't that enough? Her tormentors targeted her both in person and electronically, even creating a Facebook page called "Felicia's a Whore." "I tried to act like it didn't bother me," she said, tersely. "But it was not a lovely situation." Nor an uncommon one. The girls showed me another friend's Formspring page: a free application that allows your Facebook "friends" to ask questions or post comments about you—anonymously. That means that while the person who says "Can I see ur tits live?" or "U r a bitch!" is someone you know (or at least someone you have friended), you can never know exactly *who*. Think of it as the online equivalent of a bathroom stall with all the raunchiness and lord-of-the-flies viciousness that implies. The mind reels at the idea of such technology in the hands of teenage girls, who are already masters of—and suckers for—stealth aggression.

In the early days of the Web, people feared their daughters would be stalked by strangers online, but the far bigger threat has turned out to come from neighbors, friends, peers. In the first high-profile case of cyberbullying, a Missouri girl, Megan Meier, hung herself in her bedroom after a romance with a boy she had met on MySpace—but had never spoken to or seen in person—went sour. "You're the kind of boy a girl would kill herself over,"

Meier wrote in her final post, twenty minutes before her suicide. She was just three weeks shy of her fourteenth birthday. The boy, it was later discovered, did not exist: he had been fabricated by Meier's neighbor, forty-seven-year-old Lori Drew, to punish the girl for spreading rumors about Drew's own daughter. Four years later, in 2010, fifteen-year-old Phoebe Prince put cyberbullying back in the headlines: she hung herself after enduring months of sexual slurs in her South Hadley, Massachusetts, high school hallways, as well as via text message and on Facebook. A few months later, Alexis Pilkington, a popular seventeen-year-old soccer player from Long Island, also took her life after a series of cybertaunts, which persisted on a memorial page created after her death.

Most cases of online harassment do not go that far, but the upsurge of abuse is disturbing. A 2009 poll conducted by the Associated Press and MTV found that half of young people aged fourteen to twenty-four reported experiencing digital abuse, with girls significantly more likely to be victimized than boys. Two-thirds of those who were the target of rumors and hearsay were "very upset" or "extremely upset" by the experience, and they were more than twice as likely as their peers to have considered suicide.

Gossip and nasty notes may be painful staples of middle school and high school girls' lives, but YouTube, Facebook, instant messaging, texting, and voice mail can raise cruelty to exponential heights. Rumors can spread faster and further and, as the case of Phoebe Prince illustrates, there is nowhere to escape their reach—not your bedroom, not the dinner table, not while going out with your friends. The anonymity of the screen may also embolden bullies: the natural inhibitions one might feel face-to-face, along with any sense of accountability, fall away. It is easy, especially among young people, for behavior to spin out of control. Further, this risks exposing them to consequences they did not—or could not—anticipate.

⌀

Portraying girls as victims, particularly of other girls, is distressing, but it is also comfortable, familiar territory. What happens when girls, under the pretext of sexual self-determination, seem to victimize themselves? A 2008 survey by the National Campaign to Prevent Teen and Unplanned Pregnancy found that 39 percent of teens had sent or posted sexually suggestive messages (or "sexts"), and 22 percent of teenage girls had electronically sent or posted nude or seminude photos of themselves. At first I was skeptical of those figures: the teen sexting "epidemic" had the earmarks of media-generated hype, the kind of moral panic that breaks out whenever girls have the audacity to act sexually. Young ladies flashing skin and propositioning boys? Heavens to Betsy, hie them to a nunnery!

Then, mere days after that report was released, a friend of mine found a photo on her fourteen-year-old son's computer of one of his female classmates—a ninth-grader—naked from the waist up. She was not even a girl he knew well. "We're trying to teach our son that women are not playthings," my friend said. "How are we supposed to do that if a girl sends him something like this?"

Good question. How is one to explain such behavior? Part of me, I had to admit, was taken by the girl's bravado: that at age fourteen, she felt confident enough in her body to send a nudie shot to a boy she barely knew. Was it possible that this was a form of progress, a sign that at least some of today's girls were taking charge of their sexuality, transcending the double standard? I wanted to believe it, but the conclusion didn't sit right.

I checked in with Deborah Tolman, a professor of human sexuality studies at Hunter College who for years has been my go-to gal on all matters of girls and desire. As it happened, she had been wrestling with these very questions and had come up with a theory: girls like the one I have described are not connecting more deeply to their own feelings, needs, or desires. Instead, sexual entitlement itself has become objectified; like identity, like femininity, it, too, has become a performance, something to "do" rather than to "experience." Teasing and turning boys on might give girls a certain thrill, even a fleeting sense of power, but it will not help them understand their own pleasure, recognize their own arousal, allow them to assert themselves in intimate (let alone casual) relationships.

Previously, I mentioned that early sexualization can derail girls' healthy development, estrange them from their own erotic feelings. Ninth-graders texting naked photos may be one result. Another might be the annual "slut list" the senior girls at an affluent high school in Millburn, New Jersey, compile of incoming freshmen (which made national news after they posted it on Facebook in 2009); being chosen is at once an honor and a humiliation, marking a girl as "popular" even as it accuses her of lusting after her brother or wanting someone to "bend me over and knock me up." That detached sexuality may also contribute to an emerging phenomenon that Tolman is studying, which she called, bluntly, Anal Is the New Oral. "All girls are now expected to have oral sex in their repertoire," she explained. "Anal sex is becoming the new 'Will she do it or not?' behavior, the new 'Prove you love me.' And still, girls' sexual pleasure is not part of the equation." That is such a fundamental misunderstanding of romantic relationships and sexuality—as a mother, it plunges me into despair. I find myself improbably nostalgic for the late 1970s, when I came of age. Fewer of us competed on the sports field, raised our hands during math class, or graduated from college. No one spoke the word "vagina," whether in a monologue or not. And there was that Farrah flip to contend with. Yet in that oh-so-brief window between the advent of the pill and the fear of AIDS, when abortion was both legal and accessible to teenagers, there was—at least for some of us—a kind of *Our Bodies, Ourselves* optimism about sex. Young women felt an almost solemn, political duty to understand their desire and responses, to explore their own pleasure, to recognize sexuality as something rising from within. And young men—at least some of them—seemed eager to take the journey with us, to rewrite the rules of masculinity so they would prize mutuality over conquest. That notion now seems as quaint as a one-piece swimsuit on a five-year-old. "By the time they are teenagers," Tolman said, "the girls I talk to respond to questions about how their bodies feel—questions about sexuality or desire—by talking about how their bodies look. They will say something like 'I felt like I looked good.'" My fear for my daughter, then, is not that she will someday act in a sexual way; it is that she will learn to act sexually against her own self-interest.

Most young women, thankfully, are not out there making personalized *Playboy* centerfolds. The ones who are may well be the ones engaging in other risky behaviors offline; the statistics on sexting, for instance, are similar, demographically, to those on binge drinking. Megan Meier, the girl who committed suicide in 2006, had a history of depression, as did Alexis Pilkington. Phoebe Prince seems to have been a self-cutter. Does that make them anomalies, or canaries in a coal mine? What about the thirteen-year-old girl "in love" who sends a hot shot to her boyfriend without considering what he will do with it after she dumps him? Or the girl who one time—just one time—does a stupid, thoughtless thing. Which of us hasn't been that girl? In the old days that One Stupid Thing might have sparked ugly rumors, but it could also fade away. The bad judgment you showed when you got drunk at a party and danced topless on a table was ephemeral. But my friend's son, were he so inclined, could forward his classmate's photo to one of his friends, who could forward it to two of his friends and, as in that 1970s shampoo commercial, so on and so on, until all three thousand–plus kids at their high school had a copy—and maybe all the kids in the next town as well. And that, as much as the act itself, is the problem: the indelibility of it, the never-ending potential for replication, the loss of control over your image and identity right when, as a teenager, you need it most.

Electronic media have created a series of funhouse mirrors. They both forge greater intimacy and undermine it—sometimes simultaneously. Determining what, exactly, is going on at any given time is confusing enough for an adult, let alone a child. The ten-year-old daughter of another friend of mine recently invited a pal for a sleepover. Rather than playing in person, the girls wanted to spend the evening using the family's computers—a desktop downstairs, a laptop upstairs—to send each other messages on the virtual world Webkinz.com. Was that just a latter-day version of one of my favorite childhood activities—putting a message in a basket and lowering it down the laundry chute on a string from the second story of my house to the basement, where my best friend awaited? Or was it something else, the beginnings of alienation from living, breathing friends, from the messiness and reciprocity of authentic relationships? Watching the unparalleled social experiment being conducted on our children, it's worth considering—for boys as well as girls—how Internet use enhances their *real* lives, their *real* friendships, their contributions to the *real* world. And if we can't answer all of that in a satisfying way, maybe it is time to give their second lives some second thought.

◦────◦

So how to prepare our kids for a safe, productive life online? Late one winter afternoon I drove to Black Hawk, a gated community of multimillion-dollar houses in Danville, California. At the top of a long, twisting driveway, a building that could have been a small hotel emerged before me. It was the home of Hilary DeCesare, a former account manager at Oracle and recently divorced mom of three: twelve-year-old twins—a girl and a boy—as well as an eight-year-old girl. DeCesare's home doubled as headquarters of the soon-to-be-launched social networking site she was developing for kids aged eight to thirteen that she hopes will be as revolutionary as Facebook was. To date, there was nothing like it: a COPPA-compliant site that will allow kids to customize their profile pages, create interest groups, play games, write on one another's walls, e-mail, even video chat. A sophisticated software program will scan the site 24/7 for explicit language and the percentage of skin showing on photos and videos. Users will find regular tips posted on their walls to educate them about online safety and etiquette. Anyone caught bullying will be suspended or banished. Parents can monitor their children as closely or loosely as they see fit: approving each friend request and group membership in real time; receiving a weekly or monthly e-mail rundown of their child's activity; or, if they choose, trusting their kids to find their own way. They can restrict their children to preset "canned chat" phrases or allow them to IM one another freely. DeCesare likes to call it "the Internet with training wheels."

DeCesare, a fit blond woman dressed in a powder blue sweater and jeans, met me at the door with a plate of homemade fudge and a surprise. When we had first spoken, some months earlier, her site had been called Girl Ambition (a name that would seem more appealing to mothers than kids) and had been adamantly single-sex. She had focused on girls, she had told me, because they were adopting the social technologies more rapidly than boys. Also because she was a mom as well as an entrepreneur: one who did not like the values promoted by the commercial sites for girls her own daughters frequented. She had hoped to lure them away with a fun alternative that, P.S., would also slip in lessons on goal setting, self-esteem, and healthy body image as well as offer advice on dealing with cyberbullies. In the interim, however, she had realized it didn't make business sense to exclude half the world's kids because of their sex. So she had scaled back the educational component and renamed the company the more neutral (and potentially profitable) Everloop.

We headed into the family library, its shelves stacked with bestselling books by authors such as John Grisham and James Patterson. A volume from the *Gossip Girl* series lay on a table between two computers. A third computer sat on a desk pushed against an adjacent wall. DeCesare had asked her twins to show me around the site, so I could experience it as users would. Her son immediately sat down and began gaming. He did not say much during the rest of my visit. Her daughter Danielle, meanwhile, plopped down in another chair and turned sideways toward me, swinging her feet, her toes tipped with chipped green polish, as she showed off her home page. She had customized the background with a photo of the stars of the *Twilight* series, listed her favorite singer as Taylor Swift and her favorite show as *iCarly*. Her groups included Ro's Soccer Club (started by her little sister), *Star Wars*, and Fashion 101.

DeCesare had told me, as a selling point, that there would be no advertising on Everloop. But watching Danielle, I realized that didn't matter: product promotions are so thoroughly embedded online that ads would be redundant. In addition to groups created by the kids themselves, Everloop will feature corporate-sponsored "supergroups." Imagine an exercise group hosted by Nike, a video group hosted by Flip, a hygiene group hosted by Bonne Bell. Users will also be able to buy "stickers" of favorite products and performers to put on their home pages—a gimmick that basically convinces them to pay for advertising. All of that is in keeping with the larger "advergaming" trend on Internet sites for kids: in the popular virtual world Millsberry (owned by General Mills) users can explore the "Honey Nut Cheerios Greenhouse"; at the not-for-profit Whyville they can drive a Toyota Scion; or work at the McDonald's in Habbo Hotel; or hang out in the Cosmo-Girl lounge at There.com. Parents are often warned that, until children are six, they cannot distinguish between commercials and programming on TV. With the Internet, there is no longer a distinction to make—for them or for us. Frankly, I would prefer traditional advertising to all this embedded stuff; as a parent, I would feel less duped.

When I first met DeCesare, I was jazzed about her site, even though it seemed a little preachy. Now I felt myself beginning to turn. I appreciated the safeguards against sexual deviants, but where was the protection against other sorts of predation? How about some tips on resisting covert marketing along with the ones on combating cyberbullies? A site like Everloop may be fun, even imaginative, but it will also roll back the age at which children will create and present themselves as a brand, one composed of various products and media, most of which portray both girls and boys in stereotypical ways. If that is unhealthy for a college student, I can't see how it would be desirable for an eight-year-old.

DeCesare reminded me that parents had the option to filter any or all of that out. That may be, I said, but realistically, how long could it last? "We're not claiming we're perfect," she responded. "But it is presumed we're going to be creating an environment that's empowering to the kids."

There was that word again: "empowering." She meant that Everloop would allow kids to play online freely yet safely. But really, could any environment be truly empowering if it pushes kids—and girls in particular, since they are more active in social networks—to define themselves by what they buy, how they look, whom they idolize, what they watch? It is telling that girls' embrace of online culture is not translating into their adult ambitions. Even as the percentage of girls using the Internet has soared, the percentage of female college students majoring in computer science has plummeted, dropping by 70 percent between 2000 and 2005. The gender gap in consuming Internet culture may have closed, but the one in creating it has only grown wider.

I would like to ignore the online world of kids—the complications seem endless and overwhelming—but, like any parent today, I can't. I would rather Daisy spend her time honing her identity on an offline playground than an online one, through face-to-face relationships and real-life activities. I do not want the Web to be where she defines her femininity or asserts her independence, any more than my mom wanted me to test mine by hopping on a bus to the mall with her Shoppers Charge in hand. Yet parents also have to be realists, and, as DeCesare reminded me, this is the world in which our children are being raised. "At Everloop, we're trying to give kids unexpected freedom while giving parents like you peace of mind," she assured me. Maybe she is right. Maybe our kids do need those training wheels—and maybe recognizing that will turn DeCesare into the next Tom Anderson, one of the founders of MySpace, who sold out to Rupert Murdoch for $580 million. But for now, she said, "our goal is simple: to get kids ready for the real world, to prepare them for when they go on to other sites. Because," she added, "you know they will."

Chapter Ten

Girl Power—No, Really

i didn't like that princess," Daisy said, wrinkling her nose. "She looked funny."

It was two weeks before Christmas 2009, and that could mean only one thing: the annual release of a new animated Disney film. That year, *The Princess and the Frog* premiered amid a blitz of self-congratulatory hype about the studio's First African-American Princess (though the more impressive event will be the introduction of the *Second* or maybe the *Third* African-American Princess). America's first black president had been elected just weeks before, the news media enthused, and—as if the two were equivalent—now this! About two-thirds of the audience at our local multiplex had been African American—parents with little girls decked out in gowns and tiaras—which was undeniably strik-ing, even moving. Still, my own response, characteristically, was mixed: sure, it was about time Disney made up for the racism of *Song of the South*, *The Jungle Book*, and *Dumbo* (and *Aladdin* and *Peter Pan*), but was peddling a café au lait variation of the same old rescue fantasy in a thin-and-pretty package the best way to do that? Was that truly cause for celebration?

"But it's different for black girls," my friend Verna had told me. Verna, who is African American, is mother to a nine-year-old daughter. She is also a law professor specializing in the intersection of race, gender, and class in education law and policy. "There's a saying in our community," she continued, "'We love our sons but we raise our daughters.' Girls learn that you have to *do*. You have to be the worker bee. Princess takes black girls out of that realm. And you know, discounting the baggage of how stultifying being placed on a pedestal can be . . . " She laughed. "If you've never been on it, it looks pretty good."

I took the point, I guess. Certainly, as the mother of a biracial child myself, I identified with the constant scavenger hunt for toys and images that in *some* way resembled my kid. Take the wooden dollhouse I bought for Daisy: its choice of families spanned the skin tone spectrum, but the manufacturer's progressiveness did not extend to miscegenation (or, for that matter, to gay parents). I ended up buying two sets, one white and one Asian, so she could mix and match. It was, at best, an imperfect solution.

Scarcity breeds scrutiny. Given how few black female leads there are in G-rated animation (Anyone? Anyone?), Tiana, fairly or not, was expected to *represent*. *The Princess and the Frog* was subject to months of speculation before it opened. Outrage bubbled up when the first pass at Tiana's name was revealed: "Maddy," which sounded uncomfortably close to "Mammy." Disney also miscalculated, according to scuttlebutt, by initially making the character a chambermaid for a white woman; in the end, Tiana is a waitress at a restaurant owned by an African-American man. The texture of her hair, the shade of her skin, the fullness of her features, were all debated, as was the suspiciously indeterminate ethnicity of her prince (described as "olive-skinned," he spoke with a Brazilian accent). Disney shrewdly tried to bullet-proof the film by consulting Oprah Winfrey (who also voiced Tiana's mother, Eudora), the NAACP, and an organization called Mocha Moms. Take, *that*, critics! Of course, in the end, Tiana spent most of the film as a (shapely, long-eyelashed) amphibian, which rendered her race more or less moot.

Now here was my daughter, my very own daughter, saying that something about the princess looked off . . . *why?*

"You thought Tiana looked funny?" I asked, trying to keep my voice neutral.

She shook her head impatiently. "No," she said. "Not Tiana. The *princess.*"

"But Tiana *was* the princess," I said.

She shook her head again. "The *princess*," she repeated, then, after a moment, added, "I liked when she helped the African-American girl, though."

That was when it clicked: Daisy wasn't talking about Tiana; she was talking about Lotte, Tiana's Caucasian friend and foil. *The Princess and the Frog* opened in a flashback: the two of them, as little girls, sitting on the floor of Lotte's icing pink room, while Eudora, a seamstress, read them the story of the princess and the frog. Tiana recoiled as the plot unspooled; Lotte swooned. It was Lotte who had row upon row of pink princess gowns and a pink canopy bed; Lotte was the one who wished on stars; Lotte had the encyclopedic knowledge of fairy tales; Lotte dreamed of marrying the handsome prince and living happily ever after; Lotte, as an ingénue, swept her hair into a Cinderella 'do for the ball. And it was Lotte who, while ultimately good-hearted, was also spoiled, shallow, and ridiculous—oh, and funny-looking; whatever strides Disney has made on race, "ugly" and its stepsibling "fat" still connote stupid or evil in its films. So it was clear—to me, anyway—that the viewer was supposed to dislike, or at least disidentify with, Lotte. But I understood Daisy's confusion: Lotte was also everything that, up until now, Disney has urged our daughters to be and to buy. How was a little girl to interpret that? How were we parents to interpret it? Was Disney mocking itself? Could the studio actually be uneasy with the frenzy of acquisitiveness it had created? Was it signaling that parents should be more on guard against the very culture it had foisted on us?

Yeah, probably not, but Daisy's mix-up gave me the opening I needed to talk with her (*"with"* being the operative word) about the way the film had presented girls and women, to solicit her own ideas about it. That, in the end, is the best weapon we parents have, short of enrolling our daughters in one of those schools where kids knit all day (or moving to Sweden; marketing to children under twelve there is actually *illegal*—can you believe it?). We have only so much control over the images and products to which they are exposed, and even that will diminish over time. It is strategic, then—absolutely vital—to think through our own values and limits early, to consider what we approve or disapprove of and why.

I can't say what others' personal threshold ought to be: that depends on one's child, one's parenting style, one's judgment, one's own personal experience. It would be disingenuous to claim that Disney Princess diapers or Ty Girlz or *Hannah Montana* or *Twilight* or the latest Shakira video or a Facebook account is inherently harmful. Each is, however, a cog in the round-the-clock, all-pervasive media machine aimed at our daughters—and at us—from womb to tomb; one that, again and again, presents femininity as performance, sexuality as performance, identity as performance, and each of those traits as available for a price. It tells girls that how you look is more important than how you feel. More than that, it tells them that how you look *is* how you feel, as well as who you are. Meanwhile, the notion that we parents are sold, that our children are "growing up faster" than previous generations, that they are more mature and sophisticated in their tastes, more savvy in their consumption, and there is nothing we can (or need) do about it is—what is the technical term again?—oh yes: *a load of crap.* Today's three-year-olds are no better than their predecessors at recognizing when their desires are manipulated by grown-ups. Today's six-year-olds don't get the subtext of their sexy pirate costumes. Today's eight-year-olds don't understand that ads are designed to sell them something. And today's fourteen-year-olds are still desperate for approval from their friends—all 622 of them.

꧁꧂

I never expected, when I had a daughter, that one of my most important jobs would be to protect her childhood from becoming a marketers' land grab. I have begun to see myself as that hazel tree in the Grimms' version of Cinderella (minus the Mom-being-dead part): my branches offering her shelter, my roots giving her strength. Instead of stepsisters and stepmother, though, the new "wicked" is an amalgam of images, products, and pitches that, just as surely, threaten to limit and undermine her. I refuse to believe that parents are helpless. We can provide alternatives, especially in the critical early years when children's brains are most malleable: choices that appeal to their desire to *be girls* yet reflect parents' values, worldview, and dreams for them—which I am guessing, unless you are Billy Ray Cyrus, do not include executing squat thrusts in an oversized cage while wearing thigh-high boots and a bird costume. (Billy Ray may want to consider Chris Rock's epiphany after his wife gave birth to a girl: that, as a father, his sole task is to *keep my baby off the pole.*)

I won't lie: it takes work to find other options, and if you are anything like me, your life is already brimful with demands. I know I feel maxed out trying to be a functioning professional, a loving wife, and a fully present mother all at once—and I have only one kid. It would be so much easier to let it slide, to buy whatever it is that will make your daughter happy and keep her occupied for fifteen minutes. You can worry about the rest later, right? If it is any comfort, I have found that I get as much out of making the effort as Daisy does. It's sort of like taking the time to cook myself rather than stopping for fast food (or at *least* driving the extra mile to pick up a healthier form of takeout). In fact, the rising consciousness about kids' nutrition shows the transformative impact parents can have: organic produce is now available at many grocery stores, farmers' markets are thriving, a sweeping federal overhaul of school lunch menus is in the works. Even McDonald's has retooled its menu. If we can force change in the food industry, why not do the same for toys and media?

I wish I could tell you that I had reached my own goals: getting my daughter outside more, taking walks in the woods together, playing sports, making art. Occasionally I have—and I advocate all of that—but mostly, I have just gotten a lot more canny about how we participate in the consumer culture. For the price of one Cinderella gown, for instance, I bought a dozen Papo figurines—tiny knights, princesses, pirates, dragons, unicorns, a stray Maid Marian, a random Joan of Arc—that were not "synergistically" marketed as clothing, home decor, Web sites, DVDs, and breath mints. Perhaps because of that, the play they inspired was less rote, more creative, while still acceptably royal. (I tried slipping a Jane Austen action figure into the mix as well, but, alas, she didn't take.) At bedtime we continue to read legends, mythology, and fairy tales—all of which teem with complex female characters that fire a child's imagination—and have added, among other things, women's stories from biblical literature. Who knew that without Moses' sister Miriam, the Israelites would have died of thirst while wandering the desert?

Speaking of which, if we were stuck on a desert island with a DVD player and could have only one disc, I would want it to be a film by Hayao Miyazaki—gorgeous animation, rich stories, as much a treat for adults as they are for kids. Miyazaki is sometimes called "the Walt Disney of Japan," but that diminishes his brilliance as well as his respect for the youngest members of his audience: he never panders creatively or intellectually. The female protagonists in his films—which include *My Neighbor Totoro, Laputa: The Castle in the Sky,* and *Nausicaä of the Valley of Wind*—are refreshingly free of agenda, neither hyperfeminine nor drearily feminist. They simply *happen* to be girls, as organically as, in other directors' films, they *happen* to be boys. In one of my favorites, *Kiki's Delivery Service,* a thirteen-year-old witch must, according to custom, leave her home to find her purpose in the larger world. Her transformation ultimately hinges on self-knowledge rather than a cute makeover or love's first kiss. (Disney distributes the films in the United States and dubs them into

English. Apparently, the studio could not fully keep its paws off: Kiki wears a black witch's dress throughout the film; in this version *only* she says, "I wish it were lilac.")

It turns out, too, that, at least with younger children, "no" is a useful tactic. Your three-year-old has no interest in critical thinking, no ear for subtlety. Your attempt to deconstruct a product or sales pitch, even at its most rudimentary, sounds to her like the squawking of the grown-ups in *Peanuts.* The only thing that penetrates is PRINCESSES and TOOTHPASTE TUBE. Limiting her access to toys or media may inspire some grumbling but will not necessarily create the "forbidden fruit" effect that parents fear. According to a 1999 study, elementary school students who didn't watch violent TV at home were least interested in it in the laboratory. Meanwhile, a 2009 study found that kids that age who were shown violent film clips as part of a media literacy class later reported *more* willingness to use aggression; those taught the curriculum without the clips did not. That said, pointing out inaccurate or unrealistic portrayals of women to younger grade school children—ages five to eight—does seem to be effective, when done judiciously: talking to little girls about body image and dieting, for example, can actually *introduce* them to disordered behavior rather than inoculating them against it. I may be taking a bit of a leap here, but to me all of this indicates that if you are creeped out about the characters from *Monster High*, it is fine to keep them out of your house.

Going all Amish on your middle school or high school daughter, however, is another story. That's when kids chafe against restrictions, become skilled at finding ways around them. It is also when the eye rolling begins in earnest, when girls are exquisitely tuned to the slightest whiff of a lecture. So haranguing your twelve-year-old when she tears it up to "What I wa-wa-want is what you wa-wa-

want. Give it to me baby, like boom boom boom" is not going to reach her. However, open-minded, respectful conversation about the song's underlying message (while acknowledging its catchy beat) very well might. Lyn Mikel Brown and Sharon Lamb, whose *Packaging Girlhood* offers excellent age-appropriate "sample conversations," urge parents to ask girls questions rather than dole out opinions. Though it may sound like a big old *duh*, the best approach is to put reasonable limits on the girlz-with-a-z stuff for as long as you can and, over time, engage (without nagging) in regular dialogue with your daughter about what she consumes. Watching TV or listening to music along with your child is also a good idea, *if* you're willing to discuss the content: otherwise, your presence comes off like an endorsement. The point, according to Erica Weintraub Austin, the director of the Edward R. Murrow School of Communication at Washington State University, is not so much to raise children who are cynical about the media as ones who are skeptical.

As it happens, skepticism had marked the beginning of the end of my daughter's interest in the Disney Princesses. And it was sparked—by Disney itself! Specifically, by Daisy's embrace (with my enthusiastic approval) of Mulan, the girl who masqueraded as a male soldier and saved all of China. By rights, Mulan ought not to be in the Princess pantheon; though descended from an "honored" family, she was not herself royal, nor did she marry a prince. Plus, *Mulan II*, a straight-to-DVD sequel, portrays court life for women as little more than sumptuous slavery. In that film, Mulan and her fiancé, Shang, are charged with escorting a trio of princesses across China, where their arranged marriages will secure peace with a rival kingdom. Their showstopping musical number "Like Other Girls" expresses their longing for freedom: "No escorts / No manners / No nursemaids / No worries / No hands folded perfect, like holding a lily . . ."

"Why does she sing that?" Daisy asked one evening when she was around four.

"I suppose because it isn't easy being a princess," I said. "They don't get to decide how to live or what to do. They always have to look and act just so."

"Oh," she said.

The song continued. "I wanna be like other girls. Scrape up my knees like other girls can."

"Pause it," Daisy commanded. Then: "Why does she say *that*?"

"I don't think she really wants to get hurt," I assured her, "but she wishes she could run and jump and play. Real princesses don't have much fun."

"Oh," she said again. We continued on that way, her wanting to pause after each line so I could explain why these princesses were so unhappy being *princesses*.

"Oh," she said every time.

A few days later, as we drove home from preschool, she asked about another song in the movie, "Lesson Number One." It was one of my favorites: in it, Mulan schools a group of little girls on the yin and yang of female warriors.

"Mom?" Daisy asked. "How come in that song Mulan has to be gentle *and* strong but Shang is only strong?"

I looked into the rearview mirror and grinned as my eye caught hers.

෧෩෧

As of summer 2010, several more Princess movies were coming down the pike. Pixar was planning to release *Brave* in 2012—its first *ever* film with a female protagonist. The studio's lack of interest in the XX chromosome has been so entrenched that the original *Toy Story*, made in 1995, didn't have a *single* significant female character, not even the obligatory bookish sidekick (yes, there was the "sweet and loveable porcelain shepherdess" Bo Peep, whom the little boy occasionally uses as his "damsel in distress," but *please!*). Written by Brenda "first-woman-to-direct-an-animated-feature-which-should-be-a-source-of-industry-shame-rather-than-celebration" Chapman (who was subsequently removed from the project), *Brave* tells the story of "impetuous, tangle-haired Merida, [who,] though a daughter of royalty, would prefer to make her mark as a great archer." Sounds promising, though I cannot help but feel, after waiting patiently (and sometimes not so patiently) through twelve genre-busting films about male robots, male superheroes, male cowboys, male rats, male cars, male bugs, male fish, and a small male mailman, that it would have been nice if the movie was *not* about a princess, even a kick-ass one. Honestly, is that too much to ask? Also, my fingers are crossed that her waistline will be several pixels thicker than depicted in the early sketches that were leaked onto the Internet.

Disney, too, was busily readying its next Princess rollout, though the Magic Kingdom had hit some bumps along the royal road: it turned out that, despite the massive hoopla generated over its release, *The Princess and the Frog* was a box-office dud. Relatively speaking, that is: I personally would not sneeze at a $222 million payday. But bear in mind that *Pocahontas* grossed $346 million in 1995, when theater tickets topped out at around $4.50. And *Up*, released six months before *The Princess and the Frog*, was a $731 million jackpot. How to explain the disappointment? Disney blamed it on . . . girls. In an interview with the *Los Angeles Times*, Ed Catmull, the president of Walt Disney and Pixar Animation Studios, surmised that the word "princess" might have scared off half the ticket-buying audience (that is, boys). None of the previous femalecentric movies—not even *Cinderella*—had initially been marketed as a "Princess" film, chiefly because the concept did not yet exist. They were simply *family* movies. (Though "Disney Princess" may have become a liability at the box office, the term remains a merchandising blockbuster—seventeen thousand Tiana dolls sold during the second week of November 2009 alone, even though the film would not open nationally for another month.) Unwilling to take any chances, Disney shelved its plans to plunder Hans Christian Andersen's *The Snow Queen* and retooled its 2010 release, *Rapunzel*, to include a brand-new male character—a "bad-boy" bandit named Flynn Rider—who could be given equal billing with the lady of the locks. The project was retitled *Tangled*, which, as one Internet wag commented, was like renaming *Sleeping Beauty* "Coma."

Maybe *Tangled* will be a spectacular romp. Maybe I will adore it; it could happen. But one thing is for sure: *Tangled* will not be "Rapunzel." And that's too bad, because "Rapunzel" is an especially layered and relevant fairy tale, less about the love between a man and a woman than the misguided attempts of a mother trying to protect her daughter from (what she perceives) as the world's evils. The tale, you may recall, begins with a mother-to-be's yearning for the taste of "rapunzel," a salad green she spies growing in the garden of the sorceress who happens to live next door. The woman's craving becomes so intense, she tells her husband that if he doesn't fetch her some, she and their unborn baby will die. So he steals into the witch's yard, wraps his hand around a plant, and, just as he pulls . . . she appears in a fury. The two eventually strike a bargain: the man's wife can have as much of the plant as she wants—*if* she turns over her baby to the witch upon its birth. "I will care for it like a mother," the sorceress croons (as if that makes it all right). Then again, who would you rather have as a mom: the woman who would do anything for you or the one who would swap you in a New York minute for a bowl of lettuce?

Rapunzel grows up, her hair grows down, and when she is twelve—note that age—Old Mother Gothel, as she calls the witch, leads her into the woods, locking her in a high tower which offers no escape and no entry except by scaling the girl's flowing tresses. One day, a prince passes by and, on overhearing Rapunzel singing, falls immediately in love (that makes Rapunzel the inverse of Ariel—she is loved sight unseen *because* of her voice). He shinnies up her hair to say hello and, depending on which version you read, they have a chaste little chat or get busy conceiving twins.

Either way, when their tryst is discovered, Old Mother Gothel cries, "You wicked child! I thought I had separated you from the world, and yet you deceived me!" There you have it: the Grimms' warning to parents, centuries before psychologists would come along with their studies and measurements, against undue restriction. Interestingly, the prince can't save Rapunzel from her foster mother's wrath. When he sees the witch at the top of the now-severed braids, he jumps back in surprise and is blinded by the bramble that breaks his fall. He wanders the countryside for an unspecified time, living on roots and berries, until he accidentally stumbles upon his Love. She weeps into his sightless eyes, restoring his vision, and—voilà!—they rescue each other. "Rapunzel," then, wins the prize for the most egalitarian romance, but that is not its only distinction: it is the only well-known tale in which the villain is neither maimed nor killed. No red-hot shoes are welded to the witch's feet. Her eyes are not pecked out. Her limbs are not lashed to four horses who speed off in different directions. She is not burned at the stake. Why such leniency? Perhaps because she is not, in the end, *really* evil—she simply loves too much. What mother has not, from time to time, felt the urge to protect her daughter by locking her in a tower? Who among us doesn't have a tiny bit of trouble letting our children go? If the hazel branch is the mother I aspire to be, then Old Mother Gothel is my cautionary tale: she reminds us that our role is not to keep the world at bay but to prepare our daughters so they can thrive within it.

That involves staying close but not crowding them, standing firm in one's values while remaining flexible. The path to womanhood is strewn with enchantment, but it is also rife with thickets and thorns and a Big Bad Culture that threatens to consume them even as they consume it. The good news is, the choices we make for our toddlers can influence how they navigate it as teens. I'm not saying we can, or will, do everything "right," only that there is power—magic—in awareness. If we start with that, with wanting girls to see themselves from the inside out rather than outside in, we will go a long way toward helping them find their true happily-ever-afters.

Appendix One

A Conversation
with Peggy Orenstein

The following is an excerpt from the interview that originally aired on
The Diane Rehm Show, *January 27, 2011. Reprinted courtesy of American University*

MS. DIANE REHM

Thanks for joining us, I'm Diane Rehm. When the Disney Company began a new push to market princess products a decade ago, sales quickly soared to $300 million. Within eight years they had reached $4 billion, the largest franchise on the planet for girls aged two to six.

Now in a new book, author Peggy Orenstein talks about the impact of "princess mania" on the culture of little girlhood and on her own daughter in particular. The new book is titled *Cinderella Ate My Daughter*, and Peggy Orenstein joins me in the studio. I have the feeling that many of you have seen, been aware of, or been part of this phenomenon. Good morning, Peggy, thanks for being here.

MS. PEGGY ORENSTEIN

Thank you for having me, Diane.

REHM

Tell me about how you first became aware that this trend was materializing.

ORENSTEIN

Well, the short answer is I had a daughter. I think that before you have a child you're not really aware of what's going on in the culture of childhood. And I had my little girl, Daisy, and you know, when you have that baby—I still get teary about this—when you have that baby and you hold her in your arms, you just think you don't want her to think there's anything she *can't* do because she's a girl. And you don't want her to think that she *has* to do anything because she's a girl.

And we were going along with that and raising her that way and then she went to preschool, and within like a week, she came home and she had memorized all the gown colors and names of the Disney princesses as if by osmosis. And I had never heard of a Disney princess. I thought, What the heck is this? Meanwhile, we're going around, and the waitress—I live in Berkeley and so our waitresses are all tattooed and pierced and everything—and the tattooed, pierced waitress would give her her pancakes and say, "Here are your princess pancakes."

REHM

—wow—

ORENSTEIN

And the lady at the drugstore would say, "Would you like a balloon? I know what color you'd like!" and give her a pink one without asking. And then, finally, I took her to the pediatric dentist for her first dental appointment. And the dentist said, "Would you like to get into my princess chair so I can sparkle your teeth?" And I just thought, *Oh my God, do you have a princess drill, too?* You know, when did every little girl become a princess?

REHM

And that's the question, when did it happen?

ORENSTEIN

Well, it happened around 2000. I mean, there was always a little bit of princess play. I'm sure that you availed yourself of your mother's cast-off tiara when you were a child. And that's fine, but in 2000, for the first time, Disney took its characters and marketed them separately from a movie. So previously, like when *Cinderella* came out, it would come out of the vault—that's what they call it—and it would play for a few weeks or be out on VCR and there'd be a little bit of merchandise and then it would go away.

ORENSTEIN

So they got this idea to take all these female characters, call them princesses—some are not, some are—put them under one royal rubric and put them out there. And it was very controversial within the company. Roy Disney was against it, because he said it was mixing mythologies, and the princesses shouldn't, you know, have tea with one another because, I don't know, the world would implode or something. I'm not sure what he thought would happen.

ORENSTEIN

That's why if you look at the princess products where there are multiple princesses, they are always looking off in different directions
because none of them are supposed to know the other ones are there.
Also, I think, because princesses don't have girlfriends. And once
you notice that, it's really weird.

REHM

It sounds as though Disney found a niche, and not only did the children respond, but the parents responded.

ORENSTEIN

Yeah, obviously three-year-olds don't have credit cards, right? But
they do have a lot of begging power. And what Disney says about
this in the book is that it starts with princesses and then it just kind
of goes on—girls stick with the brand. But as part of that there's
this unprecedented way that beauty and play-sexiness are marketed
to girls at ever-younger ages. So I wanted to look at the impact of
that and how it starts with pink and sparkly, progresses to the diva,
then goes to the overtly sexualized. So it's this trajectory that girls
are put on.

REHM

And you think it begins in part with that kind of focus on
pink?

ORENSTEIN

With this gigantic focus, and what pink comes to represent is, well, it
becomes like this small box girls are put into. I remember driving—
you know how you get your best stuff when you're driving your child
around in the car and you're listening to her in the back seat? I was

driving Daisy and a friend to go to the park to scooter, and the other little girl had a pink helmet and Daisy had a fire-breathing dragon green helmet. And the other little girl looked at Daisy's helmet and said, "Why isn't your helmet pink? It's not for girls."

ORENSTEIN

And Daisy looked at her helmet and sort of furrowed her brow and said, "Well, it's for boys or for girls." And the other little girl looked very skeptical about that. And I thought there was so much in that little interchange about what was expected, about the potential exclusion if you don't follow the line, which parents worry about, and about this pink box. I mean pink is just a color, but it's a such a small slice of the rainbow, and it comes to represent this little box that gets tighter and tighter around girls that tells them that girlhood is defined by makeovers at four years old and princesses and being the fairest and ultimately the hottest of them all.

REHM

And I think the public was really exposed to that with the death of JonBenét Ramsey.

ORENSTEIN

That was a big turning point. Today's parents may not remember that so well. But the whole *Toddlers and Tiaras* phenomenon, those babies—I don't know if you watch that show—but the baby, toddler beauty pageants have become very popular to watch and be appalled by. And so I actually have a chapter in the book where I go to the toddler beauty pageants—so that you don't have to. I also go to the Miley Cyrus concert, so you don't have to.

But it would have been really easy for me to go down and attack the parents who put their daughters in those toddler pageants where they slather on the makeup and the fake tans and the big hair and the glitz and the glam. But that seemed like the easy, simple tactic and I didn't want to do that in this book. I didn't want to always take the easy attack.

So I went down and I really got to know the parents, who were really nice people. And really thought about how watching those programs distances us and lets us off the hook, because we can condemn those parents and not ask harder questions about how we're raising our own girls and where the line is, who draws it, and, you know, when you cross it.

REHM

And of course you have a seven-year-old daughter. How have you dealt with her, for example, on the helmet question?

ORENSTEIN

Well, she dealt with that herself. I was so proud of her. She was five years old by then and she just stood her ground. I write a lot about my own experience. I write about my—I mean, it's a complicated world out there and I, like any parent, am inconsistent, I'm hypocritical, I'm contradictory. I have meltdowns at Target and make my daughter cry over a Barbie, then I cry. I mean, all this stuff is in the book—our attempts to wend our way through this and navigate through. But we have found, you know, I think you can't fully avoid it. You can't censor your way out of it.

I believe in fighting fun with fun. And you can't constantly say no to your daughter and think that that's going to make her think she has more choices. I hate to tell parents who have a lot on their plate that they have to do more work. But you really have to do a little bit of digging to find fun alternatives that celebrate your daughter's girlhood without hinging it on appearance and sexiness.

REHM

Some people might think that princess mania is kind of simply a stage that kids go through, and because everybody else is doing it, because it's in the stores when the kids go in and their eyes light up at all the glitz and glitter, they, I don't know, absorb that for a while and then move on. But your concern is that rather than simply move on, they are affected by this early exposure.

ORENSTEIN

Well it's like a flume ride. You know, they're being channeled. There's this whole idea of Kids Getting Older Younger—KGOY it's called by marketers. And at the same time, adults are staying younger, older. So I have this suspicion that at some point our children are going to surpass us in age possibly. But the idea of kids getting older younger is that something that is marketed to older kids eventually becomes desirable or aspirational to younger kids. And as it ages down, the older kids give it up and the younger kids take it over.

ORENSTEIN

So when I was a girl we got our first Bonnie Bell Lip Smackers at, I don't know, age twelve. And now girls have a whole collection at four, and there's a statistic in *Cinderella Ate My Daughter* that says that nearly half of six- to nine-year-old girls wear lipstick or lip gloss regularly. And the percentage of eight- to twelve-year-olds who wear mascara and eyeliner has doubled since 2008. I don't know why the percentage of eight-year-olds wearing mascara is not zero, personally, but, you know, but whatever. So there's this way that there's this, this flume ride that . . . maybe Lip Smackers or Princesses—

—I don't know, maybe if it were just *that* it would be no big deal. But when it's Lip Smackers at four and it's Bratz dolls at six and it's *America's Top Model* at nine and it's *Keeping Up with the Kardashians* at twelve, you know . . . it's just this constant message that girls are bombarded with from an ever-younger age, and you just don't want your daughter, when she thinks about how she feels about herself, to think that what matters is the outfit she's wearing and the makeup she's wearing and she's only six years old.

REHM

On the other hand, do you think that this whole thrust has any positive effect?

ORENSTEIN

That's a really good question. What I went into it wondering was whether the pink and the princess were protective from early sexualization or whether they primed girls for it. And, you know, Disney says that it inspires imagination, but I just think it really ends up narrowing it.

Appendix Two

Beyond Princesses (Sort of):
What Girls See on Screen

Reprinted courtesy of the Geena Davis Institute on Gender in Media; the Annenberg School of Communication & Journalism; and Dr. Stacy L. Smith.

Where the Girls Aren't:
Your Neighborhood Multiplex

Across the four hundred top-grossing G, PG, PG-13 and R-rated movies released between 1990 and 2006, only 27 percent of all speaking characters were female.[1]

Little has improved since: of 5,554 speaking characters in G, PG and PG-13 films released between 2006 and 2009 only 29 percent were female.[2]

In 2007, only twenty of the top hundred grossing films featured a female lead or co-lead.[3]

Girls in Family Movies: Rated "E" for "Eye Candy"

In 2008, nearly 40 percent of female characters in movies ages thirteen to twenty were depicted wearing sexually-revealing clothing (versus 6.7 percent of males); 30.1 percent appeared partially nude (versus 10.3 percent of males); 35.1 percent had tiny waists (versus 13.6 percent of males); and 29.2 percent were overtly attractive (versus 11.1 percent of males).[4]

The percentage of females in G-rated movies wearing skimpy outfits wasn't much lower than that in movies rated R (20.3 percent and 23.5 percent, respectively). Meanwhile, females in G-rated films were actually *more* likely to have small waists or bodies with no room for internal organs—like, say, a womb. One bright spot: female characters in G-rated films are less likely than their R-rated sisters to be thin (33.1 percent versus 42.9 percent).[5]

Extreme makeovers were a key plot device for a third of female protagonists among thirteen G-rated films released between 1937 and 2005. Two thirds of heroines in those same films were in some way put on display for their beauty (or lack thereof). Three quarters wore sexy outfits. Among animated heroines, over half had improbable physical proportions.[6]

Why Your Daughter Should Go to Film School

Films directed or produced by women tend to feature a greater number of girls and women on screen. When one or more women is involved in writing the script, the percentage of female characters jumps 14.3 percent.[7]

And yet among the hundred top-grossing films of 2008, a mere 8 percent were directed by at least one woman, 13.6 percent were written by women, and 19.1 percent were produced by at least one woman.[8]

Why Going to Film School—or Pursuing Any Other Profession—Might Not Occur to Her

Among G-rated films released between 2006 and 2009 over 80 percent of characters depicted as having jobs were male.[9] Not a single woman was portrayed as an executive, a doctor, a lawyer, or a politician. Among the 101 most popular G-rated films released between 1990 and 2005, there was a near tie for the most common job held by female characters. They were (drum roll): white-collar occupations (19 percent), entertainer (16.2 percent), and . . . royalty (15.2 percent).[10]

Appendix Three

The New Girlie Girlhood
by the Numbers

The global revenue generated by Disney Princess products increased from $300 million in 2000 to $4 billion in 2009.[11]

The percentage of children ages —eight to twelve who regularly used eyeliner doubled between 2008 and 2010.[12]

Nearly half of girls between the ages of six and nine regularly use lipstick or lip gloss.[13]

Girls ages eight to twelve spend $40 million a month on beauty products. The biggest influence on their purchases is not peers or media: it's their mothers.[14]

Age of Barbie's target audience when she was introduced in 1959: nine to twelve.

Age of Barbie's target audience today: three to seven.[15]

Forty-one percent of girls ages fifteen to seventeen say they have bullied online—as opposed to 29 percent of boys.[16]

Nearly a quarter of teen girls have posted nude or semi-nude photos of themselves online.[17]

In 2009, twelve thousand Botox injections were given to children between the ages of thirteen and nineteen.[18]

In 2008, forty-three thousand children under the age of eighteen surgically altered their appearance.[19]

Forty-eight percent of girls in grades three to twelve polled in 2000 asserted that the most popular girls in school were "very thin"; by 2006 the number rose to 60 percent.[20]

Sixty percent of girls in grades nine to twelve surveyed in 2006 were attempting to lose weight; only 10 percent of these same girls were considered medically overweight.[21]

Between 1999 and 2006, the percentage of children under age twelve admitted to the hospital for eating disorders rose 119 percent. During the same period, hospital stays for eating disorders among teenagers ages twelve to nineteen increased 18 percent. Eighty-nine percent of all hospitalized patients were girls.[22]

Only 15 percent of students taking the AP computer science exam are female.[23]

Between 2000 and 2004, there was a 70 percent drop in the number of female college freshmen listing computer science as their probable major.[24]

Among fourteen thousand college students studied between 1979 and 2009, there was a 40 percent drop in empathy.[25] Age at which children express "brand consciousness": twenty-four months.[26]

Acknowledgments

t iaras all around to: my agent, Suzanne Gluck, for her fear-
less navigation of today's publishing industry; Gillian Blake,
who set this book ticking; Jennifer Barth, who skillfully saw it
through; Ilena Silverman, my enabler; my "mother superiors"
and trusted advisers—Sylvia Brownrigg, Ayelet Waldman, Ruth
Halpern, Eva Eilenberg, Peg-bo Edersheim Kalb, Elly Eisen-
berg, Barbara Lee Swaiman, Sara Corbett, Cornelia Lauf, Rachel
Silvers, Rinat Fried, Dawn Prestwich, Verna Williams; Pearlee
Coty and Lilly Krenn; Teresa Tauchi, the queen of Web design
and technology; Fred Stutzman, for saving me from myself; the
Orenstein and Okazaki clans; Danny Sager and Brian McCar-
thy for bed and board (but never bored!); Steven, my own Prince
Charming; and Daisy Tomoko, who never ceases to amaze, in-
spire, and humble me. Thanks, guys: you rule!

Notes

In the case of books, reports, articles in scholarly journals, and chapters of books, full citations will be found in the bibliography.

Chapter 1: Why I Hoped for a Boy

2   I had read about: J. T. Manning et al., "Parental Age Gap Skews Child Sex Ratio," *Nature* 389, no. 6649 (1997): 344.

6   According to the American Psychological Association: American Psychological Association, *Report of the APA Task Force on the Sexualization of Girls*, www.apa.org/pi/wpo/sexualization .html. The report defines sexualization as occurring under *any* of the following conditions: "a person's value comes only from his or her sexual appeal or behavior, to the exclusion of other characteristics; a person is held to a standard that equates physical attractiveness (narrowly defined) with being sexy; a person is sexually objectified—that is, made into a thing for others' sexual use, rather than seen as a person with the capacity for independent action and decision making; and/or sexuality is inappropriately imposed upon a person" (p. 2). According to the report, at least thirty-eight experiments, thirty-two surveys, and two interview studies have

investigated harmful connections between body dissatisfaction and the ideals of sexual attractiveness to which girls are constantly exposed (p. 23).

6   In one study: Deborah L. Tolman, Emily A. Impett, Allison J. Tracy, and Alice Michael, "Looking Good, Sounding Good." See also Emily A. Impett, Deborah Schooler, and Deborah L. Tolman, "To Be Seen and Not Heard."

6   the focus on appearance: Amy Slater and Marika Tiggemann, "A Test of Objectification Theory in Adolescent Girls"; American Psychological Association, *Report of the APA Task Force*, p. 23.

6   Even brief exposure: Duane Hargreaves and Marika Tiggemann, "The Effect of 'Thin Ideal' Television Commercials on Body Dissatisfaction and Schema Activation During Early Adolescence"; Duane Hargreaves and Marika Tiggemann, "The Effect of Television Commercials on Mood and Body Dissatisfaction"; Duane Hargreaves and Marika Tiggemann, "Idealized Media Images and Adolescent Body Image"; Paul G. Davies, Steven J. Spencer, Diane M. Quinn, and Rebecca Gerhardstein, "Consuming Images"; B. L. Fredrickson, T. A. Roberts, S. M. Noll, D. M. Quinn, and J. M. Twenge, "That Swimsuit Becomes You."

Chapter 2: What's Wrong with Cinderella?

13   They did not exist: Andy Mooney, "Remarks by Andy Mooney, Chairman, Disney Consumer Products," New York Licensing Show, New York, June 20, 2006.

13   the now-legendary story: Author's interview with Andy Mooney, Chairman, Disney Consumer Products, July 19, 2006.

13   Disney had never marketed: Author's interview with Mary Beech, Vice President, Girls Franchise Management, Disney Consumer Products, July 19, 2006.

14   It is also worth noting: Author's interview with Andy Mooney, July 19, 2006.

14   The first Princess items: Ibid.

14   By 2009: Disney Consumer Products, "Disney Consumer Products Poised to Significantly Increase Share of Boys Market," press release, June 3, 2010, www.businesswire.com/news/home/20100603005682/en/Disney-Consumer-Products-Significantly-Increase-Share.

14   more than twenty-six thousand: Author's interview with Andy Mooney, July 19, 2006.

14   "Princess" has not only: Disney Consumer Products, "Disney Consumer Products Poised."

14   To this day: Author's interview with Andy Mooney, July 19, 2006.

15   Meanwhile, by 2001: Author's interview with Sarah Buzby, Director of Barbie Marketing, Mattel, August 9, 2006.

15   Barbie sales were declining: Ibid. See also Nicholas Casey, "Mattel Profits Despite Barbie," *The Wall Street Journal*, February 1, 2008, p. A11.

15   in 2004: Author's interview with Brown Johnson, Executive Creative Director, Nickelodeon Preschool Television, August 9, 2006.

16   the more mainstream media: American Psychological Association, *Report of the APA Task Force*, pp. 27–28.

16   teenage girls and college students: Tolman et al., "Looking Good, Sounding Good"; Impett et al., "To Be Seen and Not Heard"; Anna Fels, "Do Women Lack Ambition?" *Harvard Business Review*, April 2004, www.orijen.com.au/resources/1/news-research-docs/HBR%20Do%20women%20lack%20ambition.pdf.

16   They are also less likely: American Psychological Association, *Report of the APA Task Force*, pp. 26–27; Tolman et al., "Looking Good, Sounding Good"; Impett et al., "To Be Seen and Not Heard."

17   Take the female college students: Davies et al., "Consuming Images."

17   who performed better: Fredrickson et al., "That Swimsuit Be-
      comes You."

17   a 2006 survey: Girls Incorporated, *The Supergirl Dilemma*.

18   In her brilliant book: Susan Douglas, *Enlightened Sexism*, p. 16.

21   nearly half of boys: Author's interview with Isabelle Cherney,
      Department of Psychology, Creighton University, January 25,
      2008. See also Isabelle Cherney and J. Dempsey (in press),
      "Young Children's Classification, Stereotyping, and Play Be-
      havior for Gender Neutral and Ambiguous Toys"; Isabelle
      Cherney and K. London, "Gender-linked Differences in the
      Toys, Television Shows, Computer Games, and Outdoor Ac-
      tivities of 5- to 13-Year-Old Children."

21   boys as young as four: Author's interview with Isabelle Cher-
      ney, January 25, 2008.

21   Boys were also: Cherney and Dempsey, "Young Children's
      Classification." Parents of both sexes, even today, are more
      likely to give children gender-stereotyped toys and encourage
      them to play with them. What's more, if a new toy is described
      as being liked by the other sex, it is often avoided, whereas if
      it is said to be for a child's own sex, it will be embraced. Carol
      Lynn Martin and Richard Fabes, *Discovering Childhood Devel-
      opment*, pp. 304–305.

24   That certainly fits: Author's interview with Mary Beech, July
      19, 2006.

24   Gary Cross: Cross, "Wondrous Innocence"; Cross, "Valves of
      Adult Desire."

24   They rebel against: Gary Cross, "Valves of Desire"; Cross,
      "Wondrous Innocence"; Cross, "Valves of Adult Desire"; au-
      thor's interview with Gary Cross, February 2, 2009.

25   as another cultural historian: Author's interview with Mir-
      iam Forman-Brunell, Department of History, University of
      Missouri–Kansas City, November 15, 2006.

25   Shirley Temple's film version: Ibid.

25   A mere six years old: "Biography of Shirley Temple Black," www

.kennedy-center.org/calendar/index.cfm?fuseaction=show Individual&entity_id=3814&source_type=A; see also Shirley Temple Black, *Child Star.*

25 President Franklin Roosevelt: "Biography of Shirley Temple Black."

26 the top of the box office: Ibid. See also Ken Severson, "Biography for Shirley Temple," www.imdb.com/name/nm0000073/bio.

26 She also became: Gary Cross, *Kids' Stuff*, pp. 117–118.

28 American Girl was born: "A History of Helping Girls Shine," www .americangirl.com/corp/corporate.php?section=about&id=2. See also Gretchen Morgenson, *Forbes Great Minds of Business*, pp. 123–125.

29 Pleasant Company was pulling: "Company News: Mattel Agrees to Buy Maker of American Girl Dolls," *The New York Times*, June 16, 1998, www.nytimes.com/1998/06/16/busi ness/company-news-mattel-agrees-to-buy-maker-of-ameri can-girl-dolls.html.

29 a $700 million payday: Ibid.

31 in fall 2009: Eric Noll, "Meet Gwen Thompson, the 'Homeless' American Girl," *Good Morning America*, September 26, 2009, http://abcnews.go.com/GMA/Weekend/homeless-american -girl-doll-sparks-controversy/story?id=8676579.

Chapter 3: Pinked!

35 Children weren't color-coded: Author's interview with Jo Paoletti, American Studies Department, University of Mary-land, College Park, November 16, 2006.

36 Why or when that switched: Ibid.

36 It was not until the: Ibid.

36 it was popularized: Daniel Thomas Cook, *The Commodification of Childhood*; Cook, "The Rise of 'the Toddler' as Subject and as Merchandising Category in the 1930s."

36 consider the trajectory: Daniel Thomas Cook and Susan B. Kai-ser, "Betwixt and be Tween"; Cook, "The Rise of 'the Toddler.'"

37 classic marketing bible: Daniel Acuff and Robert H. Reiher, *What Kids Buy and Why*, pp. 83–84.

37 girls become "adept": Jayne O'Donnell, "As Kids Get Savvy, Marketers Move down the Age Scale," *USA Today*, April 13, 2007, www .usatoday.com/money/advertising/2007-04-11-tween-usat_N .htm. Some marketers have even stretched "tween" to include six-year-olds. See Alicia de Mesa, "Marketing and Tweens," *Business-Week*, October 12, 2005, www.businessweek.com/innovate/con tent/oct2005/id20051012_606473.htm.

37 we now have toddlers: Acuff and Reiher, *What Kids Buy and Why*; Paul Kurnit, "Kids Getting Older Younger," interview, Advertising Education Foundation, 1999, www.aef.com/on _campus/classroom/speaker_pres/data/35.

37 thirteen- to fifteen-year-olds may still: Acuff and Reiher, *What Kids Buy and Why*, pp. 122–123.

37 children one year old and under: Kurnit, "Kids Getting Older Younger." See also Jennifer Comiteau, "First Impressions; When Does Brand Loyalty Start? Earlier than You Might Think," *Adweek*, March 24, 2003, www.adweek.com/aw/ esearch/article_display.jsp?vnu_content_id=1847851.

38 the improbable term "pre-tween": O'Donnell, "As Kids Get Savvy."

39 her presence: Tanya Barrientos, "A Rude Welcome for Abby, New Girl on *Sesame Street*," *Pittsburgh Post-Gazette*, August 30, 2006, www.post-gazette.com/pg/06242/717302-237.stm.

40 only to see them fizzle: Michael Davis, *Street Gang*, p. 324.

40 "If Cookie Monster was": Susan Dominus, "A Girly-Girl Joins the 'Sesame' Boys," *The New York Times*, August 6, 2006, www .nytimes.com/2006/08/06/arts/television/06domi.html.

40 Lulu, a shy: Ibid.

40 Zoe, who was: Davis, *Street Gang*, pp. 321–323.

40 her release fell short: Ibid., pp. 324–325.

40 With Abby, every detail: Dominus, "A Girly-Girl Joins the 'Sesame' Boys."

41   Workshop executives have denied: Ibid.

41   "If you think about": Ibid.

41   Abby's character was ideal: Ibid.

42   consciously developed: Author's interview with Brown Johnson, August 9, 2006.

42   In 2009, Nick introduced: Marysol Castro and Taylor Behrendt, "Dora the Explorer Updates Her Look," *Good Morning America Weekend*, March 8, 2009, http://abcnews.go.com/GMA/Weekend/story?id=7033295&page=1.

44   I'm projecting my own: See Brian Sutton-Smith, *Toys as Culture*, pp. 247–253.

44   playthings were expressly intended: Cross, *Kids' Stuff*, pp. 9, 24, 50–53.

45   couples no longer felt compelled: Ibid., p. 78.

45   less than 25 percent: Miriam Forman-Brunell, *Made to Play House*, p. 30.

45   campaign against "race suicide": Cross, *Kids' Stuff*, p. 78.

45   When women "feared motherhood": Theodore Roosevelt, *The Strenuous Life*, p. 4.

45   Baby dolls were seen: Cross, *Kids' Stuff*, pp. 77–78.

45   Miniature brooms, dustpans: Ibid., pp. 11, 16, 51.

45   "companion" dolls: Ibid., pp. 75–76.

45   Boys, by contrast: Ibid., p. 4.

45   That division continued: Ibid., p. 9.

45   when she was introduced: Ibid., p. 171.

47   baby boomers and Gen Xers: Author's interview with Gary Cross, February 2, 2009.

47   A headline-grabbing: Alexandra Frean, "Barbarism Begins with Barbie, the Doll Children Love to Hate," *The Times*, December 19, 2005, www.timesonline.co.uk/tol/news/uk/article767739.ece. See also University of Bath, "'Babyish' Barbie Under Attack from Little Girls, Study Shows," press release, December 19, 2005, www.bath.ac.uk/news/articles/archive/barbie161205.html.

48   the lower her sales fell: Nicholas Casey, "Mattel Profits De-

spite Barbie," *The Wall Street Journal*, February 1, 2008, p. A11. See also Joseph Woelfel, "Mattel Earnings Fall 46%, Sales Drop 11%," *The Street*, February 2, 2009, www.thestreet.com/story/10461260/mattel-earnings-fall-46-sales-drop-11.html.

49   gobbling up a full 40 percent: Margaret Talbot, "Little Hotties," *The New Yorker*, December 4, 2006, p. 74.

49   in 2008, Mattel struck back: "Barbie's Mattel Sues Maker of Bratz Dolls," *Morning Edition*, NPR, June 3, 2008, www.npr.org/templates/story/story.php?storyId=91098062.

50   With Bratz on ice: Andrea Chang, "Mattel Earnings Rise on Robust Sales and New Product Lines," *Los Angeles Times*, April 17, 2010, http://articles.latimes.com/2010/apr/17/business/la-fi-mattel17-2010apr17.

50   MGA rolled out Moxie Girlz: Ruth La Ferla, "Losing the Limo: New Fashion Dolls," *The New York Times*, November 8, 2009, p. ST1.

52   an annual survey: Lloyd B. Lueptow, Lori Garovich-Szabo, and Margaret B. Lueptow, "Social Change and the Persistence of Sex Typing: 1974–1997."

Chapter 4: What Makes Girls Girls?

55   "X: A Fabulous Child's Story": Lois Gould, "X: A Fabulous Child's Story," *Ms.*, December 1972, pp. 74–76, 105–106.

56   a Swedish couple: Lydia Parafianowicz, "Swedish Parents Keep 2-Year-Old's Gender Secret," *The Local*, June 23, 2009, www.thelocal.se/20232/20090623/.

57   rocking a blanket-wrapped Tonka: As early as age two and a half children have absorbed basic stereotypes about the sexes, including those involving appearance and activities. That influences not only how they see themselves but their assumptions about other children's behavior and preferences. What's more, children often distort or misremember information to conform to their stereotypes: over half of five- to nine-year-old children, after watching a TV commercial in which a boy

played with a doll and a girl with a truck, later recalled the reverse. So merely exposing children to examples that counter their expectations does not change stereotypes; more proactive measures have to be taken. Carol Lynn Martin and Richard Fabes, *Discovering Childhood Development*, p. 304.

57   Several cited the classic: For more on David Reimer, see Lise Eliot, *Pink Brain, Blue Brain*, pp. 33–34; John Colapinto, *As Nature Made Him*.

58   more like Canadians and Americans: Or, as Kathryn Dindia, Professor of Communications, University of Wisconsin–Milwaukee, put it in an article of the same name, "Men are from North Dakota, women are from South Dakota."

59   Male fetuses, she explained: Author's interview with Lise Eliot, Associate Professor, Department of Neuroscience, Chicago Medical School, May 13, 2009; see also Eliot, *Pink Brain, Blue Brain*, pp. 45–48.

59   There is another hormonal spike: Ibid.

59   in the beginning: Author's interview with Lise Eliot, May 13, 2009; see also Eliot, *Pink Brain, Blue Brain*, p. 107.

59   Then the whole concept: Author's interview with Lise Eliot, May 13, 2009; see also Eliot, *Pink Brain, Blue Brain*, pp. 117–118.

60   There is a legendary story: Jeremy is the son of Sandra Bem, professor of psychology at Cornell University. She writes about this incident in her book *The Lenses of Gender*, p. 149. It has become a favorite anecdote among women's studies and psychology professors everywhere. Eliot also relates this story; see Eliot, *Pink Brain, Blue Brain*, p. 118. See also Judith Elaine Owen Blakemore et al., *Gender Development*, p. 234.

60   until around age five: Psychologists call that gradual revelation "gender stability." It is also sometimes called "gender continuity." The recognition that others don't change sex by changing superficial appearance, which children arrive at around six or seven, is called "gender consistency," "gender constancy," or "gender immutability." Eliot, *Pink Brain, Blue Brain*, p. 116; au-

thor's interview with Carol Lynn Martin and Richard Fabes, Department of Family and Human Development, Arizona State University, June 25, 2009; Diane N. Ruble et al., "The Role of Gender Constancy in Early Gender Development"; Martin and Fabes, *Discovering Childhood Development*, p. 302; Blakemore et al., *Gender Development*, pp. 205–206, 236–242.

61   That's why four-year-olds: Author's interview with Carol Lynn Martin and Richard Fabes, June 25, 2009.

62   boys hopped: Vivian Gussin Paley, *Boys and Girls*, pp. ix, 19.

62   the Big Kahuna: Martin and Fabes, *Discovering Childhood Development*, pp. 304–305; Blakemore et al., *Gender Development*, pp. 125–126.

62   You even see it: Satoshi Kanazawa, "Why Do Boys and Girls Prefer Different Toys?" *Psychology Today*, April 17, 2008, www.psychologytoday.com/node/447.

63   that finding was replicated: Ibid. See also Janice M. Hassett et al., "Sex Differences in Rhesus Monkey Toy Preferences Parallel Those of Children."

63   girls who are born: Eliot, *Pink Brain, Blue Brain*, p. 126.

63   Toy choice turns out: Ibid., p. 106; author's interview with Carol Lynn Martin and Richard Fabes, June 25, 2009.

64   A child's brain: Author's interview with Lise Eliot, May 13, 2009.

64   their brains are also: Ibid.

64   Boys from more egalitarian homes: Judith Elaine Owen Blakemore, "The Influence of Gender and Parental Attitudes on Preschool Children's Interest in Babies."

64   a study of more than five thousand: John Rust et al., "The Role of Brothers and Sisters in the Gender Development of Preschool Children."

65   mathematically inclined girls: Janis E. Jacobs et al., "'I Can, But I Don't Want To': Impact of Parents, Interests, and Activities on Gender Differences in Math."

65   David was nearly two: Eliot, *Pink Brain, Blue Brain*, pp. 34–35.

66   a third of girls aged seven to eleven: Author's interview with Carol Lynn Martin and Richard Fabes, June 25, 2009.

68   the church-and-state separation: Author's interview with Carol Lynn Martin and Richard Fabes, June 25, 2009. See also Carol Lynn Martin and Richard A. Fabes, "The Stability and Consequences of Young Children's Same-Sex Peer Interactions"; Eleanor E. Maccoby, "Gender and Group Process"; Eleanor E. Maccoby, "Gender and Relationships"; Blakemore et al., *Gender Development*, pp. 306–315.

68   By the end of the first year: Author's interview with Carol Lynn Martin and Richard Fabes, June 25, 2009. See also Blakemore et al., *Gender Development*, pp. 306–315.

68   When they do have cross-sex friendships: Author's interview with Carol Lynn Martin and Richard Fabes, June 25, 2009. See also Blakemore et al., *Gender Development*, pp. 322–323.

68   self-segregation, like toy choice: Author's interview with Carol Lynn Martin and Richard Fabes, June 25, 2009. See also Maccoby, "Gender and Relationships."

68   The threat of cooties: Author's interview with Carol Lynn Martin and Richard Fabes, June 25, 2009. See also Martin and Fabes, "The Stability and Consequences of Young Children's Same-Sex Peer Interactions."

68   Every cliché I have: Author's interview with Carol Lynn Martin and Richard Fabes, June 25, 2009. See also Martin and Fabes, "The Stability and Consequences of Young Children's Same-Sex Peer Interactions"; Maccoby, "Gender and Group Process"; Maccoby, "Gender and Relationships"; Blakemore et al., *Gender Development*, pp. 306–308. All that said, there are cultural differences in children's sex-typed behaviors, such as conflict resolution. At ages four and five, African-American and Latina girls tend to speak more directly than Caucasian or Asian-American girls. Girls in mainland China at that age also have a more assertive communication style; see Blakemore et al., *Gender Development*, p. 311.

69   children who have friends of the other sex: Children who have

friends of the other sex in elementary school also appear to have better social skills. Blakemore et al., *Gender Development*, p. 323.

70   boys hear less well: Elizabeth Weil, "Teaching Boys and Girls Separately," *The New York Times Magazine*, March 2, 2008, www.nytimes.com/2008/03/02/magazine/02sex3-t.html. See also Leonard Sax, *Why Gender Matters*, pp. 16–18, 24.

70   Girls, by contrast: Weil, "Teaching Boys and Girls Separately."

71   sex-based hearing and vision differences: In their ground-breaking work *The Psychology of Sex Differences*, Eleanor Maccoby and Carol Nagy Jacklin write that one of the most serious problems with research on sex differences is that it is, in fact, skewed toward *differences*: research showing how slight differences are, or that shows similarities where differences were expected, does not get published; see Blakemore et al., *Gender Development*, p. 35, and Eliot, *Pink Brain, Blue Brain*, pp. 61–64.

71   assigning kids to classrooms: Weil, "Teaching Boys and Girls Separately."

71   the number of single-sex: www.singlesexschools.org/schools -schools.htm.

Chapter 5: Sparkle, Sweetie!

82   in 2007, we spent: Jayne O'Donnell, "As Kids Get Savvy, Marketers Move down the Age Scale," *USA Today*, April 13, 2007, www.usatoday.com/money/advertising/2007-04-11-tween-usat_N.htm.

82   Close to half: NPD Group, "NPD Reports Tween Girls Increase Their Beauty Usage," press release, April 29, 2010, www.npd.com/press/releases/press_100429.html.

82   the percentage of: Ibid.

82   "Tween" girls now spend: Ibid.

82   No wonder Nair: Andrew Adam Newman, "Depilatory Market Moves Far Beyond the Short-Shorts Wearers," *The New York*

Times, September 14, 2007, www.nytimes.com/2007/09/14/business/media/14adco.html.

82 And who, according to: NPD Group, "NPD Reports Tween Girls Increase."

82 As a headline: "How Many 8-Year-Olds Have to Get Bikini Waxes Before We Can All Agree the Terrorists Have Won?" Weblog entry, Jezebel, March 27, 2008, http://jeze bel.com/373096/how-many-8+year+olds-have-to-get-bikini -waxes-before-we-all-agree-the-terrorists-have-won.

83 it was conceived of: Sree Roy, "Very Important Princesses," *Display and Design Ideas*, March 1, 2005, www.allbusiness .com/retail-trade/miscellaneous-retail/4165383-1.html; Susan Chandler, "Retailer Courts the 'Princess Set,'" *Chicago Tribune*, February 10, 2002, http://articles.chicagotribune.com/2002 02-10/business/0202100006_1_tween-girls-american-girl -place-chain; "Saks Incorporated Acquires Club Libby Lu," *Business Wire*, May 6, 2003, www.allbusiness.com/retail/ retailers-general-merchandise-stores-department/5774038-1 .html.

84 Marketers call that KGOY: Paul Kurnit, "Kids Getting Older Younger," interview, Advertising Education Foundation, 1999, www.aef.com/on_campus/classroom/speaker_pres/data/35; Lisa Bannon, "Little Big Spenders," *The Wall Street Journal*, October 13, 1998, p. A1.

84 That's why the cherry-flavored: O'Donnell, "As Kids Get Savvy."

84 girls are going through puberty: Denise Grady, "First Signs of Puberty Seen in Younger Girls," *The New York Times*, August 9, 2010, p. A11; Tara Parker-Pope, "Earlier Puberty in European Girls," *The New York Times*, May 4, 2009, http:// well.blogs.nytimes.com/2009/05/04/earlier-puberty-in -european-girls/?scp=1&sq=Aksglaede&st=cse; Susan Brink, "Modern Puberty," *Los Angeles Times*, January 21, 2008, p. F1.

84 pediatricians no longer consider it: Brink, "Modern Puberty."

84 although they are physically more advanced: Ibid.

85   imposing any developmental task: Stephen Hinshaw with Rachel Krantz, *The Triple Bind*, p. 112. For more on academically
accelerated kindergarten and preschool, see Edward Miller
and Joan Almon, *Crisis in Kindergarten.*

85   the ways pageant moms: Martha Heltsley and Thomas C. Calhoun, "The Good Mother."

86   The routine sparked: *Fox and Friends*, May 15, 2010, http://
video.foxnews.com/v/4197785/sexual-dance-sparks-contro
versy; Michael Winter, " 'Single Ladies' Dance by Young Girls
Is Kicking Up a Storm," Weblog entry, "On Deadline," *USA
Today*, May 14, 2010, www.usatoday.com/communities/on
deadline/post/2010/05/single-ladies-dance-by-young-girls
-is-kicking-up-a-storm/1; *Rick's List*, May 13, 2010, http://
edition.cnn.com/video/#/video/showbiz/2010/05/14/sbt.too
.sexy.too.soon.cnn?iref=allsearch.

86   best known for the faux pas: DeNeen L. Brown, "First Lady
Assails Use of Daughters' Images for Dolls," *The Washington
Post*, January 25, 2009, www.washingtonpost.com/wpdyn/
content/article/2009/01/24/AR2009012401854.html.

90   Historically, girls' bodies: Joan Jacobs Brumberg, *The Body
Project.*

91   Back in the 1960s: Kareen Nussbaum, "Children and Beauty
Pageants," 2002, www.minorcon.org/pageants.html.

91   A woman who did not: Camille Sweeney, "Never Too Young for
That First Pedicure," *The New York Times*, February 28, 2008,
www.nytimes.com/2008/02/28/fashion/28Skin.html. See also
Camille Sweeney, "A Girl's Life, with Highlights," *The New
York Times*, April 3, 2008, www.nytimes.com/2008/04/03/
fashion/03SKIN.html.

91   Parents in San Francisco: Meredith May, "Kids Escape to Spa
Camp," *The San Francisco Chronicle*, August 12, 2007, p. B1.

94   One prominent former: Andrea Canning and Jessica Hoff-
man, "Former Child Beauty Queen Speaks Out," *Good Morning America*, August 13, 2009, http://abcnews.go.com/GMA/

beauty-queen-takes-gma-scenes-pageants/story?id=8315785; for video, see http://jezebel.com/5336807/former-child-beauty -queen-says-pageants-led-to-emotional-problems.

Chapter 6: Guns and (Briar) Roses

98   there is virtually no research: Author's interview with Diane Levin, Department of Education, Wheelock College, Boston, May 18, 2009. See also Diane E. Levin and Nancy Carlsson-Paige, *The War Play Dilemma*, p. 30.

98   violent play is useful: Author's interview with Diane Levin, May 18, 2009. Levin and Carlsson-Paige, *The War Play Dilemma*, pp. 25–28, 37–39, 46.

98   children's television advertising: Author's interview with Diane Levin, May 18, 2009; Levin and Carlsson-Paige, *The War Play Dilemma*, pp. 3–5, 15–17.

99   rather than engaging in creative play: Author's interview with Diane Levin, May 18, 2009; Levin and Carlsson-Paige, *The War Play Dilemma*, pp. 3–5.

100 Allied commanders banned: Thomas O'Neill, "Guardians of the Fairy Tale: The Brothers Grimm," *National Geographic*, December 1999, www.nationalgeographic.com/grimm/article .html.

100 we avoid the Grimms' grimness: Bruno Bettelheim, *The Uses of Enchantment.*

100 the brothers' gore: Ibid., p. 19.

100 John Locke, disagreed: Ruth B. Bottigheimer, "Fairy Tales and Folk-Tales," p. 154; John Locke, *Some Thoughts Concerning Education*, pp. 189–190.

100 fairy tales and *only*: Bettelheim, *The Uses of Enchantment*, pp. 35–41.

100 In their tiny minds: Ibid.; see, e.g., pp. 24–27, 39–40, 57–58.

100 the solutions to life's struggles: Ibid., pp. 4–5, 25–26.

102 Calling the Grimms': Maria Ibido, "Reading the Grimms' *Children's Stories and Household Tales*," pp. xxvii–xlvii.

102 Before the Grimms: Ibid., pp. xlii–xliii; Giambattista Basile, "Sun, Moon, and Talia."

102 the porn of their day: Maria Tatar, *The Hard Facts of the Grimms' Fairy Tales*, pp. xiii–xiv.

102 They were also rife: Ibid., pp. 10–11, 20.

102 The brothers' delicacy: Ibid.

103 There are at least: Some scholars put the number at 345, others at "thousands." For a list of some of them (and links to online texts), see "Tales Similar to Cinderella" at www.surlalune fairytales.com/cinderella/other.html.

103 The Chinese Yeh-Shen: This is the first known recorded version of a Cinderella story. See also Jacob Grimm and Wilhelm Grimm, *The Annotated Brothers Grimm*, p. 114.

104 splitting the mother: Tatar, *The Hard Facts*, p. 223.

105 she demands that he: Joan Gould, *Spinning Straw into Gold*, p. 70.

107 In the Andersen version: Hans Christian Andersen, *Hans Christian Andersen: Eighty Fairy Tales*, pp. 46–63.

108 the heroine shrewdly foiled: Jacob Grimm and Wilhelm Grimm, "The Robber Bridegroom," in Grimm and Grimm, *The Annotated Brothers Grimm*, pp. 187–193.

108 a feisty girl saved her sisters: Grimm and Grimm, *The Annotated Brothers Grimm*, pp. 201–207.

108 a princess fearlessly: Ibid., pp. 291–300.

109 a seven-year vow of silence: Ibid., pp. 224–231.

109 I loved Diane Wolkstein's: Diane Wolkstein, *The Glass Mountain*.

109 an Algonquin Indian legend: Katrin Tchana and Trina Schart Hyman, "Nesoowa and the Chenoo," in Tchana and Hyman, *The Serpent Slayer*, pp. 13–18.

109 imagined in a "vivid dream": Stephenie Meyer, "The Story Behind Twilight," www.stepheniemeyer.com/twilight.html.

109 more than 100 million copies: John A. Sellers, "New Stephenie Meyer Novella Arriving in June," *Publisher's Weekly*, March 30, 2010. The Harry Potter series has sold more than three times

as many volumes, but though the books are fantasy, I do not consider them to be fairy tales.

109 films based on the first two: Global grosses for *New Moon*, which broke opening-day records, were nearly $710 million as of June 8, 2010. Global grosses for *Twilight* were nearly $410 million. http://boxofficemojo.com/movies/?id=newmoon.htm; http://boxofficemojo.com/movies/?id=twilight.htm.

109 No wonder it has been: Sara Vilkomerson, "Why Is *Twilight* Such Crack for Girls?" *The New York Observer*, November 20, 2008, www.observer.com/2008/o2/why-twilight-such-crack-girls; Sarah Hepola, "'Twilight' of Our Youth," *Salon*, November 16, 2009, www.salon.com/life/feature/2009/11/16/twilight_of_our_youth; Tracee Sioux, "Empowering Girls: Twilight, Female Crack Cocaine."

111 "some fear they can't": Cited in Hepola, "'Twilight' of Our Youth."

111 "some things, it seems": Laura Miller, "Touched by a Vampire," *Salon*, July 30, 2008, www.salon.com/books/review/2008/07/30/Twilight.

Chapter 7: Wholesome to Whoresome: The *Other* Disney Princesses

114 Until the publication: Bruce Handy, "Miley Knows Best," *Vanity Fair*, June 2008, www.vanityfair.com/culture/features/2008/06/miley200806.

114 Miley was quoted: Ibid.

114 releasing a formal: Brooks Barnes, "Revealing Photo Threatens a Major Disney Franchise," *The New York Times*, April 28, 2008, p. C1.

115 Bruce Handy asked: Handy, "Miley Knows Best."

116 Anne Sweeney: Karl Taro Greenfeld, "How Mickey Got His Groove Back," *Portfolio*, May 2008, www.portfolio.com/news-markets/national-news/portfolio/2008/04/14/Disneys-Evolving-Business-Model; Julia Boorstin, "Disney's 'Tween

Machine," *Fortune*, September 29, 2003, http://money.cnn.com/magazines/fortune/fortune_archive/2003/09/29/349896/index.htm.

116   Within a year: Boorstin, "Disney's 'Tween Machine."

117   Duff quit: Stephen M. Silverman, "Lizzie McGuire Star Divorces Disney," *People*, May 27, 2003, www.people.com/people/article/0,26334,626089,00.html.

117   Disney simply replicated: Boorstin, "Disney's 'Tween Machine"; Greenfeld, "How Mickey Got His Groove Back."

118   200 million viewers globally: Stephen Armstrong, "Teen Queen Is a Global Brand," *The Sunday Times*, May 21, 2009, cited on www.dispatch.co.za/article.aspx?id=316998.

118   *Billboard*'s top five: Ibid.

118   some were later scalped: Stephen M. Silverman, "Possible *Hannah Montana* Ticket Scalping Probed," *People*, October 4, 2007, www.people.com/people/article/0,,20137827,00.html.

118   The limited-release: http://boxofficemojo.com/movies/?id=hannahmontanaconcert.htm.

118   more than $155 million worldwide: http://boxofficemojo.com/movies/?id=hannahmontanamovie.htm.

118   Cyrus is on track: Greenfeld, "How Mickey Got His Groove Back."

119   By age eleven: Kristin Mcmurran, "Shirley Temple Black Taps Out a Telling Memoir of Child Stardom," *People*, November 28, 1988, www.people.com/people/archive/article/0,,20100608,00.html.

120   MGM forced: Christopher Finch, *Rainbow*, pp. 134–135.

120   a navel-baring swimsuit: There is a picture of said event at www.beachpartymoviemusic.com/TheMythoftheHidden Navel.html.

120   Hilary Duff appeared: See the cover of *Maxim*, August 2007.

120   "your favorite witch": Stephen Schaefer, "Tarted-up Hart Draws 'Sabrina' Fire," *USA Today*, November 17, 1999, www.usatoday.com/life/enter/leps004.htm.

120 she has been accused: TMZ Staff, "Vanessa Hudgens Attacks over Naked Pics," August 6, 2009, www.tmz.com/2009/08/06/vanessa-hudgens-nude-photos/.

120 a film starring: Roger Ebert, "Review: Freaky Friday," *Chicago Sun-Times*, August 6, 2003, http://rogerebert.suntimes.com/apps/pbcs.dll/article?AID=/20030806/REVIEWS/308060301/1023.

121 "a sleazy, inept and worthless": William Booth, "Critics Everywhere Agree: These Were the Stinkers of Summer," *The Washington Post*, September 12, 2007, www.washingtonpost.com/wp-dyn/content/article/2007/09/11/AR2007091102208.html.

121 Lohan, who admitted to drug use: Jennifer Vineyard, "Lindsay Lohan Admits Eating Disorder, Drug Use in *Vanity Fair* Interview," MTV News, January 4, 2006, www.mtv.com/news/articles/1519731/20060104/lohan_lindsay.jhtml.

122 publicly insisted on her chastity: "Britney's Boast Busts Virgin Myth," July 9, 2003, http://news.bbc.co.uk/2/hi/entertainment/3052143.stm.

122 she appeared on the cover: www.mirror.co.uk/celebs/news/2009/05/28/lady-gaga-appears-semi-naked-on-rolling-stone-and-more-controversial-nude-front-covers-from-the-last-twenty-years-115875-21396496/; see also John Harris, "Britney Spears: This Baby Doll Means Business," *The Independent*, May 14, 2000, www.independent.co.uk/news/people/profiles/britney-spears-this-baby-doll-means-business-717538.html.

122 in an *Esquire* interview: Chuck Klosterman, "Bending Spoons with Britney Spears," *Esquire*, October 1, 2008, www.esquire.com/women/women-we-love/britney-spears-pics-1103?click=main_sr.

123 "slore": Melanie Lowe, "Colliding Feminisms: Britney Spears, 'Tweens,' and the Politics of Reception," *Popular Music and Society* 26, no. 2 (2003): 123–140.

123   Over the course: See "Britney Spears Biography," www.people .com/people/britney_spears/biography.

126   she chooses clothing that: Tim Nudd, "Miley Cyrus: Being a Role Model Starts with the Clothes," *People*, December 20, 2007, www.people.com/people/article/0,,20167543,00 .html.

127   "any parent's antidote": *The Barbara Walters Special*, ABC, February 24, 2008, video at www.youtube.com/ watch?v=NfJOwV6TjL8.

127   Once again, controversy: See, e.g., Katherine Thomson, "Miley Cyrus' Teen Choice Pole Dance (Video)," *The Huffington Post*, August 10, 2009, www.huffingtonpost.com/2009/08/10/mi ley-cyrus-teen-choice-p_n_255338.html.

127   lying on a table: Holly Millea, "Miley Cyrus Cover Shoot," *Elle*, July 27, 2009, www.elle.com/Pop-Culture/Cover-Shoots/Mi ley-Cyrus2/Miley-Cyrus-Cover-Shoot.

128   Bridgit Mendler: Belinda Luscombe, "Making New Mileys: Disney's Teen-Star Factory," *Time*, October 22, 2009, www .time.com/time/business/article/0,8599,1930657,00.html.

129   A *Wall Street Journal* profile: Amy Chozick, "Creating the Next Teen Star," *The Wall Street Journal*, August 28, 2009, http:// online.wsj.com/article/SB10001424052970203706604574374 561767358856.html.

129   Although she is actually: Ibid.

129   "true love waits" ring: Katherine Thomson, "Miley Cyrus on God, Remaking 'Sex and the City' and Her Purity Ring," Weblog entry, *The Huffington Post*, July 15, 2008, www .huffingtonpost.com/2008/07/15/miley-cyrus-on-god -remaki_n_112891.html; "Disney Tween Selena's Vow of Ab- stinence," *Extra*, June 9, 2008, http://extratv.warnerbros .com/2008/06/disney_tween_selenas_vow_of_ab.php.

Chapter 8: It's All About the Cape

135 nearly half of girls: For an overview of research on preadoles-
cent girls' body image, see Dohnt and Tiggemann, "Body Image Concerns in Young Girls." See also Jessica Bennett, "Say
'Cheese!' and Now Say 'Airbrush!'" *Newsweek*, February 16,
2008, www.newsweek.com/2008/02/16/say-cheese-and-now
-say-airbrush.html; Peggy Orenstein, *Schoolgirls*, p. 97.

136 pinups of mid-nineteenth-century: Peter N. Stearns, *Fat History*, p. 9.

136 Those not blessed: Ibid., p. 80.

136 Children were considered sickly: Ibid., pp. 140–148.

136 overweight was first linked: Ibid., pp. 25–47.

136 Fat did not take on: Ibid., pp. 48–70.

138 has become the single: Orenstein, *Schoolgirls*, p. 94; Brown et
al., "Changes in Self-Esteem in Black and White Girls Between
the Ages of 9 and 14 Years."

138 must be derived: Self-esteem is defined as "the value an individual attaches to the mental picture of himself or herself."
Patterns of self-esteem are made up of combinations of compe-
tence and worthiness: Carol Lynn Martin and Richard Fabes,
Discovering Childhood Development, p. 301. If what makes a girl
feel "high worth" is looking sexy and she achieves that, her
self-esteem may be great but perhaps not derived from the most
appropriate or most sustainable of sources. What's more, as the
psychologist Jean Twenge has pointed out, self-esteem without basis breeds narcissism. "Study Sees Rise in Narcissism
Among Students," *Day to Day*, NPR, February 27, 2007, www
.npr.org/templates/story/story.php?storyid=7618722&ps=rs.

138 an article I recently saw: "Stars Who Make over 40 Look Fab,"
More, October 2009, www.more.com/2049/9377-stars-who
-make-over-40#1. To be fair, the magazine also ran ground-
breaking pictures of the famously fit actress Jamie Lee Curtis,
then forty-three, posed in her underwear, without benefit of
stylists, makeup, or Photoshop. She looked as bulgy as any of

us. The next page showed Curtis glammed up like a star—a transformation, she said, that took thirteen people three hours to achieve. Amy Wallace, "Jamie Lee Curtis: True Thighs," *More*, September 2002, www.more.com/2049/2464-jamie -lee-curtis-true-thighs.

138 "Should women simply": Cited in Catherine Saint Louis, "Appreciating Your Value as You Age," *The New York Times*, March 18, 2010, p. E3.

139 Most of the 9.3 million: American Society for Aesthetic Plastic Surgery, *Cosmetic Surgery National Data Bank Statistics*.

139 a new picture book: Michael Salzhauer, *My Beautiful Mommy*; the recommended reading level for this book on Amazon .com is four to eight years of age; www.amazon.com/Beautiful -Mommy-Michael-Alexander-Salzhauer/dp/1601310323.

139 Nearly 43,000 children: American Society for Aesthetic Plastic Surgery, *Cosmetic Surgery National Data Bank Statistics*.

139 That does not include: Ibid.

139 the 12,000: Catherine Saint Louis, "This Teenage Girl Uses Botox. No, She's Not Alone," *The New York Times*, August 12, 2010, p. E1.

140 for girls growing up: Joan Jacobs Brumberg, *The Body Project*, p. xxi.

141 try not commenting: A 2004 survey of 3,000 women in ten countries commissioned by Dove's "Real Beauty" campaign found that only 2 percent of women said they would describe themselves as beautiful, while two-thirds said they avoided basic activities—including going to work or school and voicing opinions—on days they felt unattractive. Nancy Etcoff, Susie Orbach, Jennifer Scott, and Heidi D'Agostino, "The Real Truth About Beauty: A Global Report," www.cam paignforrealbeauty.com/uploadedfiles/dove_white_paper_ final.pdf.

142 I took the quandary: Author's interview with Catherine Steiner-Adair, director of eating disorders education and pre-

vention at the Klarman Eating Disorders Center at McLean Hospital, Belmont, Mass., May 2, 2010.

146 Consider a 2007 survey: Catalyst, *The Double-Bind Dilemma.*

147 40 percent of men: J. Walter Thompson, "Millennial Women Face Gender Issues," press release, April 24, 2008.

148 "Excellent question!": Marc Santora, "Pointed Question Puts McCain in Tight Spot," *The New York Times*, November 14, 2007, www.nytimes.com/2007/11/14/us/politics/14mccain.html.

148 Rush Limbaugh declared: Ellen Goodman, "Eek! It's a Wrinkle!" December 19, 2007, www.truthdig.com/report/item/20071219_eek_its_a_wrinkle/.

148 "aging and resentful female": Christopher Hitchens, "Identity Crisis," *Slate*, January 7, 2008, www.slate.com/id/2181460/.

148 the novelist Susanna Moore: Susan Morrison, ed., *Thirty Ways of Looking at Hillary. New York Times* reviewer Michiko Kakutani commented that the book underscored "this willful focus on the personal" in the analysis of Clinton; see "Candidate Clinton Scrutinized by Women," *The New York Times*, January 15, 2008, www.nytimes.com/2008/01/15/books/15kaku.html.

148 "The mind . . . strays": Robin Givhan, "Wearing the Pants," *The Washington Post*, December 9, 2007, www.washingtonpost.com/wp-dyn/content/article/2007/12/08/AR2007120801502.html.

148 she used her position: Jo Becker, Peter S. Goodman, and Michael Powell, "Once Elected, Palin Hired Friends and Lashed Foes," *The New York Times*, September 14, 2008, p. A1; Katie Couric, "One-on-One with Sarah Palin," *CBS Evening News*, September 24, 2008, www.cbsnews.com/stories/2008/09/24/eveningnews/main4476173.shtml.

149 Palin had been dubbed: Carolyn Lockhead, "Who's Sarah Palin? She's Hot Where He's Not," Weblog entry, "Below the Beltway," *San Francisco Chronicle*, March 1, 2008, www.sfgate.com/cgi-bin/blogs/nov05election/detail?blogid=14&entry_id=24593.

149   a woman at a firehouse: Tony Plohetski, "Defacing at Fire Station Unsolved," *The Austin American-Statesman*, January 10, 2007, www.freerepublic.com/focus/f-news/1765197/posts.

151   the culture ultimately offers: Sharon Lamb and Lyn Mikel Brown, *Packaging Girlhood.*

153   the movement went alt-rock: Hole, in turn, paved the way for Alanis Morissette, whose 1995 album, *Jagged Little Pill*, a sometimes scathing—but endlessly catchy—ode to female coming-of-age, was one of the decade's top sellers.

154   something called "girlie feminism": See Jennifer Baumgardner and Amy Richards, *Manifesta (10th Anniversary Edition)*, p. 80.

Chapter 9: Just Between You, Me, and My 622 BFFs

160   A digital divide was looming: Matthew DeBell and Chris Chapman, *Computer and Internet Use by Children and Adolescents in 2003*, p. v.

160   35 million kids: Ibid., p. iii.

161   Girls spend the same: Ibid., p. v.

161   Girls, meanwhile, are: Amanda Lenhart, Mary Madden, Aaron Smith, and Alexandra Macgill, *Teens and Social Media.*

161   Doll sales have declined: Lini S. Kadaba, "Girls Abandon Dolls for Web-based Toys," *The Philadelphia Enquirer*, March 31, 2010, www.philly.com/inquirer/magazine/89579552.html #axzz0nvMSGtfF.

162   It chilled me: Ibid.

162   Children's Online Privacy Protection Act: For more on COPPA, see www.coppa.org/coppa.htm.

163   3.7 million teens: Mike Shields, "Kids' Virtual Worlds Gain Traction," *Mediaweek*, May 22, 2009, www.adweek.com/aw/content_display/news/digital/e3i9659c5aa3ebf28066173d de9ce1c5366.

165   young people's real-life identities: Author's interview with Adriana Manago, Department of Psychology and Children's Digital Media Center, UCLA, May 7, 2010; Adriana Manago,

Michael B. Graham, Patricia M. Greenfield, and Goldie Salimkhan, "Self-Presentation and Gender on MySpace."

166 scores of the 16,475: "Study Sees Rise in Narcissism Among Students," *Day to Day*, February 27, 2007, www.npr.org/tem plates/story/story.php?storyId=7618722&ps=rs; Associated Press, "College Students Think They're *So* Special," February 27, 2007, www.msnbc.msn.com/id/17349066/.

166 empathy, too, seems: "Empathy: College Students Don't Have as Much as They Used to, Study Finds," *Science Daily*, May 29, 2010, www.sciencedaily.com/releases/ 2010/05/100528081434.htm.

167 provocative photos: Author's interview with Adriana Manago; Manago et al., "Self-Presentation and Gender on MySpace."

168 the first high-profile case: Jennifer Steinhauer, "Verdict in MySpace Suicide Case," *The New York Times*, November 27, 2008, p. A25.

169 Phoebe Prince: Brian Ballou and John Ellement, "9 Charged in Death of South Hadley Teen, Who Took Life After Bullying," *The Boston Globe*, March 29, 2010, www.boston.com/news/ local/breaking_news/2010/03/holding_for_pho.html.

169 Alexis Pilkington: Oren Yaniv, "Long Island Teen's Suicide Linked to Cruel Cyberbullies, Formspring.me Site: Police," *Daily News*, March 25, 2010, www.nydailynews.com/news/ ny_crime/2010/03/25/2010-03-25_li_teens_suicide_linked_ to_cruel_cyberbullies_police.html; "Cyber Bullies Harass Teen Even After Suicide," *The Huffington Post*, March 24, 2010, www.huffingtonpost.com/2010/03/24/alexis-pilking ton-faceboo_n_512482.html.

169 half of young people: Associated Press and MTV, "A Thin Line: Executive Summary," MTV, December 2009, www.athinline .org/MTV-AP_Digital_Abuse_Study_Executive_Summary .pdf. A report by the Pew Internet and American Life Project put the rates of cyberbullying at one-third of teens; 38 percent of girls in that survey experienced harassment versus 26 per-

cent of boys. Amanda Lenhart, *Cyberbullying*, www.pewinter
net.org/reports/2007/cyberbullying.aspx.

170　39 percent: The National Campaign to Prevent Teen and Unplanned Pregnancy, *Sex and Tech: Executive Summary.*

171　the annual "slut list": Tina Kelley, "A Rite of Hazing Now Out
in the Open," *The New York Times*, September 18, 2009, p. A13;
Tina Kelley, "When the Cool Get Hazed," *The New York Times*,
September 27, 2009, p. WK5.

172　Megan Meier, the girl: Steinhauer, "Verdict in MySpace Suicide Case"; "Cyber Bullies Harass Teen Even After Suicide."

172　Phoebe Prince seems to have: Emily Bazelon, "What Really
Happened to Phoebe Prince?" *Slate*, July 20, 2010, www.slate
.com/id/2260952.

Chapter 10: Girl Power—No, *Really*

180　café au lait variation: While young black women are not affected by exposure to idealized images of white women, they report higher levels of body dissatisfaction after viewing those of
African-American women. Cynthia Frisby, "Does Race Matter?"
See also Taneisha S. Buchanan et al., "Testing a Culture-Specific
Extension of Objectification Theory Regarding African American Women's Body Image."

180　the first pass: Bobbi Misick, "Controversy over 'The Princess
and the Frog,'" Weblog entry, *Essence*, November 30, 2009,
www.essence.com/entertainment/film/critics_dispute_prin
cess_and_the_frog.php.

180　Disney also miscalculated: Ibid.

181　by consulting Oprah Winfrey: Chuck Barney, "Disney's First
Black Princess Has Parents Excited," *Contra Costa Times*, December 11, 2009, www.popmatters.com/pm/article/117751
-disneys-first-black-princess-has-parents-excited.

182　marketing to children under twelve: Sarah Ellison, "Marketing to Children Sparks Criticism in Europe," *The Wall Street
Journal*, December 18, 2000, p. 1. Denmark, meanwhile, bans

ads aimed at children within ninety seconds of children's pro-gramming. State broadcasters in Belgium can't air ads di-rected at kids for five minutes on either side of a children's show. In Greece, there are no toy advertisements before 10 P.M. Norway, the Netherlands, Ireland, and Austria all have some restrictions.

184 squat thrusts in an oversized cage: See Miley Cyrus "Can't Be Tamed" video, released May 2010, www.youtube.com/watch?v=sjSG6z_13-Q. Cyrus also made headlines in 2010 for kissing a female backup dancer during an onstage rendition of that song. "Girl-on-girl" action between straight women is an-other example of female sexuality as a performance for others' pleasure.

186 Your attempt to deconstruct: Author's interview with Sahara Byrne, Department of Communications, Cornell University, May 28, 2010. See also Sahara Byrne and Philip Solomon Hart, "The Boomerang Effect"; Sahara Byrne, Daniel Linz, and James W. Potter, "Test of Competing Cognitive Explana-tions for the Boomerang Effect in Response to the Deliberate Disruption of Media-Induced Aggression."

186 the "forbidden fruit" effect: Amy I. Nathanson, "Identifying and Explaining the Relationship"; Nathanson, "The Unintended Effects of Parental Mediation of Television on Adolescents."

186 Meanwhile, a 2009 study: Byrne, Linz, and Potter, "Test of Competing Cognitive Explanations."

186 pointing out inaccurate: Nathanson, "The Unintended Effects."

186 talking to little girls: Byrne et al., "Test of Competing Cogni-tive Explanations."

186 Going all Amish: Nathanson, "The Unintended Effects"; Byrne and Hart, "The Boomerang Effect."

187 Lyn Mikel Brown: Lamb and Brown, *Packaging Girlhood*, pp. 263-294.

187 otherwise, your presence: Nathanson, "Identifying and Ex-plaining the Relationship."

187   ones who are skeptical: Author's interview with Erica Weintraub Austin, Edward R. Murrow School of Communication, Washington State University, May 8, 2010.

189   The studio's lack of interest: Manohla Dargis and A. O. Scott, "Memos to Hollywood," *The New York Times*, May 3, 2009, p. MT1.

189   *The Princess and the Frog*: Dawn C. Chmielewski and Claudia Eller, "Disney Restyles 'Rapunzel' to Appeal to Boys," Weblog entry, "Company Town," *Los Angeles Times*, March 9, 2010, http://articles.latimes.com/2010/mar/09/business/la-fi-ct-disney9-2010mar09.

189   *Pocahontas* grossed $346 million: http://boxofficemojo.com/movies/?id=pocahontas.htm.

189   *Up*, released six months before: Chmielewski and Eller, "Disney Restyles 'Rapunzel.'"

189   Ed Catmull: Ibid.

190   merchandising blockbuster: "Disney's 'The Princess and the Frog' Merchandise in High Demand Weeks Before Film's Debut," November 18, 2009, http://fefwww.istockanalyst.com/article/viewiStockNews/articleid/3647634#.

190   Disney shelved its plans: Chmielewski and Eller, "Disney Restyles 'Rapunzel.'"

191   neither maimed nor killed: See Bettelheim, *The Uses of Enchantment*, p. 149.

Appendix 2: Beyond Princesses (Sort of): What Girls See on Screen

1   Smith, S. L., and Cook, C.A. (2008). *Gender Sterotypes: An Analysis of Popular Films and TV*. Paper prepared for the Geena Davis Institute for Gender and Media conference in Los Angeles, CA.

2   Smith, S. L., and Choueiti, M. (2010). *Gender on Screen and Behind the Camera in Family Films: The Executive Report*. Paper prepared for the Geena Davis Institute on Gender in Media.

Notes

3 Smith, S. L., Weber, R., and Choueiti, M. (2010). *Female Characters and Financial Performance: An Analysis of 100 Top-Grossing Films at the Box Office and DVD Sales.* Poster presented at the Association for Education in Journalism and Mass Communication.

4 Smith, S. L., and Choueiti, M. (2011). *Gender Inequality in Cinematic Content? A Look at Females on Screen and Behind-the-Camera in Top-Grossing 2008 Films.* Los Angeles, CA: Annenberg School for Communication & Journalism.

5 Smith, S. L., and Cook, C. A. (2008). Op. cit.

6 Ibid.

7 Smith, S. L., and Choueiti, M. (2011). *Gender Inequality in Cinematic Content? A Look at Females on Screen and Behind-the-Camera in Top-Grossing 2008 Films.* Los Angeles, CA: Annenberg School for Communication & Journalism.

8 Ibid.

9 Smith, S. L., Choueiti, M., and Stern, J. (2011). *Occupational Aspirations: What Are G-Rated Films Teaching Children about the World of Work?* Paper prepared for the Geena Davis Institute on Gender in Media conference in Los Angeles, CA.

10 Smith, S. L., Pieper, K. M., Granados, A., and Choueiti, M. (2010). "Assessing Gender-Related Portrayals in Top-Grossing G-Rated Films." *Sex Roles, 62,* 774–86.

Appendix 3: The New Girly Girlhood by the Numbers

11 Disney Consumer Products Corporate Information, 2009.

12 NPD Group, *Insight into the Youth Beauty Market,* 2010.

13 Ibid.

14 *Newsweek,* March 30, 2009.

15 *The New Yorker,* December 4, 2006.

16 Pew Internet & American Life Project, *Cyberbullying,* 2007.

17 The National Campaign to Prevent Teen and Unplanned Pregnancy, *Sex and Tech,* 2008.

18 *The New York Times,* August 12, 2010.

Notes

19   American Society for Aesthetic Plastic Surgery, *Cosmetic Surgery National Data Bank Statistics*, 2009.

20   Girls Incorporated, *The Supergirl Dilemma*, 2006.

21   Ibid.

22   Zhao, Yafu and William Encinosa, "Statistical Brief #70," Healthcare Cost and Utilization Project, April 2009.

23   National Center for Women & Information Technology, "NCWIT Scorecard 2007."

24   *Computerworld* "Special Report, Careers: IT Professions 2010."

25   University of Michigan, "Research at U-M," May 28, 2010.

26   *Adweek*, March 24, 2003.

Bibliography

Acuff, Daniel, and Robert H. Reiher. *What Kids Buy and Why*. New York: Simon and Schuster, 1997.

American Psychological Association, Task Force on the Sexualization of Girls. *Report of the APA Task Force on the Sexualization of Girls*. Washington, D.C.: American Psychological Association, 2007. www.apa.org/pi/wpo/sexualization.html.

American Society for Aesthetic Plastic Surgery. *Cosmetic Surgery National Data Bank Statistics*. New York: American Society for Aesthetic Plastic Surgery, 2008.

Andersen, Hans Christian. *Hans Christian Andersen: Eighty Fairy Tales*, tr. R. P. Keigwin. New York: Pantheon, 1982.

Basile, Giambattista. "Sun, Moon, and Talia." In *Stories from the Pentamerone*, ed. E. F. Strange. London: Macmillan & Co., 1911. www.surlalunefairytales.com/pentamerone/29sunmoontalia1911.html.

Baumgardner, Jennifer, and Amy Richards. *Manifesta (10th Anniversary Edition)*. New York: Farrar, Straus and Giroux, 2010.

Bem, Sandra. *The Lenses of Gender*. New Haven, Conn.: Yale University Press, 1994.

Bettelheim, Bruno. *The Uses of Enchantment: The Meaning and Importance of Fairy Tales*. New York: Vintage Books, 1989.

Bibliography

Black, Shirley Temple. *Child Star.* New York: McGraw-Hill, 1998.

Blakemore, Judith Elaine Owen. "The Influence of Gender and Parental Attitudes on Preschool Children's Interest in Babies: Observations in Natural Settings." *Sex Roles* 38 (1998): 73–94.

Blakemore, Judith E. Owen, Sheri A. Berenbaum, and Lynn S. Liben. *Gender Development.* New York: Psychology Press, 2009.

Bottigheimer, Ruth B. "Fairy Tales and Folk-Tales." In *International Companion Encylopedia of Children's Literature,* ed. Peter Hunt and Sheila G. Bannister Ray. London: Routledge, 1996.

Brown, K. M., et al. "Changes in Self-Esteem in Black and White Girls Between the Ages of 9 and 14 Years: The NHLBI Growth and Health Study." *Journal of Adolescent Health* 23, no. 1 (1998): 7–19.

Brumberg, Joan Jacobs. *The Body Project: An Intimate History of American Girls.* New York: Vintage, 1998.

Buchanan, Taneisha S., et al. "Testing a Culture-Specific Extension of Objectification Theory Regarding African American Women's Body Image." *The Counseling Psychologist* 36, no. 5 (2008): 697–718.

Byrne, Sahara, and Philip Solomon Hart. "The Boomerang Effect: A Synthesis of Findings and a Preliminary Theoretical Framework." In *Communication Yearbook 33,* ed. Christina Beck. Mahwah, N.J.: Lawrence Erlbaum Associates, 2009, pp. 33–37.

Byrne, Sahara, Daniel Linz, and James W. Potter. "Test of Competing Cognitive Explanations for the Boomerang Effect in Response to the Deliberate Disruption of Media-Induced Aggression." *Media Psychology* 12, no. 3 (2009): 227–248.

Catalyst. *The Double-Bind Dilemma for Women in Leadership: Damned if You Do, Doomed if You Don't.* New York: Catalyst, 2007.

Cherney, Isabelle D., and J. Dempsey (in press). "Young Children's Classification, Stereotyping, and Play Behavior for Gender Neutral and Ambiguous Toys." *Journal of Educational Psychology.*

Cherney, Isabelle, and K. London. "Gender-linked Differences in the Toys, Television Shows, Computer Games, and Outdoor Activities of 5- to 13-Year-Old Children." *Journal of Sex Roles* 54 (2006): 717–726.

Colapinto, John. *As Nature Made Him*. New York: HarperCollins, 2001.

Cook, Daniel Thomas. *The Commodification of Childhood: The Children's Clothing Industry and the Rise of the Child Consumer*. Durham, N.C.: Duke University Press, 2004.

———. "The Rise of 'the Toddler' as Subject and as Merchandising Category in the 1930s," in *New Forms of Consumption: Consumers, Culture, and Commodification*, ed. Mark Gottdiener. Lanham, Md.: Rowman and Littlefield, 2000, pp. 111–130.

Cook, Daniel Thomas, and Susan B. Kaiser. "Betwixt and be Tween: Age Ambiguity and the Sexualization of the Female Consuming Subject." *Journal of Consumer Culture* 4, no. 2 (2004): 203–227.

Cross, Gary. *Kids' Stuff: Toys and the Changing World of American Childhood*. Cambridge, Mass.: Harvard University Press, 1997.

———. "Valves of Adult Desire: The Regulation and Incitement of Children's Consumption." In *Childhood and Consumer Culture*, ed. David Buckingham and Vebjørg Tingstad. London: Palgrave, 2010, pp. 17–30.

———. "Valves of Desire: A Historian's Perspective on Parents, Children, and Marketing." *Journal of Consumer Research* 29, no. 3 (2002): 441–447.

———. "Wondrous Innocence: Print Advertising and the Origins of Permissive Child Rearing in the U.S." *Journal of Consumer Culture* 4, no. 183 (2004): 183–201.

Davies, Paul, Steven J. Spencer, Diane M. Quinn, and Rebecca Gerhardstein. "Consuming Images: How Demeaning Commercials That Elicit Stereotype Threat Can Restrain Women Academically and Professionally." *Personality and Social Psychology Bulletin* 28, no. 12 (2002): 1615–1628.

Davis, Michael. *Street Gang: The Complete History of Sesame Street*. New York: Penguin, 2009.

Bibliography

DeBell, Matthew, and Chris Chapman. *Computer and Internet Use by Children and Adolescents in 2003.* Washington, D.C.: National Center for Education Statistics, 2006. http://nces.ed.gov/pubs2006/2006065.pdf.

Dohnt, Hayley, and Marika Tiggemann. "Body Image Concerns in Young Girls." *Journal of Youth and Adolescents* 35, no. 2 (2006): 135–145.

Douglas, Susan J. *Enlightened Sexism: The Seductive Message That Feminism's Work Is Done.* New York: Henry Holt, 2010.

Eliot, Lise. *Pink Brain, Blue Brain: How Small Differences Grow into Troublesome Gaps—and What We Can Do About It.* New York: Houghton Mifflin, 2009.

Finch, Christopher. *Rainbow: The Stormy Life of Judy Garland.* New York: Ballantine, 1975.

Forman-Brunell, Miriam. *Made to Play House: Dolls and the Commercialization of American Girlhood, 1830–1930.* New Haven, Conn.: Yale University Press, 1993.

Fredrickson, B. L., T. A. Roberts, S. M. Noll, D. M. Quinn, and J. M. Twenge. "That Swimsuit Becomes You: Sex Differences in Self-Objectification, Restrained Eating, and Math Performance." *Journal of Personality and Social Psychology* 75, no. 1 (1998): 269–284.

Frisby, Cynthia M. "Does Race Matter? Effects of Idealized Images on African American Women's Perceptions of Body Esteem." *Journal of Black Studies* 34, no. 3 (2004): 323–347.

Girls Incorporated. *The Supergirl Dilemma: Girls Grapple with the Mounting Pressure of Expectations, Summary Findings.* New York: Girls Incorporated, 2006.

Gould, Joan. *Spinning Straw into Gold: What Fairy Tales Reveal About the Transformations in a Woman's Life.* New York: Random House, 2006.

Grimm, Jacob, and Wilhelm Grimm. *The Annotated Brothers Grimm,* ed. Maria Tatar. New York: W. W. Norton, 2004.

Hargreaves, Duane, and Marika Tiggemann. "The Effect of Television Commercials on Mood and Body Dissatisfaction: The Role of Appearance-Schema Activation." *Journal of Social and Clinical Psychology* 21, no. 3 (2002): 287–308.

———. "The Effect of 'Thin Ideal' Television Commercials on Body Dissatisfaction and Schema Activation During Early Adolescence." *Journal of Youth and Adolescence* 32, no. 5 (2003): 367–373.

———. "Idealized Media Images and Adolescent Body Image: 'Comparing' Boys and Girls." *Body Image* 1, no. 4 (2004): 351–361.

Hassett, Janice M., et al. "Sex Differences in Rhesus Monkey Toy Preferences Parallel Those of Children." *Journal of Hormones and Behavior* 54, no. 3 (2008): 349–364.

Heltsley, Martha, and Thomas C. Calhoun. "The Good Mother: Neutralization Techniques Used by Pageant Mothers." *Deviant Behavior* 24, no. 2 (2003): 81–100.

Hinshaw, Stephen, with Rachel Krantz. *The Triple Bind: Saving Our Teenage Girls from Today's Pressures.* New York: Random House, 2009.

Impett, Emily A., Deborah Schooler, and Deborah L. Tolman. "To Be Seen and Not Heard: Feminine Ideology and Adolescent Girls' Sexual Health." *Archives of Sexual Behavior* 35, no. 2 (2006): 129–142.

Jacobs, Janis E., et al. "'I Can, but I Don't Want To': Impact of Parents, Interests, and Activities on Gender Differences in Math." In *Gender Differences in Mathematics: An Integrative Psychological Approach*, ed. Ann M. Gallagher and James C. Kaufman. Cambridge, England: Cambridge University Press, 2005, pp. 246–263.

Lamb, Sharon, and Lyn Mikel Brown. *Packaging Girlhood: Rescuing Our Daughters from Marketers' Schemes.* New York: St. Martin's Press, 2006.

Lenhart, Amanda. *Cyberbullying.* Washington, D.C.: Pew Internet & American Life Project, 2007.

Lenhart, Amanda, Mary Madden, Aaron Smith, and Alexandra Macgill. *Teens and Social Media*. Washington, D.C.: Pew Internet & American Life Project, 2007. www.pewinternet.org/Reports/2007/Teens-and-Social-Media.aspx.

Levin, Diane E., and Nancy Carlsson-Paige. *The War Play Dilemma: Balancing Needs and Values in the Early Childhood Classroom*. New York: Teachers College Press, 2005.

Locke, John. *Some Thoughts Concerning Education*. Cambridge, England: Cambridge University Press, 1989 (first published 1693).

Lueptow, Lloyd B., Lori Garovich-Szabo, and Margaret B. Lueptow. "Social Change and the Persistence of Sex Typing: 1974–1997." *Social Forces* 80, no. 1 (2001): 31–35.

Maccoby, Eleanor E. "Gender and Group Process." *Current Directions in Psychological Science* 11, no. 2 (2002): 54–59.

———. "Gender and Relationships: A Developmental Account." *American Psychologist* 45, no. 4 (1990): 513–520.

Manago, Adriana, Michael B. Graham, Patricia M. Greenfield, and Goldie Salimkhan. "Self-Presentation and Gender on MySpace." *Journal of Applied Developmental Psychology* 29, no. 6 (2008): 446–458.

Martin, Carol Lynn, and Richard Fabes. *Discovering Childhood Development*, 2nd ed. Belmont, Calif.: Wadsworth, 2008.

———. "The Stability and Consequences of Young Children's Same-Sex Peer Interactions." *Developmental Psychology* 37, no. 3 (2001): 431–446.

Miller, Edward, and Joan Almon. *Crisis in Kindergarten: Why Children Need to Play in School*. New York: Alliance for Childhood, 2009.

Morgenson, Gretchen. *Forbes Great Minds of Business*. New York: John Wiley & Sons, 1997.

Morrison, Susan, ed. *Thirty Ways of Looking at Hillary*. New York: Harper, 2008.

Nathanson, Amy I. "Identifying and Explaining the Relationship Between Parental Mediation and Children's Aggression." *Communication Research* 26, no. 2 (1999): 124–133.

———. "The Unintended Effects of Parental Mediation of Television on Adolescents." *Media Psychology* 4, no. 3 (2002): 207–230.

National Campaign to Prevent Teen and Unplanned Pregnancy. *Sex and Tech: Executive Summary.* Washington, D.C.: National Campaign to Prevent Teen and Unplanned Pregnancy, December 2009.

Orenstein, Peggy. *Schoolgirls: Young Women, Self-Esteem, and the Confidence Gap.* New York: Anchor, 1995.

Paley, Vivian Gussin. *Boys and Girls: Superheroes in the Doll Corner.* Chicago: University of Chicago Press, 1984.

Roosevelt, Theodore. *The Strenuous Life: Essays and Addresses.* Mineola, N.Y.: Dover Books, 2009 (originally published 1900).

Ruble, Diane N., et al. "The Role of Gender Constancy in Early Gender Development." *Child Development* 78, no. 4 (2007): 1121–1136.

Rust, John, et al. "The Role of Brothers and Sisters in the Gender Development of Preschool Children." *Journal of Experimental Child Psychology* 77, no. 4 (2000): 292–303.

Sax, Leonard. *Why Gender Matters: What Parents and Teachers Need to Know about the Emerging Science of Sex Differences.* New York: Broadway, 2006.

Slater, Amy, and Marika Tiggemann. "A Test of Objectification Theory in Adolescent Girls." *Sex Roles* 46, no. 9 (2002): 343–349.

Stearns, Peter N. *Fat History.* New York: New York University Press, 1997.

Sutton-Smith, Brian. *Toys as Culture.* New York: Gardner Press, 1986.

Tatar, Maria. *The Hard Facts of the Grimms' Fairy Tales,* 2nd ed. Princeton, N.J.: Princeton University Press, 2003.

———. "Reading the Grimms' *Children's Stories and Household Tales.*" In Jacob Grimm and Wilhelm Grimm, *The Annotated Brothers Grimm,* ed. Maria Tatar. New York: W. W. Norton, 2004.

Bibliography

Tchana, Katrin, and Trina Schart Hyman. *The Serpent Slayer*. New York: Little, Brown, 2000.

Tolman, Deborah, Emily A. Impett, Allison J. Tracy, and Alice Michael. "Looking Good, Sounding Good: Femininity Ideology and Adolescent Girls' Mental Health." *Psychology of Women Quarterly* 30 (2006): 85–95.

Wolkstein, Diane. *The Glass Mountain*. New York: Morrow, 1999.

Index

Abby Cadabby, 39, 40–41, 43, 51

advertising, 17, 91, 98, 176–77, 183, 202*n*–3*n*

  restrictions on, 182, 221*n*

Advertising Educational Foundation, 37–38

African-American females, 179–81, 205*n*, 220*n*

aging, 138–39, 148

Aguilera, Christina, 120

American Girl collection, 26–32, 140, 144

American Girl Place, 8, 27, 29, 31–32

American Psychological Association, 6, 195*n*

Andersen, Hans Christian, 107–8, 190

Anglund, Joan Walsh, 165

Ariel, 14, 20, 107, 124, 162, 191

Arizona State University, 66, 67

"Aschenputtel" (Brothers Grimm), 103–5, 111

Austin, Erica Weintraub, 187

Ava (five-year-old classmate), 133–35, 136–37, 143, 151

avatars, 159, 160, 161, 162, 167

baby dolls, 45, 52

" . . . Baby One More Time," 121

Barbie, 7, 15, 28, 39, 42, 44, 45–48, 49, 50, 63, 84, 88, 97

Barbie.com, 161, 162

Barney and Friends, 128

Batgirl, 145

BBC, 75, 94

Beanie Babies, 86

beauty pageants, 8, 73–82, 89–94, 125

  gowns and outfits of, 74, 75, 77, 82, 89

  hair and makeup in, 73, 74, 75, 77, 91

beauty pageants *(cont.)*
  media coverage of, 75–76, 81, 89, 94
  prizes of, 74, 75, 76, 91, 92, 93
  parents of contestants, 74–76, 78–82, 85, 90–91
beauty products, 34, 73, 74, 75, 77, 91, 155, 156
  for preschoolers and "pre-tween" girls, 7, 38, 42, 52, 82, 83–84, 85, 91
  for "tween" girls, 29, 37, 91, 156
Bella Swan (char.), 109–12
Belle, 14, 124, 162
Bem, Jeremy, 60, 203n
Bem, Sandra, 203n
Berkeley, Calif., 4, 21, 147
Bettelheim, Bruno, 100, 102, 105, 106, 108, 109, 145
Beyoncé, 86
Bible, 135
Bikini Kill, 153
biological determinism, 52, 56–61, 62–64, 69, 70
board games, 7, 34, 49–50, 152
body image issues, 2, 6, 8, 88, 133–43, 158, 175, 186, 196n
  African-American women and, 220n
  self-loathing and, 6, 18, 134, 137, 141–42, 216n
Body Project, The (Brumberg), 140
Bonne Bell, 37, 84, 176
Botox, 138, 139
boyhood culture, 16, 19–22, 35–36, 38, 43, 57, 62, 97
  gender segmentation of toys and, 21–22, 38, 43, 45, 50, 51, 97, 98–99
  Internet use in, 160–61, 174, 175

nature vs. nurture in, 53–54, 55–61, 62–65, 69–71, 98, 145
  playtime patterns in, 67–69, 98, 99, 145, 157–58
  segregation of girl culture from, 51–53, 65, 66, 67–72, 156–58
brain development, 59, 60–61, 64–65
Bratz, 48–49, 50, 51, 84, 86, 91, 153, 155, 161
Brave, 188–89
Brown, Lyn Mikel, 151–52, 187
Brumberg, Joan Jacob, 140
Buffy the Vampire Slayer, 112
Burmeister, Jamara, 89–90, 92–93
Burmeister, Jason, 89, 92
Burmeister, Tammi, 89–90, 93
Burnett, Frances Hodgson, 25

California, University of (Berkeley), 84–85
Catmull, Ed, 189
Chapman, Brenda, 189
Cheetah Girls, The, 117
Cherney, Isabelle, 21
childhood consumerism and marketing, 24, 30–43, 49, 79, 98–99, 136–39, 153–56, 187
  of beauty products, 7, 29, 34, 37, 38, 42, 52, 82, 83–84, 85, 155, 156
  of fashion and clothing, 36, 38, 82, 86, 117, 119, 139, 143, 152
  of fictional female characters and role models, 15, 36, 39–43, 46, 50, 117, 118
  gender segmentation and color coding in, 7, 35–36, 38–39,

43, 51–52, 53, 58, 63, 70, 72, 98–99

gender stereotyping in, 91, 155, 202*n*–3*n*

Kids Getting Older Younger in, 47, 48, 84–85, 91, 139, 183

materialism and narcissistic values emphasized in, 16, 30, 32, 34, 42, 46, 48, 49–50, 83, 88, 104, 155, 156, 161–62

online, 176–77

pink-and-pretty trend in, 33–35, 36, 38–43, 51, 52, 125, 155

in princess culture, 13–16, 23, 24–25, 26, 32, 36, 41, 61–62, 116, 189–90

protecting girls from influence of, 182–85, 192

restrictions on, 182, 221*n*

of "sexiness" and "cool," 47, 48–49, 50, 52, 84, 85–88, 91, 183

television commercials and, 98

of toys and merchandising, 3, 7, 15, 16, 26–32, 33–35, 39–43, 45–52, 70, 85–88, 91, 98–99, 155, 180, 185, 190

of young female celebrities, 26, 114, 115–31

Children's Digital Media Center, 165

children's literature, 23, 28–30, 100–112, 140, 211*n*

female protagonists in, 12, 20–21, 101, 102, 104–5, 108–12, 149–50, 185, 190–92

rescue-fantasy and landing-a-prince theme in, 12, 20, 23, 101, 102, 103, 107, 110, 111

Twilight series in, 109–12, 211*n*

see also fairy tales

Children's Online Privacy Protection Act (COPPA), 162, 174

child stars, 25–26, 113–31, 221*n*

squeaky-to-skanky transformations in, 113–15, 120–24, 126–28, 129, 130

Cinderella, 3, 6, 9, 14, 17, 20–21, 23, 24, 36, 44, 48, 58, 61–62, 89, 102, 111, 114, 115, 116, 123, 124, 152, 162, 182, 185

Brothers Grimm version of, 103–5, 183

Cinderella, 13, 190

Cinderella Complex, The (Dowling), 111

Clarissa Explains It All, 116, 118–19, 120

Clinton, Hillary, 147–48, 149, 217*n*

Club Libby Lu, 83–84

Cook, Daniel, 36

Cookie Monster, 40, 43

cosmetic surgery, 138–40

Couric, Katie, 149

Cross, Gary, 24

cross-sex play, 50, 66, 67–70, 72, 158, 205*n*–6*n*

Curtis, Jaime Lee, 215*n*–16*n*

cyberbullying, 168–70, 172–73, 174, 175, 177, 219*n*–20*n*

Cyrus, Billy Ray, 114–15, 118, 127, 184

Cyrus, Miley, 8, 117–19, 121, 129, 130, 138, 153, 155

concert tours of, 118, 124, 125–26, 128, 130–31

sexualization of, 113–15, 126–28, 221*n*

Index

Damned if You Do, Doomed if You Don't (Catalyst), 146
Dangerous Book for Boys, The (Iggulden and Iggulden), 155
Daring Book for Girls, The (Buchanan and Peskowitz), 155, 156–57
DeCesare, Danielle, 175–76
DeCesare, Hilary, 174, 175–78
depression, 6, 16, 18, 76, 172
dieting, 8, 135, 143, 186
Diller, Vivian, 138–39
Disney, 8, 13, 14, 16, 22, 23, 24, 32, 36, 41, 51, 87–88, 102, 103, 107, 111, 144, 185–86
child stars launched and marketed by, 113–15, 116–19, 120, 124–25, 128–30
first African-American Princess of, 15, 179–82, 189–90
Disney, Roy, 13
Disney, Walt, 116, 120
Disney Channel, 7, 114, 116, 117, 128
Disneyland, 41
Disney Princesses, 3, 7, 8, 19, 20, 23, 31, 32, 33, 48, 49, 61, 62, 85, 111, 114, 115, 124, 135, 138, 142, 143–44, 153, 155, 187
marketing of, 13–15, 16, 23, 24, 26, 36, 104, 116, 125, 182, 189–90
Web site for, 162
Dora the Explorer, 7, 15, 42–43, 51, 161–62
Duff, Hilary, 115, 116–17, 118, 120, 129

eating disorders, 6, 76, 137, 141
education reform, 70–71, 85
Elenita (Campbell and Juan), 149–50

Eliot, Lise, 59, 60–61, 62–63, 64, 65, 69, 71
Eschberger, Tallon, 80–82
Eschberger, Taralyn, 73–75, 78, 79–81, 84, 89, 92, 93–94
Eschberger, Todd, 80, 82, 93, 94
Eschberger, Traci, 74–75, 79–82, 89, 90, 91, 92, 93
Everloop, 174–78

Fabes, Richard, 66, 67–68, 69, 71–72, 158, 215n
Facebook, 24, 163, 164–65, 166, 168, 169, 171, 174, 182
Face It (Diller and Muir-Sukenick), 138–39
fairy tales, 8, 12, 13, 14, 20–21, 23, 25, 101, 108–9, 115, 139, 145, 149, 181, 185, 190, 211n
by Brothers Grimm, 100, 101–7, 108–9, 183, 190–92
emotional development aided by, 100, 102, 104
rescue-fantasy and landing-a-prince theme in, 12, 20, 23, 101, 102, 103, 107, 144, 182
violent and gruesome imagery in, 100, 102–3, 105, 106–9, 191–92
Fairytopia Barbie, 88
fashion, 82, 86, 91, 117, 119, 123, 125, 139, 143, 152
female heroines and role models, 14, 36, 180–82, 187–91
in fairy tales, 12, 14, 20–21, 101, 102, 104–5, 107, 108–9, 185, 190–92
independent and nontraditional examples of, 30, 42, 46, 50, 101, 108–9, 112, 128, 144–45, 148, 149–50, 153, 185–86
marketing and merchandising

of, 15, 36, 39–43, 46, 117, 118

rescue-fantasy and landing-a-prince theme in fiction of, 12, 20, 23, 101, 102, 103, 107, 144, 180, 182

sexualization of, 113–15, 120–24, 125, 126–28, 129–31, 144–45, 149, 221n

in TV shows for tweens, 116–20, 128–29, 130

in *Twilight* series, 109–12

femininity, female identity, 7, 8, 9, 19, 22, 57, 58, 61, 62, 72, 87, 96, 138–39, 155, 156–58

culture's emphasis on beauty in, 5, 6, 9, 16, 18, 19–20, 22, 23, 34, 50, 94, 101, 119, 134, 135, 137–39, 140–41, 142–44, 145, 148–49, 152, 158, 183

digital media in shaping of, 159, 160, 162, 163, 165–68, 173, 177

exposure to stereotypes in shaping of, 16–17, 63–64, 91, 150, 198n, 202n–3n

fashion and, 17, 18, 148, 152

"Girl Power" movement in, 7, 153–55

materialistic values and, 32, 46, 49–50, 77

persisting tensions around power and, 146–49, 150–52

pink-and-pretty trend in defining of, 7, 34, 35, 36, 43, 44, 61, 67, 125

pleasing behavior as cultural trait of, 16, 17, 18, 112

and pressure to be "perfect," 17–18, 94, 111, 140

sexiness equated with, 112, 125, 130, 134, 167, 183

"tomboys" and, 66–67

two cultural models of, 151–52

see also girlhood culture

feminism, 4, 19, 22, 46, 51, 56–58, 82, 101, 154–58, 185

princess tales inspired by, 101, 149

Fisher-Price, 51, 53

"Fitcher's Bird" (Brothers Grimm), 108

Formspring, 168

Free to Be You and Me, 150

Friend Is Someone Who Likes You, A (Anglund), 165

Funicello, Annette, 120

"Furrypelts" (Brothers Grimm), 108

Garland, Judy, 120

gender development and identity, 55–72, 203n, 205n, 206n

brain development and, 59, 60–61, 64–65, 69, 70

nature vs. nurture in, 53–54, 55–61, 62–65, 69–71, 98, 145

playtime patterns in, 67–69, 98, 145, 157–58

segregation of sexes and, 65–72, 157–58

toy preferences and, 57, 62–64, 68

see also femininity, female identity

gender segmentation, 52, 72

color coding and, 7, 35–36, 38–39, 43, 50, 51, 63

as marketing strategy, 35–36, 38, 43, 51–52, 53, 58, 98–99

of toys, 3, 7, 21–22, 38–39, 43, 45, 50, 51–52, 63, 70, 97, 98–99, 198n

gender segregation, 51–53, 59, 65–72, 157

in playtime, 50, 66, 67–70, 72, 156–58

General Mills, 176
girlhood culture:
  African Americans and,
    179–81, 205n, 220n
  beauty and appearance em-
    phasized in, 5, 6, 8, 16, 18,
    19–20, 22, 23, 34, 42–43,
    49, 82, 94, 101, 119, 134,
    135, 137–39, 140–41,
    142–44, 145, 149, 152, 158,
    180, 183
  beauty and sexuality as
    sources of power in, 7,
    121–22, 134, 139, 143, 149,
    167, 171
  color coding of, 7, 35–36,
    38–39, 43, 50, 51, 63, 152
  cosmetics marketed to, 7,
    29, 34, 37, 39, 42, 52, 82,
    83–84, 85, 155, 156
  cute-to-cool trajectory in,
    24–25, 47, 48
  cyberbullying in, 168–70,
    172–73, 174, 175, 177, 219n–
    20n
  distorted expectations of inti-
    mate relationships in, 6, 16,
    85, 110–12, 171, 172
  fashion and clothing in, 38, 82,
    86, 117, 119, 125, 139, 143,
    152
  female celebrities marketed in,
    26, 113–31, 153–55, 221n
  "Girl Power" movement in, 7,
    153–55
  Internet use in, 159–71, 172–78
  Kids Getting Older Younger
    trend in, 47, 48, 84, 139, 183
  literature and fairy tales in, see
    children's literature; fairy
    tales
  materialism and narcissis-
    tic values emphasized in,
    16, 23, 30, 32, 42, 46, 48,
    49–50, 77, 83, 88, 104, 117,
    155, 156, 161–62
  nature vs. nurture in, 53–54,
    55–61, 62–65, 69–71, 98,
    145
  playtime patterns in, 41, 42,
    43, 44, 67–69, 98, 99, 145–
    46, 150, 156–58, 162, 185
  premature sexualization in,
    6–7, 8, 24–25, 32, 52, 75,
    76, 79, 84–86, 91, 113–14,
    123, 125, 167–68, 170–72,
    183, 184, 215n
  and protecting from influence
    of media and marketing,
    182–87, 192
  protecting innocence in, 6,
    24, 25, 26, 32, 49, 52, 81,
    85–88, 114, 119, 125
  segregation of boy culture
    from, 51–53, 65, 66, 67–72,
    156–58
  self-loathing in, 6, 18, 137,
    141–42, 216n, 220n
  self-objectification and per-
    formance in, 6–7, 8, 76, 78,
    85, 123–24, 129–30, 142,
    166–67, 171–72, 183, 195n
  toys and merchandise targeted
    to, 15, 21–22, 26–32, 33–35,
    38–39, 40–43, 44–52, 84,
    86–88, 91, 97, 98, 117, 118,
    144, 152, 155, 180, 185, 190
  two models of female identity
    in, 151–52
  violent play and imagery in,
    96–98, 99–100, 102–3, 105,
    106–9, 191–92
  see also femininity, female iden-
    tity; specific age groups
"girlie feminism," 154–55, 157
"Girl Power Index" (GPI), 83

Index

"Girl Power" movement, 7, 153–55

Girls' Book, The: How to Be the Best at Everything (Foster), 155, 156, 157

Gomez, Selena, 128–29, 130

Good Luck Charlie, 128

Good Morning America, 75, 86

Gould, Joan, 105

Great Depression, 25

Grimm, Jacob and Wilhelm, 100, 101–9, 115, 183, 191

Groovy Girls, 88

Grover (Muppet), 40, 43

guns, toy, 96–98, 99, 102

Handy, Bruce, 115

Hannah Montana, 117–19, 128, 130, 131, 154, 182

Hannah Montana: The Movie, 118

Hannah Montana 2/Meet Miley Cyrus, 118

Happily Ever After Stories, 23

Harry Potter series, 211*n*

Hawkgirl, 144

Hello Kitty, 38, 126

High School Musical, 117, 120

Hill, Annette, 77, 78, 92, 93

Hinshaw, Stephen, 84–85

Hitchens, Christopher, 148

Hole, 153, 218*n*

Hot Wheels, 22, 46

Hunter College, 6, 171

I Know Who Killed Me, 120–21

Internet, 8, 100, 114, 120, 149, 159–71, 172–78, 189

  avatars and online personas on, 159–60, 165–68

  cyberbullying on, 168–70, 172–73, 174, 175, 177, 219*n*–20*n*

narcissistic tendencies and, 165–66

premature sexualization and, 167–68, 170–71, 172

preparing kids for safer and more responsible use of, 163, 174–78

sexually suggestive messages sent on, 170–71, 172

in shaping girls' identities, 159, 160, 162, 163, 165–68, 173, 177

social networking sites on, 159, 161, 163, 164–70, 172–73, 174–78

teenage girls' use of, 162–71, 172–73, 219*n*–20*n*

Jacklin, Carol Nagy, 206*n*

Jasmine, 6, 14

Javits Center, 33, 44

Jezebel.com, 82

Jordan, Michael, 37

Julie (preschool mother), 19, 21, 22

Kakutani, Michiko, 217*n*

Kids Getting Older Younger (KGOY), 84–85, 91

Kiki's Delivery Service, 185–86

Klarman Eating Disorders Center, 142

Lamb, Sharon, 151–52, 187

LeapFrog, 43

Legos, 38, 39, 46

Levin, Diane, 98, 99

Limbaugh, Rush, 148

Lip Smackers, 38, 84

Little Mermaid, 4

Little Mermaid, 20, 107

"Little Mermaid, The" (Andersen), 107–8

Index

Little Orphan Annie, 25
Little Princess, A (Burnett), 25
Lizzie McGuire, 116–17, 118–19
Lizzie McGuire Movie, The, 117
Locke, John, 100
Lohan, Lindsay, 25, 115, 120–21, 127, 129
Lord & Taylor, 36
Los Angeles Times, 1, 189
Lovato, Demi, 128
Love, Courtney, 153

McCain, John, 148
McDonald's, 176, 184
Madonna, 121–22
mainstream media culture, 16–17, 83, 137, 153, 211n
  advertising in, 17, 91, 98, 176–77, 182, 183, 202n–3n, 221n
  beauty emphasized in, 5, 6, 16, 23, 42–43, 119, 138, 145, 148, 149, 180, 183
  child stars in, 25–26, 113–31
  female sexualization in, 6–7, 16, 113–15, 120–24, 125, 127–28, 129–31, 144–45, 149, 167, 183, 184, 221n
  gender stereotypes in, 16–17, 91, 147–48, 150, 155, 202n–3n
  girlish innocence celebrated in, 24–26, 123, 129, 130
  "Girl Power" movement in, 7, 153–55
  materialism and narcissistic values emphasized in, 16, 23, 30, 46, 104, 117, 155, 156, 161–62
  premature sexualization and, 86, 113–14, 123, 124–25, 167, 183, 184

  princess movies in, 104, 107, 179–82, 187–90
  rescue-fantasy and landing-a-prince theme in, 12, 20, 23, 102, 103, 107, 110, 111, 180, 182
  sexuality commodified and marketed in, 121–24, 129, 130
  squeaky-to-skanky celebrity transformations in, 120–24, 127–28, 129, 130
  standards of beauty and idealized images of women in, 6, 17, 111, 134, 135, 137, 138, 144, 145, 148, 149, 196n, 220n
  superheroines in, 144–46
  see also childhood consumerism and marketing; Internet
Manago, Adriana, 165, 167
Martin, Carol, 66–67, 68–70, 71, 158, 215n
Mary Poppins, 36
Mary Tyler Moore Show, The, 41
Mattel, 15, 29, 32, 42, 49, 50–51
Maxim, 120, 123
Meier, Megan, 168–69, 172–73
Mendler, Bridgit, 128
Meyer, Stephenie, 109
MGA, 48, 49, 50, 51
MGM, 120
Miller, Laura, 111
mixed-sex play, 66, 67–70, 72, 158, 205n–6n
Miyazaki, Hayao, 185–86
Monster High, 50, 144, 186
Mooney, Andy, 13, 14, 15, 16, 22, 41, 88, 116
Moore, Susanna, 148, 217n
More, 138, 215n–16n

Moxie Girlz, 50, 91, 138, 155, 161
Mr. Mopp's, 95–96
Ms., 55
MTV, 75, 116, 122, 169
Muir-Sukenick, Jill, 138–39
Mulan, 14, 187–88
Mulan II, 187–88
Muppets, 39, 40, 43
Muppet Show, The, 39
Murdoch, Rupert, 178
My Beautiful Mommy (Salz-
    hauer), 139, 216n
MySpace, 165, 168, 178

NAACP, 181
Narcissistic Personality Inven-
    tory, 166
National Campaign to Prevent
    Teen and Unplanned Preg-
    nancy, 170
National Institute of Mental
    Health, 71
New York Post, 121
New York Times, The, 1, 71, 217n
New York Times Magazine, The,
    4
Nickelodeon, 15, 42, 116, 127
Nike, 13, 37, 176

Obama, Barack, 148
Obama, Malia and Sasha, 86
OfficeMax, 129
Ouija boards, 49
Oz, Frank, 39

Packaging Girlhood (Lamb and
    Brown), 151–52, 187
"Painted Babies" (BBC docu-
    mentary), 94
Palin, Sarah, 148–49
Paoletti, Jo, 35
Paper Bag Princess, The (Munsch
    and Martchenko), 101

Parente, Carol-Lynn, 40
parents:
    advice on curtailing body
        image issues for, 137, 141,
        142–43, 186
    of beauty pageant contestants,
        74–76, 78–82, 85, 90–91
    princess culture as viewed by,
        19–21, 22–23, 24
    in protecting girlhood inno-
        cence, 6, 24, 25, 26, 32, 52,
        85–88, 114, 119, 125
    in protecting girls from media
        and marketing influence,
        182–87, 192
    and safer and responsible In-
        ternet use, 163, 174–78
    undue restrictions by, 186,
        191–92
Perrault, Charles, 103
Pilkington, Alexis, 169, 172–73
pink-and-pretty trend, 4, 6, 32,
    33–36, 38–45, 51, 52, 61, 83,
    136, 144, 152, 181
    in board games, 7, 34, 49–50,
        152
    in fictional female characters
        and role models, 39–43,
        47–48
    innocence symbolized in, 34,
        49, 52, 125
    as marketing strategy, 35–36,
        38, 40, 41–43, 52, 155
    narcissism and materialism in,
        42, 46, 48, 49–50
    in toys and merchandise,
        33–35, 38–39, 40–43, 44,
        47–48, 49–50, 98, 152
Pink Brain, Blue Brain (Eliot),
    59
Pink Yahtzee, 49
Pixar Animation Studios,
    188–90

play, 145–46, 158, 161–62, 185
  gender segregation in, 50, 66,
    67–70, 72, 156–57
  violent themes in, 96–98, 99,
    102
Pocahontas, 14, 31, 124
Pop (pseudonym), 56–58, 63
Portfolio, 118
Power Rangers, 16
preschool girls, 2–4, 5, 37, 58,
    142
  beauty pageants for, 73–82, 85,
    89, 90, 93–94, 125
  cosmetics targeted to, 7, 52,
    84, 85
  premature sexualization of, 75,
    76, 79, 85–86
  princess culture of, 3–6, 18–21,
    22, 23, 24, 25, 61–62, 64,
    124, 186
  toys targeted to, 3, 34, 38, 51,
    86–88
"pre-tween" girls, 38
  beauty pageants for, 73–82,
    89–94, 125
  cosmetics marketed to, 42, 82,
    83–84, 91
  materialistic and narcissistic
    values marketed to, 16, 23,
    30, 32, 42, 46, 48, 49–50, 83,
    88, 104, 155, 156, 161–62
  online sites aimed at, 161–62,
    164
  premature sexualization of, 75,
    78, 79, 91, 123, 125, 183
  see also preschool girls; "tween"
    girls
Prince, Phoebe, 169, 172–73
Princess and the Frog, The, 179,
    180–82, 189–90
princess culture, 3–6, 8, 13–16,
    18–21, 22–25, 26, 41, 58, 64,
    75, 83, 96, 99, 101, 115, 124,
    138, 143–44, 150, 153, 155,
    186, 187–92
  Disney's marketing of, 13–15,
    16, 23, 24, 26, 36, 104, 116,
    125, 182, 189–90
  first mainstream African-
    American character in, 15,
    179–82, 189–90
  materialistic values in, 16,
    23
  mothers' perspectives on,
    19–21, 22–23, 24
  movies in, 104, 107, 179–82,
    187–90
  as protecting girls' innocence,
    6, 24, 25, 32, 49, 81, 114,
    119, 125
  rescue fantasies and landing
    Prince Charming empha-
    sized in, 4, 6, 12, 14, 16, 20,
    23, 111, 144, 180, 182
  toys and merchandise of,
    15–16, 26, 33–34, 35, 48,
    61–62, 85, 182, 186, 190
  see also fairy tales
Princess Smartypants (Cole),
    101
Psychology of Sex Differences, The
    (Maccoby and Jacklin), 206
Pussycat Dolls, 83, 119

Ramona and Beezus, 128
Ramsey, JonBenét, 72, 90
Rapunzel, 102
"Rapunzel" (Brothers Grimm),
    190–92
Reimer, David, 57, 65
Riot Grrrl movement, 153, 154,
    155, 218n
"Robber Bridegroom, The"
    (Brothers Grimm), 108
Rolling Stone, 122
Roosevelt, Franklin, 25

Roosevelt, Theodore, 45
Rowland, Pleasant, 28, 32
"Rumpelstiltskin" (Brothers Grimm), 105–6

Saks Fifth Avenue, 27, 32, 83
Salon, 111
same-sex play, 67–69
Sanford Harmony Program, 66–67, 71–72, 158
Sax, Leonard, 70, 71
Scholastic, 156
Schoolgirls (Orenstein), 140–41
Scrabble, 7, 152
self-esteem, 6, 16, 22, 76, 137, 138, 175, 215*n*
Sesame Street, 39–41
Sesame Workshop, 40–41
"sexting," 170, 172
sexuality, female, 7, 8, 85, 112, 121–24, 129–31, 167
    detachment in, 6–7, 16, 85, 121, 123–24, 171–72
    objectification and perfor-
        mance in, 6–7, 8, 76, 85, 123–124, 129–130, 167, 171–172, 183, 195*n*, 221*n*;
        see also sexualization, female
    in toys marketed to children, 47, 48–49, 84, 85–88, 91
sexualization, female, 8, 75, 76, 121–22, 129, 167, 195*n*–96*n*
    femininity equated with, 112, 125, 130, 134, 167, 183
    mental health and, 6, 16, 76, 85, 137, 138, 196*n*
    of superheroines, 144–45
    of women in power, 149
    of young female celebri-
        ties, 113–15, 120–24, 125, 126–28, 129–31, 221*n*

sexualization, premature, 75, 76, 84–86, 91, 171, 184, 215*n*
    detached sexuality as result of, 6–7, 16, 85, 123–24, 129–30, 171–72
    digital media and, 167–68, 170–71, 172
    fashion and, 86, 91, 123, 125
    female celebrities and, 113–15, 123, 124–25, 221*n*
    mainstream media's role in, 86, 113–14, 123, 124, 125, 167, 183, 184
    princess and pink culture in protecting from, 6, 24–25, 32, 52, 81
    sibling effect, 64–65
"Single Ladies (Put a Ring on It)," 86
"Six Swans, The" (Brothers Grimm), 108–9
Sleeping Beauty, 5, 14, 23, 24, 36, 62, 102, 115, 144, 162
Sleeping Beauty, 190
Snow Queen, The (Andersen), 190
Snow White, 3, 12, 14, 15, 16, 20, 21, 23, 115, 120
"Snow White" (Brothers Grimm), 100
social networking sites, 159, 161, 163, 164–70, 182
    cyberbullying on, 168–70, 172–73, 174, 175, 177
    for "tweens," 174–78
Sonny with a Chance, 128
Sophie (ten-year-old girl), 27, 31–32
Spears, Britney, 115, 121–23, 127, 129, 130, 153
Spears, Jamie Lynn, 127
Spice Girls, 153–55
Spider-Woman, 144

Spinning Straw into Gold
(Gould), 105
Steiner-Adair, Catherine, 142
stereotypes, gender, 63–64, 97,
146–47, 198*n*
in mainstream media, 16–17,
91, 147–48, 150, 155,
202*n*–3*n*
Steven (author's husband), 2, 15,
88, 97, 99
Stewart, Kristen, 112
suicide, 18, 169, 172–73
Supergirl, 144–45
superheroines, 144–46, 148,
150, 158
*Superstar: The Karen Carpenter
Story*, 46

Talking Elmo, 51
Tangled, 190
Target, 42, 88
teenage girls, 122, 137–41, 166,
167, 183, 192, 215*n*
body image issues and self-
loathing in, 6, 18, 137, 139,
141
cyberbullying of, 168–70,
172–73, 174, 219*n*–20*n*
depression in, 16, 18, 172
detached sexuality in, 6–7, 16,
123, 171–72
Internet use of, 162–71,
172–73, 219*n*–20*n*
premature sexualization of,
6–7, 16, 113–15, 123–24,
130, 167–68, 170–72, 183,
215*n*, 221*n*
suicide and, 18, 169, 172–73
Teen Choice Awards, 127
television, 50, 91, 100, 144, 186,
187
commercials on, 27, 98,
202*n*–3*n*, 221*n*

for tweens and pretweens,
116–20, 127, 128–29, 130
Temple, Shirley, 25–26, 79,
119–20
text messaging, 161, 169
sexually suggestive, 170–71,
172
That's So Raven, 117
Thelma & Louise, 101
Thirty Ways of Looking at Hillary
(Moore), 148, 217*n*
Tiana (char.), 15, 180–81,
190
Tinker Bell, 14, 144
TinkerToys, 7, 38, 45
toddlers, 5, 36–37, 38, 39, 95,
116, 192
Toddlers & Tiaras, 75, 77, 89
Tolman, Deborah, 6–7, 171–72
"tomboys," 66–67
Tonka, 38, 57, 202*n*
Toy Fair (Jacob Javits Center),
33–35, 51, 53
toys and merchandise, 13,
15–16, 20, 26–32, 45–52, 57,
95–96, 144, 155, 180, 184,
185
Barbie line of, 7, 15, 28, 39, 42,
44, 45–48, 49, 50, 63, 84,
88, 97
board games, 7, 34, 49–50,
152
Bratz line of, 48–49, 50, 51, 84,
86, 91, 153, 155
of fake guns, 96–98, 99,
102
gender and inborn preferences
in, 57, 62–64, 68
gender color coding of, 7, 21,
35, 38–39, 43, 50, 51, 63,
152
as gender role propaganda,
44–45, 52

gender segmentation of, 3, 7,
21–22, 38–39, 43, 45, 50,
51–52, 63, 70, 97, 98–99,
198*n*

materialistic and narcissistic
values in, 32, 42, 46, 48,
48–51, 88, 155

pink-and-pretty trend in,
33–35, 38–39, 40–43, 44,
47–48, 49–50, 51, 152

for preschool girls, 3, 34, 38,
51, 86–88

princess culture of, 15, 26,
33–34, 35, 48, 61–62, 182,
186, 190

"sexiness" and "cool" marketed
in, 47, 48–49, 50, 52, 85–88,
91

Ty Girlz line of, 86–88, 155,
161, 182

Toys "R" Us, 8, 39, 118

Toy Story, 39, 189

Triple Bind, The (Hinshaw), 84–85

"tween" girls, 5, 135, 183

beauty products marketed to,
29, 37, 42, 82, 83, 156

celebrity role-models marketed to, 113–31

clothing marketed to, 82, 91,
125

elastic age span in categoriza-
tion of, 37, 42

materialistic values marketed
to, 30, 49–50, 83, 117, 155,
156

premature sexualization of, 6,
7, 84–86, 91, 123, 125

social networking site for,
174–78

see also "pre-tween" girls

Twenge, Jean, 215*n*

Twilight series (Meyer), 6,
109–12, 182, 211*n*

Twitter, 24, 166

Ty Girlz, 86–88, 155, 161,
182

Universal Royalty Texas State
Beauty Pageant, 73–75,
76–78, 79–80, 89–91,
92–94

Up, 189

Uses of Enchantment, The (Bettelheim), 100

Vanity Fair, 114, 115, 121, 127,
130

Verna (African-American
mother), 180

Viacom, 15

violence:
in fairy tales, 100, 102–3, 105,
106–9, 191–92
in media, 98, 186
in play, 96–98, 99–100

Vogue, 149

Wall Street Journal, The, 129

Walmart, 86, 119, 124

Walters, Barbara, 127

War Play Dilemma, The (Levin),
98

Washington Post, The, 148

Webkinz.com, 173

What Kids Buy and Why (Acuff
and Reiher), 37

"What's Wrong with Cinderella?" (Orenstein), 4–5

Why Gender Matters (Sax),
70

Whyville, 159–60, 176

Winfrey, Oprah, 126, 181

Wizard of Oz, The, 120

Wizards of Waverly Place,
128–29

Wolkstein, Diane, 109

Wonder Woman, 144, 145–46,
148, 150, 158
Wonder World Tour, 124,
125–26, 130–31
Wood, Eden, 78, 79, 89, 90, 92
Wood, Mickie, 78, 90
World War II, 100

"X: A Fabulous Child's Story,"
55–56

Yeh-Shen, 103
YouTube, 46, 144, 161, 169

Zoe (Muppet), 40